DATE DUE

CHRISTIAN
FAITH
and
MODERN
DEMOCRACY

FRANK M. COVEY, JR.
Loyola Lectures in Political Analysis

THOMAS S. ENGEMAN
General Editor

Our late colleague Richard S. Hartigan founded the Frank M. Covey, Jr., Lectures in Political Analysis to provide a continuing forum for the reanimation of political philosophy. The lectures are not narrowly constrained by a single topic nor do they favor a particular perspective. Their sole aim is to foster serious theoretical inquiry, with the expectation that this effort will contribute in essential ways to both human knowledge and political justice.

CHRISTIAN
FAITH
and
MODERN
DEMOCRACY

God and Politics in the Fallen World

ROBERT P. KRAYNAK

UNIVERSITY OF NOTRE DAME PRESS
Notre Dame, Indiana

Manufactured in the United States of America

Library of Congress Cataloging-in-Publication Data
Kraynak, Robert P., 1949–
    Christian faith and modern democracy : God and politics in the fallen
world / Robert P. Kraynak.
        p.   cm.—(Frank M. Covey, Jr. Loyola lectures in political analysis)
    Includes bibliographical references and index.
        ISBN 0-268-02265-8 (cloth : alk. paper)— ISBN 0-268-02266-6 (pbk. :
alk. paper)
        1. Democracy—Religious aspects—Christianity.   2. Christianity and
politics.   I. Title.   II. Series.
    BR115.P7 K66   2001
    261.7—dc21
    2001001292

∞ *This book is printed on acid-free paper.*

Dedicated to my parents,

GEORGE, JR.
&
SOPHIA KRAYNAK

CONTENTS

Preface and Acknowledgments   xi

INTRODUCTION
Challenging the New Consensus in Christian Politics
1

CHAPTER ONE
Why Modern Liberal Democracy Needs God
9

CHAPTER TWO
The Illiberal and Undemocratic Christian Tradition
45

CHAPTER THREE
The Opening of Christianity to Democracy and Human Rights
107

CHAPTER FOUR
Rethinking Christian Politics: The Two Cities in the Modern Age
165

CHAPTER FIVE

The Earthly City: Constitutional Government under God

203

CONCLUSION

The Spiritual Significance of the Modern Democratic Age

269

Notes   275
Select Bibliography   297
Index   309

"In relation to the true ends of human beings here on earth . . . the state structure is of secondary significance."

Alexander Solzhenitsyn, *From Under the Rubble* (1974)

PREFACE
AND
ACKNOWLEDGMENTS

This book is an expanded version of the Covey Lectures that I delivered at Loyola of Chicago in 1998 on Christian faith and modern liberal democracy. The topic, of course, is a controversial one that has been addressed by many theologians and political philosophers before me. It is part of an ancient debate about religion and politics—the question of how the spiritual and moral teachings of Christianity might be translated into forms of government and political institutions. It is also a vital part of American history, a source of inspiration and conflict since the time of the early Puritans and the American founders. And it remains a lively topic today because Christians of all denominations are taking an active part in politics, and thoughtful participants have wondered how it is possible to reconcile Christian faith with the norms of modern liberal democracy.

What I would like to contribute to the debate is an analysis that takes nothing for granted about this relationship—an analysis that does not assume from the outset that there must be a necessary harmony between Christianity and modern liberal democracy just because many people happen to love both ideals. What is needed is a return to fundamentals that enables us to reexamine the entire relationship. We need to ask honestly: Do Christianity and modern liberal democracy share a common moral vision, or are they opposed and even hostile to each other? Are they inherently compatible or incompatible?

For those who are distrustful of all religion in politics—the confirmed secularists—the answer to these questions is obvious: The two are incompatible. Christianity (and religion in general) are the enemies of liberty and democracy. On the other side, most Christian believers today emphasize compatibility. They see the conflicts of the past as misunderstandings that have been overcome; they welcome modern liberal democracy as a friend and an ally, even though they may criticize some of its features as misguided or downright immoral.

The position that I will take is somewhere between the two conventional views—though I write not as a secular intellectual but as a believing and practicing Catholic. I seek to challenge both the secularists and the committed believers by posing a dilemma that is extremely difficult to resolve. On the one hand, modern liberal democracy needs the Christian religion to support its social and political institutions and to provide a grounding for its deepest moral claims—especially its claims about the innate worth and dignity of every individual. On the other hand, Christianity is not necessarily a liberal or a democratic religion, nor does it make the support of a political order its highest priority. The implications of this dilemma are that the secularists are wrong if they think religion should be kept out of the 'public square'; but religious believers are also mistaken if they think that it is easy to reconcile their faith with the principles and practices of modern liberal democracy.

Regarding the first part of the dilemma, I argue that modern liberal democracy needs a religious basis because its moral claims cannot be vindicated by secular and rational means alone. The weakness of the secular and rational approach can be seen in the philosophers of liberalism (from Locke and Kant to Rorty and Rawls) who have tried to vindicate those claims: They insist on respect for the rights and dignity of everyone, while denying that objective knowledge of the highest good is possible to attain. They also have spread their skeptical views to the general public under the banner of enlightened thinking, badly damaging the moral fabric of democratic society. The lesson I draw is that the secular and rationalist version of modern liberal democracy is the cause of its own decline because it is driven by a 'culture of disbelief' that continuously undermines its foundations. As a corrective, modern democracy needs the faith and morals of Christianity to sustain its deepest assumptions about responsible freedom and human dignity.

The difficulty is that modern democracy's need for a religious basis is no guarantee that one is readily available. As disturbing as it might be for modern believers to admit, the critics of religion have a legitimate point: Christian faith is derived from a revealed book, the Bible, and from church traditions that are not necessarily liberal or democratic in their teachings. The Christian notion of human dignity, for example, is derived from the biblical idea that human beings are made in the image and likeness of God. But it is not clear if the Bible's idea of the divine image in man—the *Imago Dei*—entails political notions like democracy and human rights; in fact, many great theologians of the past understood it to be compatible with kingship, hierarchy, or authoritarian institutions. The Christian view of human dignity is also qualified by a severe view of human sinfulness and by other difficult doctrines—such as, divine election, the hierarchical authority of the church, and the priority of duties to God and neighbor over individual rights. These doctrines are not always easy to square with democratic norms of freedom and equality, nor are they easily discarded without removing the core of the Christian faith.

Thus, we must face the disturbing dilemma that modern liberal democracy needs God, but God is not as liberal or as democratic as we would like Him to be.

My aim in this book is to analyze this dilemma and to suggest a possible solution. In doing so, I try to convey a sense of the many important issues at stake. Most studies have not done so, I believe, because they tend to view the relation between Christianity and democracy as essentially harmonious once the two ways of life are properly understood. And most studies do not ask if democracy is the form of government that best suits the Christian religion, or if it is the only legitimate political system. Because such issues are generally avoided, we lack adequate means for answering crucial questions about faith and politics. I have tried to bring all of the relevant issues together in five lectures, now expanded into five chapters and presented in the form of an 'essay of opinion'—a boldly argued thesis with a minimum of scholarly references that stimulates people to rethink a fundamental issue.

In chapters one and two, I begin by exploring the complex and often troubled relation between Christian faith and modern liberal democracy. I argue that liberalism needs the biblical God for its moral foundations; but I also remind readers that the authors of the Bible and many of the greatest Christian theologians were not particularly liberal or democratic in their political views (in most cases, they supported monarchy, theocracy, and hierarchical institutions). I try to explain the reasons for their views and argue that they cannot be dismissed as readily as they are today. In chapter three, I explain how the Christian tradition evolved from its monarchical and hierarchical past to an acceptance of democracy and human rights in the contemporary world. The most controversial thesis I advance is that contemporary Christians have embraced liberal democracy too closely. They now view it as an unconditional imperative of Christian ethics—as the only form of government compatible with the dignity of man in his full moral maturity—rather than as a conditional good or as the best available option for the present age. I trace the new attitude to the influence of Kant on Christian theology and argue that a 'Kantian imperative' has led modern Christians to exaggerate the ethical and spiritual significance of liberal democracy and to ignore the dangers of democratic tyranny. The net effect has been to soften many of the radical demands of the Christian faith in order to fit the mold of political liberalism.

In chapters four and five, I attempt to restore the proper balance between the spiritual and political realms by recovering St. Augustine's doctrine of the Two Cities—the distinction between the city of God and the earthly city—and applying it to the modern age. Augustine's teaching reminds us that God has divided the created world into two realms that are distinct but not entirely separate from each other. On the one side is the spiritual realm or "city of God," which consists of the entire supernatural order of charity, holiness, and grace, including, though by no means restricted to, the institutional church. This realm is governed by divine law which, in the Christian teaching, is more spiritual than political because it directs man to eternal happiness and does not require a specific political regime or code of civil law. On the other side is the temporal realm or "earthly city" consisting of the state, the economy, the arrangement of social classes, the military, and the rules of warfare; it is secondary to the spiritual realm because it serves the lesser ends of temporal happiness. The point largely forgotten today is that Christianity does not derive political imperatives, either for or against democracy, from divine law but leaves them to prudence guided by a realistic view of man's fallen nature. From the perspective of the Two Cities, the entire modern age of democracy—spanning the last three or four hundred years of historical development—may be nothing more than a temporary blip or transient phase in the rise and fall of the earthly city rather than a significant stage in salvation history or a step toward building the kingdom of God on earth.

This sobering insight about our democratic age does not mean, as some have charged, that Christianity is indifferent to the political world; nor does it imply that Christians are in any way exempt from the duties and responsibilities of citizens, soldiers, and statesmen. Rather, it implies, as Alexander Solzhenitsyn has said (in words expressing my own viewpoint), that "in relation to the true ends of human beings here on earth . . . the state structure is of secondary significance." The meaning of Solzhenitsyn's provocative statement will be elaborated in the pages that follow. But, on a preliminary level, it means that man's spiritual life is higher, nobler, and more permanent than the state's concerns and sets limits on political power while also upholding the legitimate authority of the state as a provider of civil peace and moral order. Following this insight, Solzhenitsyn revives a very old Christian view (the Augustinian view sketched above) that sees the state as an authority instituted by God for the limited and secondary but necessary and important ends of the temporal realm—an approach to politics that I call 'limited government under God' and that I develop into a Christian theory of constitutionalism. My principal contention is that a Christian theory of constitutionalism, derived from the distinction of the Two Cities rather than from the liberal doctrine of private rights, is the best way to resolve the dilemma posed at the beginning. It provides a religious foundation for constitutional government, including certain forms of constitutional democracy, while protecting Christianity from the influence of liberalism and other political ideologies that threaten to turn a lofty spiritual tradition into nothing more than a mirror image of the modern world.

I hope and expect that this thesis will be controversial to secular intellectuals and Christian believers alike. I am therefore extremely grateful for the opportunity to present my case to the general public—an opportunity provided to me by Thomas S. Engeman and John W. Danford, the directors of the Frank M. Covey, Jr., Loyola Lectures in Political Analysis. I thank them warmly for taking a chance on me, a relatively obscure professor from upstate New York, to deliver the Covey Lectures in 1998. During my stay at Loyola of Chicago, Professor Danford and his wife, Karen, were gracious hosts, as were the faculty at Loyola and the graduate students in the political science department (especially Will Jordan and Doug Davis). I hope this book retains some of the freshness and spontaneity of the original lectures, while benefiting from their comments and criticisms.

In addition, I would like to express my gratitude to the Earhart Foundation for supporting the initial research as well as the writing of the book manuscript.

I appreciate as well the generosity of Colgate University's Dean of the Faculty, Jane Pinchin, and the Faculty Development Council at Colgate for providing leave time to work on the Covey Lectures; and I thank Cindy Terrier, our department secretary, for her help in preparing the manuscript and bibliography.

Numerous colleagues and friends also deserve recognition for helping me along the way with this project—Kenneth L. Grasso, Mark C. Henrie, John C. McCarthy, Robert K. Faulkner, Arthur M. Melzer, Barry A. Shain, Stanley C. Brubaker, Thomas L. Pangle, Timothy L. Burns, Peter A. Lawler, Daniel J. Mahoney, Werner J. Dannhauser, Ernest L. Fortin, Thomas G. West, James Wetzel, and James V. Schall, S.J.

CHALLENGING
THE NEW CONSENSUS
IN CHRISTIAN POLITICS

A striking feature of contemporary Christianity is the new consensus that has emerged about politics. Almost all churches and theologians now believe that the form of government most compatible with the Christian religion is democracy. This consensus is so powerful that the only serious debate in Christian politics today is not whether democracy should be preferred to other forms of government, such as monarchy or aristocracy or theocracy, but which kind of democracy is best—liberal democracy based on principles of human rights or socialist democracy based on more radical notions of human liberation. For Christians in the contemporary world, it seems obvious that the Gospel message of care for the poor and universal love requires democratic equality and freedom in one fashion or another.

And yet, what is obvious today has not always been so obvious. One should not forget that the writers of the New Testament, as well as many great Christian theologians of the past, never drew the logical inferences of today. As a result, the Christian tradition for much of its two-thousand-year history has been indifferent to or hostile to democracy and to the various forms of liberalism that have arisen over the centuries. A few general observations will serve as reminders of this sometimes disturbing fact.

In the first place, the Gospels and Epistles hardly speak of politics, let alone democracy (though written in Greek, the New Testament never uses the common term, *democratia*). The few words uttered by

1

Christ on the subject of politics were to distinguish the duties to God from the duties to Caesar—an implicit acceptance of the authority of the Roman emperor in the political realm, without specifying very precisely what that entails beyond paying taxes and treating Caesar as a human authority instead of a god. The ambiguity of the Christian message lay in the clear preference shown by Christ for the poor and the humble over the rich and the powerful, combined with an apparent acceptance of the social and political hierarchies of the day. Not surprisingly, we find Paul and Peter saying in the Epistles—"Let every soul be subject to the governing authorities" (Rom. 13:1) and "Be subject for the Lord's sake to every human institution" (1 Pet. 2:13)—which are general admonitions to obey the established authorities. While these New Testament admonitions do not preclude the distinction between just and unjust authority, they do not point specifically to the superiority of one form of government or social order over another.

For centuries, theologians interpreted the words of Christ and the admonitions of Paul and Peter to support kingship and hierarchical institutions. Consider the views of some of the most influential Christian theologians—St. Augustine, St. Thomas Aquinas, Martin Luther, John Calvin, Richard Hooker, and the early American Puritans. Augustine was basically neutral regarding forms of government, sometimes praising the Roman republic and sometimes praising Christian emperors, while believing that authority as such was necessary to restrain man's sinful nature. Aquinas was more definite about the best form of government; he favored mixed or constitutional monarchy. Luther was an Augustinian authoritarian in his politics, with a strong emphasis on obedience and an aversion to rebellion. John Calvin was distrustful of kings but favored theocracy governed by a spiritual aristocracy. Richard Hooker was an Anglican conservative, a supporter of monarchy and episcopacy against Puritan insurgents. And even many Puritans could agree with the American divine, John Cotton, who said in 1636, "Democracy, I do not conceive that God ever did ordain as a fit government for church or for commonwealth." It is astonishing for us to read these great Christian theologians and to see how far they are from our automatic assumptions that liberal democracy is the best form of government and the one closest to Christian ethics.

In addition to recalling the New Testament and the views of past theologians, one might consider the historical practices of the churches. Here, the record is complex, with many different currents flowing between church and state. I will venture a few generalizations about church history at this point to set the stage for my argument. Regarding the oldest Christian church, the Roman Catholic Church, I would observe that it supported emperors and kings throughout much of its history; and although it also resisted them on many occasions to defend the freedom of the church and the needs of the people, it did not really accept liberal democracy until very recently, when the Second Vatican Council (1962–65) endorsed a qualified version of democratic human rights. The second oldest church, the Eastern Orthodox, was more consistently friendly to emperors and kings than the Western or Roman church because its ideal of Byzantine harmony assumed a close collaboration—sometimes called "Caesaro-Papism"—between monarch and patriarch which lasted into the twentieth century in orthodox nations such as Russia and Greece. The younger Protestant churches are a diverse group; but according to the conventional historical wisdom, only the radical offshoots of the Reformation developed liberal or democratic practices, such as the toleration of Roger Williams or the self-governing "free churches" of Anabaptists and Congregationalists who carried democratic models of church organization into the political realm.[1] And only a few, short-lived millenarian sects, such as the early-sixteenth-century revolutionaries led by Thomas Muntzer, pursued militant visions of radical democracy.

From this brief survey, one is led to a startling conclusion: Today's condition, where most Christian theologians and churches accept democratic politics, is a historical anomaly, a peculiarity of modern times. Even those scholars who have carefully examined earlier periods of Christianity for evidence of democratic and liberal movements that might have existed but were suppressed or ignored—such as, Elaine Pagels, who claims that the Gnostic Gospels advanced democratic social ideals, or Brian Tierney, who finds the origin of natural rights in twelfth-century canon law—concede the basic point: that the Christian tradition has been rather illiberal and undemocratic for much its history.[2] The present democratic consensus is thus quite recent and, I might add, quite astonishing!

If we accept this conclusion, then two obvious questions follow: What caused the change in attitude toward democratic politics by Christian believers? And, was the change justified?

The first question leads to an interesting story in intellectual history about the 'democratization' of Christianity. Many factors have been cited by scholars—late medieval ideas of representation; Protestant ideas of individual conscience and covenanting communities; neo-Scholastic notions of popular sovereignty; the impact of the Enlightenment and the democratic revolutions in America and France on church politics; the impact of rationalistic movements within Christianity, such as Unitarianism and Deism; the struggles of the churches against colonialism, slavery, and the industrial exploitation of workers; the experience of totalitarianism in the twentieth century. All of these factors played a role in democratizing Christianity; and they will be analyzed in chapter three below. But the historical analysis of the causes of change, while enormously fascinating, is ultimately of secondary importance compared to the question: Was the change justified?

This is a momentous question that is extremely difficult to answer. For it is not enough to pull passages from Scripture and draw political lessons, either in favor of kingship or of democracy. Instead, one most investigate a more subtle question that I would formulate as follows: Does Christianity require a specific form of government or political ideology as a direct consequence of divine law or as a moral imperative of its ethical teachings? Or, does Christianity require a prudential approach to all political matters, thereby permitting a variety of legitimate regimes depending on how well they attain the ends of the temporal realm in the given circumstances of time and place?

This distinction between a 'politics of moral imperatives' (to borrow from Kant) and a 'politics of prudence' (to borrow from Russell Kirk) is crucial in trying to make a judgment about the present relation of Christianity and modern democracy. For, as I shall argue, the main difference between the older and the more recent theologians is not simply a difference between monarchists and democrats. Rather, the older theologians adopted a prudential approach because their view of politics was largely shaped by the Augustinian doctrine of the Two Cities—the distinction between the city of God and the earthly city. They did not think that the spiritual order of God directly determined the political order of the earthly city. Instead, they made their political judgments by using prudence, guided by natural law (the predominantly Catholic approach) or by a notion of the limited ends of the state in the sinful world (the predominantly Protestant approach). By contrast, modern theologians have closed the gap between the Two Cities. They argue that the spiritual and ethical teachings of Christianity have a political dimension that necessarily entails one specific form of government, namely, democracy and especially liberal democracy founded on human rights.

If we ask how modern Christians justify closing the gap between their faith and a specific form of government or political ideology, the answer, I believe, lies in a *heightened sensitivity to the demands of human dignity in the modern age.* One can detect this heightened sensitivity in many church leaders, theologians, and lay scholars who have argued that an intimate connection exists between Christianity and modern liberal democracy.

For example, among Catholics, the influential figure Jacques Maritain has written numerous books arguing that democracy is evangelical—inspired by the Gospel and its teaching that every human being has equal spiritual dignity before God, which led over many centuries in the West to the rights of man and eventually to Maritain's teaching that the dignity of the human person requires democracy. Similarly, the "Declaration on Religious Freedom" by the Second Vatican Council begins with the statement that "a sense of the dignity of the human person has been impressing itself more and more on the consciousness of contemporary man" and infers from this dignity that the "human person has a right to religious freedom." One might also cite Catholic neoconservatives, such as Michael Novak, George Weigel, and Paul Johnson, who believe, as Johnson says, that "Christianity, with its stress on the individual, did carry with it the notion of inalienable rights, slowly though it matured."[3]

Among Protestants, a similar convergence is supported by a long tradition of scholarship that links the leading theological ideas of the Reformation—the priesthood of all believers and the sanctity of unmediated conscience—with modern democracy and religious freedom.[4] Sometimes it is argued that the American political tradition, from the congregationalism of the early Puritans to the Declaration of Independence to the United States Constitution, is an exercise in the practical application of Protestant ideas—in what H. Richard Niebuhr has called the "constructive Protestantism" of the American churches.[5] Sometimes the whole Bible, from the Hebrew prophets to Jesus and the early Christians, is seen as the source of modern democracy because it established the "exalted individual" or "the infinite value of the personality" as the spiritual center of Western politics.[6] Further developments by Protestant ministers such as Martin Luther King, Jr. and Archbishop Desmond Tutu of South Africa have deeply influenced the Christian conception of civil rights. As Bishop Tutu said in "Religious Human Rights and the Bible": It was the "egalitarianism of the Bible . . . that fired our struggle against apartheid—the incredible sense of the infinite worth of each person created in the image of God . . . inviolate, possessing a dignity that is intrinsic . . . that is what invests them with preciousness and from this stems all kinds of rights."[7]

One might add to this list of influential Christian leaders the names of more secular thinkers and philosophers who have argued for the religious roots of modern democratic politics. Secularized Christians, such as Alexis de Tocqueville, as well as post-Christians, like Georg W. F. Hegel, and even anti-Christians, like Friedrich Nietzsche, could all agree with Nietzsche's statement that "the democratic movement is the heir of the Christian movement."[8]

The powerful thought that runs through all of these thinkers is that Christianity introduced a revolutionary idea into world history—the equal dignity and infinite worth of every human being in the eyes of God—and that the full social and political implications of this idea were hidden by prejudice and intolerance for many centuries until they emerged in the modern age as the democratic idea of equality and the liberal idea of respect for individual human rights. According to this view, Christianity and modern democracy share a common moral vision and, when properly understood, mutually support each other. They are like two sides of the same coin—the sacred and secular aspects of a common conception of human dignity.

But now we must raise the difficult question: Is this interpretation true, or, is it merely a form of wishful thinking, generated by people who love two noble ideals, Christianity and democracy, which they have mistakenly fused together in their hearts and minds? To this question, a cautious person with some historical perspective might respond that such a grand convergence is highly improbable. It sounds too sweeping to say that Judaism and the Hebrew prophets, Christianity in its Catholic, Orthodox, and Protestant forms, as well as the American and French Revolutions are all converging toward a common conception of freedom and dignity. A less cautious person might say that such a theory is cowardly because it denies the reality of exclusive choices in life. The formula I prefer reflects many of the doubts about a grand convergence theory or even a common moral vision, without abandoning hope for a practical accommodation. In my view, we are confronted with a perplexing dilemma whose first part is the proposition that modern liberal democracy needs the Christian religion to support its basic moral claims, and whose second part is the disturbing proposition that Christianity is not inherently a liberal or democratic religion nor a religion that offers a direct political message.

I shall now turn to the first part of the dilemma and attempt to explain why modern democracy needs a religious foundation to support its claims about freedom and human dignity. After that, I will explain why the Bible and many great Christian theologians understood these terms in radically different ways than modern liberals and democrats. Finally, I will suggest how Christianity and modern democracy can establish a practical working relation that does not foster the illusion of convergence but accepts the enduring tensions that exist (and will continue to exist until the end of time) between the demands of the heavenly and earthly cities.

CHAPTER ONE

WHY MODERN
LIBERAL DEMOCRACY
NEEDS GOD

Democracy is a form of government in which the people hold the supreme power rather than a single person or a few privileged elites. Throughout history, this form of government has come in many different sizes and shapes, but most have been short-lived and relatively powerless. Among the ancient Greeks, democracies flourished in Athens and a few other city-states during the fifth and fourth centuries B.C. and then permanently disappeared after they were overthrown by foreign conquerors. During the Italian Renaissance, democracies or small republics were established in Florence and other cities but were dissolved after brief periods by factionalism. More enduring democratic traditions were established by the Swiss cantons and Dutch republics, though they played a minor role in world history. On the whole, the ancient democracies and the republics of the free city-states have been weak and transient phenomena compared to the kings and emperors who ruled the world.

In the past few centuries, however, a new species of democracy has appeared—modern liberal democracy—that has changed the course of history and made the democratic form of government the most powerful in the world. It arose in the seventeenth and eighteenth centuries among the nations of Western Europe and America by advancing new ideas of freedom and equality that challenged the old regimes of absolute monarchy, aristocracy, and theocracy. By the end of the nineteenth century, the successes of liberal democracy over its traditional rivals led many to believe that it was destined to sweep the world by the inevitable forces of historical progress. But the devastation of world wars and the rise of totalitarianism in the twentieth century shattered that naive illusion; and liberal democracy was embattled for most of that century. It was almost defeated by fascism in World War II; and shortly thereafter in the Cold War, it struggled to maintain its resolve in an apparent stalemate against communism. And yet, surprisingly, liberal democracy emerged victorious from all these struggles and stands at the beginning of the twenty-first century as the dominant force in the world.

From this success story, some scholars have drawn the conclusion that liberal democracy has permanently triumphed over all other political ideologies and that its principles provide the only source of legitimacy for governments in the modern world.[1] In my judgment, this thesis is vastly overstated and tends to hide the weaknesses and anxieties that underlie the liberal democracies of the modern Western world. Those weaknesses and anxieties are reflected in the fact that most political leaders and citizens are unsure about the overall purpose and direction of modern democracy, and the most influential thinkers are uncertain about how to defend its fundamental principles. Surely it is a sign of confusion and loss of purpose when the most common argument that one hears today in defense of liberal democracy derives from moral relativism—from the denial of objective truth about good and evil which seems to suggest that liberal democracy is preferable because it permits any kind of behavior within the limits of the law. As Pope John Paul II has observed, "Nowadays there is a tendency to claim that agnosticism and skeptical relativism are the philosophy and the basic attitude which correspond to democratic forms of political life. Those who are convinced that they know the truth and firmly adhere to it are considered unreliable from a democratic point of view. [But] . . . if there is no ultimate truth to guide and direct political activity, then ideas and convictions can easily be manipulated for reasons of power."[2]

In this climate of opinion, it is necessary to return to fundamentals and to rethink the entire justification for liberal democracy, first, by identifying its essential moral claims and then, by asking if they are defensible on rational or on religious grounds. My procedure will be to begin with a comparison of ancient and modern democracy in order to show that the distinctive feature of modern liberal democracy is a notion of justice whose fundamental assumptions are the intrinsic worth and dignity of every human being and the preeminence of the human species in the natural universe. I will then show that liberal democracy is unable to vindicate these lofty claims about human dignity, either on the practical level of daily living in a modern mass society or on the theoretical level in the arguments of the liberal philosophers. Hence, I shall conclude, liberal democracy cannot stand on its own and needs support from the biblical claim that human beings are made in the image and likeness of God.

Ancient Greek Democracy

In order to see the distinctive claims of modern liberal democracy, it is useful to compare it with democracy in the ancient world. Such comparisons have been a major theme of political philosophers and historians for centuries.[3] In most cases, the analysis consists in pointing out differences between ancient and modern democracies (or republics) on such issues as the optimal size of the state, the use of representative institutions, and the underlying ethos or culture of democracy, leading to a judgment about which kind of democracy is better. The following account will be a brief distillation of this great debate, with special attention paid to the way that ancient and modern democracies justify their claims to rule.

In the ancient Greek world, the prime example of democracy was Athens, a relatively small city-state in which citizens participated directly in political deliberations and held office through frequent rotation. Citizenship was restricted to free adult males of Athenian parentage, which meant that only about 30,000 inhabitants were Athenian citizens and another 200,000 were noncitizens of differing status. The citizens exercised their power through various deliberative bodies—in the Assembly where every citizen could speak and participate in lawmaking, in the Council of 500 selected by lot for administration, and in the people's courts, also selected by lot.[4] Although citizenship was restricted to a small circle, that circle was egalitarian and participatory in nature, making Athens the model of a direct democracy.

In trying to understand the ethos or culture of Athenian democracy, one should beware of simple characterizations. While its admirers emphasize an ethos of civic virtue and patriotism, few are willing to acknowledge that its elevation of public concerns over private life was not motivated primarily by altruism or self-sacrifice. The spirit of virtue in the ancient democracies is best captured by the word "manliness"—meaning admiration for toughness and strength, love of dominating and exploiting others, and a zest for competing unabashedly for honors in public activities. Virtue was the manly contest to be the greatest in war, oratory, office holding, and public spectacles. As Paul Rahe says in his magisterial history of ancient and modern republics: "To be great and brilliant, to shine . . . this was the desire that animated the Greek *polis.* . . . Political liberty was the opportunity to do or say something of note . . . [which] the poet Simonides [explained by saying] that 'man is distinguished from other animals by his desire for honor . . . [a desire that] grows up only in those judged to be real men (*andres*).'"5

Scholars who are less admiring of Greek democracy also point out that this ethos of virtue was combined with a hard-nosed brand of class politics. The economic and social basis of Athenian democracy was the lower middle class: the small farmers, craftsmen, free laborers, shopkeepers, and sailors of the Athenian navy. These were "the people"—the *demos*—of Athenian democracy. They acquired supreme power in the city of Athens through the reforms of Cleisthenes in 508 B.C. and maintained their dominance over the upper classes of noble birth and new wealth for almost one hundred eighty years (except for two brief periods of oligarchic reaction). Cleisthenes empowered the people not only by making them citizens and giving them equality under the law but also by instituting the practice of "ostracism"—the official act of voting to expel citizens from Athens if they were thought to be too great or powerful. Ostracism was a weapon of class warfare, although it could be considered mild because the usual banishment was temporary (typically ten years) and much milder than other forms of class warfare, such as the guillotining of aristocrats after the French Revolution. Moreover, the Athenians continued to trust select members of old aristocratic families for leadership roles, such as Cleisthenes himself and great generals like Pericles and Alcibiades. The historian Thucydides even notes that under Pericles, the leader of Athenian democracy during its golden age (from about 450–430 B.C.), Athens was really a government of one man. Nevertheless, Pericles governed by maintaining his popularity among the masses and broadening the democratic basis of the regime.[6]

Class politics and the cult of manly virtue, however, were not the only ingredients of Athenian culture; it was also shaped by a sense of ethnic superiority and religious tribalism. The Greeks believed they were superior to the barbarians; and the Athenians believed they were superior to other Greeks, specially protected by the goddess Athena. The Athenian superiority complex was partly due to the legend that they were the only indigenous Greeks—the only Greeks who had always occupied their land (in contrast, it was said, to the Spartans, who came from outside and conquered the indigenous people, the Helots, making them their slaves). The Athenians also believed in their superiority because of the more substantial claim that they led all the Greeks in defeating the Persians, a feat that Herodotus specifically attributes to the pride of the Athenians as freemen who no longer worked for a master but for themselves.[7]

As a result of their sense of superiority, the Athenians felt they were justified in seeking an empire over other Greeks after the Persian wars. In their imperial policy, the Athenians frequently imposed democracy on their colonies, which may sound like an early version of modern American idealism: spreading a universal ideal of democracy and bringing the blessings of freedom to all. But the truth is much less idealistic. The Athenians spread democracy out of self-interest and desire for dominance, creating groups of democratic partisans in the colonies who would be loyal to their Athenian masters. As one classical scholar notes in comparing ancient and modern democracy: "The openness of domination in antiquity [meant] the absence of ideological cover for empire. Pericles boasted to the Athenians that 'no subject of ours can complain of being ruled by unworthy people.' That is as near to an ideological statement as [one] can find about empire."[8]

In sum, Athenian democracy was not only a public assembly for the exercise of virtue and self-governance; it was also a blood-and-soil tribe of warriors, united as a defensive brotherhood against the powerful elites of the city and as an imperialistic army against other cities, races, and gods.[9] The ethos of Athenian democracy, we may therefore infer, was entirely shaped from instinctive drives and popular beliefs—about class solidarity, manliness, and a form of patriotism derived from ethnic superiority and quasi-religious tribalism—rather than from philosophical theories; it was a prerational culture, arising from practical needs and primordial instincts rather than from theoretical reflection.

This fact is particularly striking because the Greek city-states, and Athens especially during the democratic period, were full of philosophers, some living as citizens and some as outsiders. Yet, the great philosophers of antiquity were almost uniformly opposed to democracy and highly critical of Athenian democracy in particular. As one classical scholar notes in astonishment: "The greatest democracy of Greece [produced] no statement of democratic political theory. All the Athenian political philosophers . . . were in various degrees oligarchic [i.e., elitist] in sympathy. . . . Socrates, so far as we can trace his views . . . was at least highly critical of democracy. Plato's [antidemocratic] views . . . are too well known to need stating. Isocrates in his earlier years wrote panegyrics of Athens, but [later in] his more philosophical works became increasingly embittered against the political regime of his native city. Aristotle is the most judicious, and states the pros and cons, but his ideal was a widely based oligarchy [i.e., aristocracy]. With the historians, the same bias is evident . . . Thucydides is hostile: In one of the few passages where he reveals his personal views he expresses approval of a regime which disenfranchised about two-thirds of the citizens, [including] those who manned the fleet on which the survival of Athens depended. Xenophon was an ardent admirer of the Spartan regime. Aristotle, in the historical part of the Constitution of Athens, followed, rather uncritically, a source with a marked oligarchic bias. Only the fourth century orators [such as Demosthenes] were democrats; and their speeches, being mostly concerned with practical political issues . . . have little to say on the basic principles of democracy, which they take for granted."[10]

It is hard for us living in the modern world, where many democratic revolutions have been inspired by philosophical theories, to understand the world of classical antiquity where the philosophers and the people diverged so markedly in their political views. The people, and even many of the statesmen of Athenian democracy, simply did not need philosophical theories to justify their rule or to give legitimacy to a regime that was so deeply rooted in instinctive power relations among classes and races—in the common people's sense of being a band of brothers united against common foes (against the rich above, the slaves below, and the foreigners outside). The closest the people came to possessing a democratic ideology was in using slogans about equality: *isonomia,* equality under the law, and *isegoria,* equality of speech. But these slogans originally were applied to aristocrats and only later were extended to accommodate the growing sense of power among the people.[11]

Thus, when Socrates says in Plato's *Republic* (563b) that democracy is governed by the "law of equality and freedom" or when Aristotle in his *Politics* (1280a, 1310a) describes the democratic view of justice as "the equality of free-born citizens," we may wonder if these accounts are not already a kind of abstract and rationalized version of what typical Athenian citizens felt about their regime. The philosophers use words like equality and freedom and make them sound as if they were universal principles, describing the form of democracy itself. But the Athenians never intended to apply them universally and cannot be accused of hypocrisy (as modern democrats may be accused) when they granted citizenship only to adult males of pure Athenian ancestry who, although not rich, were not born as slaves.

Even after rationalizing the implicit democratic view of justice, the classical philosophers were not impressed with its claims. The main objection of Socrates, Plato, Aristotle, and others was that democracy was hostile to real virtue—understood, not merely as manly competition for greatness, but as a rationally ordered soul, in which reason ruled the irrational desires, that was perfected above all by the philosopher and secondarily by liberally educated gentlemen. The classical philosophers saw in the democratic notion of equality, not the equal opportunity to compete for honors that Pericles praised and Athenians cherished, but the leveling effect of common people on the manners of educated gentlemen and on the rationality of the philosophers. And they saw in the democratic practice of freedom an indulgence of lower, animal pleasures or an indiscriminate indulgence of both higher and lower pleasures that prevented the full development of reason, the highest faculty of the human soul.

Thus, the classical philosophers judged democracy to be contrary to human dignity as they understood it—contrary, that is, to the elevation of man above the other animals through the perfection of the unique human capacity for rational discourse (*logos*). From this point of view, democracy is either prerational or subrational; and any attempt to enhance its dignity would require changing it into an aristocracy of wisdom and virtue.

MODERN LIBERAL DEMOCRACY

How strange this account of democracy sounds to modern ears! Both the description of ancient democracy and the attitude of the philosophers toward the democratic way of life are alien to us. That is because the kind of democracy familiar to us—modern liberal democracy, embodied above all in the American republic and in British parliamentary government—is radically different from ancient Greek democracy. Hence, the common saying that 'Athens is the birthplace of democracy' is true only in the narrow sense that democracy first arose in ancient Athens. It is false as an account of the origins of modern democracy. The genus may be the same, but the species are different.

In other words, the term 'democracy' may be applied to both ancient and modern kinds because the regimes in question are based on the rule of the people. Moreover, certain external similarities exist, such as the common terminology of equality, freedom, and citizenship as well as the classical style of architecture which the American founders employed in our government buildings. But none of the external resemblances changes the fact that ancient and modern democracy are two distinct species of government, differing significantly in matters of scale, institutional arrangements, and ethos or culture.

Unlike the democracies that existed in the ancient Greek city-states or in some of the Italian city-states during the Renaissance, modern liberal democracy arose in the great nation-states of modern Western Europe and America. Comparatively speaking, the democracies of the modern nations have been large in scale, covering vast territories and incorporating hundreds of thousands and eventually millions of citizens. It is often remarked by scholars, and proclaimed in *The Federalist Papers* (no. 9), that this difference in size or scale is made possible by the device of representation—the delegation of authority by the people to a few persons through elections—which was unknown to the ancients and must be regarded as an invention of modern political science. Such a claim would be boastful exaggeration if it were understood to mean that an institutional device like representation was inconceivable to the dim-witted ancients. After all, the delegation of authority to a few is not hard to imagine, if one is so inclined. One could even argue that representation existed in some fashion in Athens when, contrary to the normal practice of choosing officials by lot, the Athenians elected their generals, on the assumption that decisions about military strategy required special expertise as well as accountability. It can also be found in the office of the Tribune among the Romans, whose republic was dominated by the patricians of the Senate but which allowed popular representation by two tribunes selected to defend the interests of the common people.

One may infer, then, that it was not the inconceivability of a specific institutional device that prevented the ancients from developing representative democracy. Rather, the very notion of representation seemed undesirable to them because only direct or participatory democracy permitted the competition for public honors by all citizens. Size and institutional arrangements are therefore not the decisive factors in determining the character of a democratic regime; something more fundamental is at work. The large-scale representative democracies of the modern age were made possible by a new ethos or culture whose ingredients must now be identified.

The most common view equates the culture of ancient democracy with virtue and that of modern liberal democracy with commerce. In the unforgettable words of Rousseau, "Ancient politicians talked incessantly about morals and virtue, those of our time talk only of business and money."[12] For Rousseau, the ancients were citizens, while the moderns are bourgeois—the former inspired by patriotism to subordinate private interest to the public good, the latter concerned primarily with middle-class status and motivated by enlightened self-interest. Rousseau's portrait, of course, is a caricature, which must be qualified by pointing out that America has a strong ethos of civic virtue and participation in local self-government and noble traditions of military service. After making such corrections, however, one must acknowledge that displays of civic and military virtue are the exception and that the dominant moral qualities of modern democracies are in fact *bourgeois* virtues—the habits of industry, rationality, and peaceful self-absorption that are required for successful careers in business and other middle-class professions. The channeling of most energies into middle-class careerism means that private life takes precedence over public life, which requires the delegation of political responsibilities to representatives.

Despite this emphasis, the ethos of modern liberal democracy contains a passion for justice which, if not comparable to ancient virtue, is also not reducible to bourgeois careerism or a life of private retirement. The inspiring idealism of liberal democracy arises from its foundation on bold principles that claim to be rational and universal in their appeal. Those principles, of course, are *the rights of man, otherwise known as natural rights or human rights* because they are inherent in human nature. Though embryonic notions of rights may be found in medieval sources (a point I will discuss later), they were not given a systematic rational defense until the philosophers of the Enlightenment did so in the seventeenth and eighteenth centuries. Their doctrine was later called liberalism, which combined the liberal principle of securing the rights and liberties of individuals with the democratic principle of government by consent of the people, producing a new political phenomenon, 'liberal democracy.'

Herein lies the major difference between ancient and modern democracy. Whereas the ethos of ancient democracy was shaped by instinctive drives and popular beliefs rather than by teachings of philosophers (most of whom opposed democracy), the ethos of modern democracy has been decisively shaped by the theoretical doctrines of philosophers or intellectuals who became the greatest champions of democracy. As a result, Hegel could say of the most dramatic democratic revolution of his age, "The [French] Revolution received its first impulse *from philosophy*."[13] This point was also made in critical fashion by Edmund Burke who adamantly opposed the influence of philosophical doctrines in politics, which he considered theoretical abstractions that were inherently revolutionary and dangerous. Burke analyzed the three great democratic revolutions of the modern age—the Glorious Revolution of 1688 in England, the American Revolution of 1776, and the French Revolution of 1789—and came to the conclusion that the English and American Revolutions were justified because they were based on custom, tradition, and practical experience rather than the abstract theory of the rights of man which inspired the French Revolution. Yet, even Burke may have underestimated the influence of theoretical doctrines on the English and American Revolutions and on modern liberal democracy in general.

One only has to notice that all three of these revolutions were accompanied by official proclamations or "declarations"—the English Declaration of Rights passed by the British Parliament shortly after the Glorious Revolution, the American Declaration of Independence proclaiming the colonies to be free and independent states, and the French Declaration of the Rights of Man and of the Citizen passed by the National Assembly shortly after it assumed sovereign power. These declarations showed the need of all three nations to publicly proclaim and rationally justify their revolutions by appealing to the basic principles of liberal democracy—namely, the rights of individuals and government by consent of the governed.

Consider the case of England's Glorious Revolution. While its immediate effect was to replace a Catholic king, James II, with a Protestant king and queen, William and Mary, and to require a Protestant succession, the revolution also had two long-term effects. One was to change the constitutional balance in favor of parliamentary sovereignty. Though Burke insists that Parliament declined to assert its sovereignty at this moment, its written act indicates that it did. The Declaration of Rights passed in 1688 not only settles the monarch's religion "by authority of the present parliament . . . forever"; but Parliament more generally states that "*for vindicating . . . ancient rights and liberties* . . . the pretended power of suspending laws or execution of laws, by regal authority, *without consent of parliament*, is illegal."[14] Beyond this affirmation of rights and of parliamentary consent, the revolution marked a shift away from the whole notion of divine right. The belief that kings are divinely ordained to rule was being replaced by the liberal democratic notion that legitimate authority inheres in the representatives of the people as the most trusted protectors of individual rights.

In the American Declaration, the same principles are presented in more sweeping terms. Liberty is clearly spelled out in terms of the inalienable natural rights to life, liberty, and the pursuit of happiness. Equality is asserted as a self-evident truth and refers not only to the enumerated rights but also to the principle that "governments are instituted among men, deriving their just powers from the consent of the governed." Equality is linked to government by consent because, as Lincoln later explained, the fundamental meaning of equality is that "no man is good enough to govern another man, without that other's consent."[15] Equality, therefore, supplies the premise of democratic consent and liberty denotes the end, the exercise of inalienable rights.

When understood in this fashion, the principles of the English and American Revolutions are similar (though not identical) to those of the French Revolution. Shortly after the Third Estate proclaimed itself the National Assembly and the representative of the French nation, beginning the revolution, it passed its famous Declaration of the Rights of Man which states that all "men are born and remain free and equal in their rights" and the end of every political association is to secure these rights. It then adds that the nation as a whole is the sovereign authority and that "law is the expression of the general will . . . [in which] every citizen has a right to participate personally, or through his representative."[16] Thus, the official doctrine of the French Revolution asserts notions of freedom and equality that justify the sovereignty of the nation or general will of the people (expressed directly or through representatives) and the rights of man.

This survey of public declarations illustrates the self-consciously ideological nature of modern democracy in comparison to ancient democracy. Even though it suggests that Burke understated the role of abstract principles in the English and American cases (he never mentions Jefferson and Paine in connection with the American Revolution), it does not deny Burke's comparative judgment of the three revolutions: the English was the least ideological, the American was more ideological, and the French was the most ideological democratic revolution. Nor does it deny that other factors besides philosophical principles were at work in the modern democratic revolutions— factors such as class warfare, personal honor and love of military glory, ethnic pride and nationalism, and other prerational motives that shaped ancient democracy. Nor does it rule out the influence of religion, particularly, Protestant Christianity in shaping notions of political authority (although this influence is often misunderstood, as we shall see). After making all of these qualifications, however, the fact remains that modern liberal democracies have been shaped by philosophical doctrines in a way that previous regimes never were; and the decisive doctrine is the philosophy of liberalism.

If we probe the foundations of this philosophy, we reach the deepest level of modern liberal democratic culture: the new notion of *human dignity* that underlies individual rights and democratic consent. The modern notion of human dignity has many dimensions. The first is the dignity of the individual, meaning the inherent worth of every person as a responsible moral agent, possessing independent judgment and free will. This could be called rational autonomy, for it implies the capacity of individuals to make rational choices for themselves; it could also be called willful autonomy, for it often involves raw assertions of the will in creating a unique personal identity. The second dimension of human dignity is political, the dignity of a people or a nation that freely chooses its destiny. This is sometimes referred to (in the language of the United Nations) as national self-determination or (in the American tradition) as republican self-government.

If we search for the common basis of these two dimensions of human dignity, the personal and the political, it may be found in the underlying metaphysical and cosmological view that is most characteristic of the modern mind—the belief that the universe is ordered by scientific laws that are indifferent to man, requiring human beings to assert their own dignity by showing that they are autonomous beings and masters of their fate. In the modern view of human dignity, God and nature may exist as causes of order in the universe but man's rational constructions and willful creations take precedence as sources of human dignity or worth. Though this view of human dignity may not be stated explicitly by every liberal philosopher, it is present in some fashion in all versions of philosophical liberalism.[17] And though it may not be recognized in such grand theoretical terms by ordinary citizens of democratic nations, it is present in everyone who finds a sense of dignity in his or her independent judgment, in self-reliant living, in a unique personal identity, and in the pride of participating in national self-determination. In short, a specific view of human dignity is the underlying assumption of the individual rights and self-government of modern liberal democracy.

Consider how it animates the exercise of rights. What individuals call their natural or human rights are the claims they make against authority for protections and entitlements. Rights are designed to prevent authorities of all kinds (political, religious, paternal) from interfering in one's life in the name of superior wisdom and virtue or to assert their arbitrary power. 'Don't tread on me!' was the slogan of the Sons of Liberty during the American Revolution that expressed this view of rights. Such rights demand a zone of privacy that is off-limits to the state. They may even go further and demand goods and services from political authorities. Rights, in other words, are claims for protections and immunities or for entitlements that put authority on the defensive. But claims against authority are only half of the argument for rights—the negative or defensive half that aims at protecting people from the violence of tyrants and the persecutions of self-righteous crusaders. In addition, rights presuppose individuals who are capable of enlightened thinking and independent judgment that frees their minds from the intellectual slavery that Thomas Hobbes called the "kingdom of darkness." This project of enlightening the people shows great confidence in ordinary citizens to think for themselves—an affirmation of their freedom and dignity that is more fundamental than the fear and selfishness that Hobbes also attributes to them. The same confidence in the independent judgment of the people was later developed into a theory of rational autonomy by Kant and eventually into a theory of willful autonomy by the romantic theorists of individuality. In all cases, the affirmation of independent thinking confers a status on individuals that raises their rights claims from defensive protections to a near-sacred principle of human dignity.

The same may be said of democracy's principle of government by consent. Its premise is a basic equality among people, which the Declaration of Independence asserts to be self-evident but which later generations of Americans had to explain and to justify. As we noted, Lincoln explained the meaning of equality by saying that no one is good enough to govern others without their consent. The flip-side of this proposition is that, even though human beings are unequal in many respects, everyone has a sufficient moral capacity to govern himself. In Lincoln's eyes, the question of "the capability of a people to govern themselves" had universal significance; indeed, he sometimes spoke as if it had cosmic significance—that the American experiment in republican self-government was "the last best hope of earth."

Why did it matter so much? The most plausible answer, which Lincoln did not develop philosophically, is that republican self-government is the ultimate test of human dignity. If the people could not meet the challenge, even when led by great statesmen like himself, and the nation spun out of control, driven by the destructive passions for expansion, slavery, and secession, then the logical conclusion would be that the people and their elected leaders needed a master of some kind to control them. The capability of a people to govern themselves is a test of human dignity because it is a test of moral responsibility—of the ability of the human race to progress to the point where people can take charge of their lives and act like mature adults rather than like children or slaves who were forever dependent on a self-appointed authority figure to govern them. Lincoln's words resonate with modern democratic citizens precisely because they mean that, if government by the people perishes from this earth, then the dignity of man would be lost; and humanity would be thrown back to a condition where all but a few were kept in child-like dependence and servitude.

This is a remarkable claim that raises some difficult questions. Does it mean that, prior to the democratic revolutions in England, America, and France, people lacked human dignity—that they were not, in a sense, human, or were even subhuman? Does it mean that the success of certain political experiments is required to vindicate the dignity of man? Such thoughts seem to be implied in the statements of two other great American statesmen, Jefferson and Hamilton. At the beginning of *The Federalist Papers*, Hamilton equates passage of the newly written Federal Constitution with a historic test: "Whether societies of men are really capable or not of establishing good government from reflection and choice, or whether they are forever destined to depend . . . on accident and force." Hamilton's warning is that a wrong decision at this historic moment would be considered "the general misfortune of mankind."[18] His reasoning is that subjection to the arbitrary dictates of accident and force—fatalism, in other words—is the greatest insult to human dignity, while mastery of one's fate through rational choice is the greatest tribute to human dignity. Hamilton's description of the deliberation about the Constitution raises the event to a world-historic test of human dignity.

A more radical statement of the same idea can be found in Jefferson's shocking defense of the Jacobin Terror of the French Revolution. Although the Terror led to the deaths of thousands in the name of the rights of man, Jefferson cooly argues that it was worth the price, even if most were innocent victims. They died like noncombatants in a great war, Jefferson says, and then adds, in a very revealing choice of words: "Rather than [the French Revolution] should have failed, I would have seen half the earth desolated. Were there but *an Adam and an Eve left in every country and left free*, it would be better than it now is."[19] The implication is that the human race begins anew, or rather for the first time, with the French Revolution. Hence, it does not matter if many people were killed, so long as one man and one woman were left, who, now being free for the first time in history, would repopulate the world with free human beings. Like a new Adam and Eve, they would become the true originators of humanity. The implication is that before the rights of man were proclaimed, people were barely recognizable as human beings because their minds were enslaved to superstition and the mystifications of authority; but after the American and French Revolutions, they attained their human dignity for the first time by exercising their independent judgment and taking responsibility for their lives.

Following Jefferson, those who see republican self-government as the decisive test of human dignity oppose any authority that stands above the will of the people, including the chiefs and village elders of most tribal societies, or the kings and priests of feudal societies, or

Plato's philosopher-kings. These 'higher authorities' are almost as great an insult to the modern notion of human dignity as the tyrants, dictators, and slave-masters of the world. For even though the traditional authorities may be benevolent, they are essentially paternalistic and threaten the autonomy, independence, or sense of cosmic responsibility required for the modern democratic sense of human dignity.

This sense is so deep and pervasive in modern culture that it can be found in other realms besides ethics and politics. It underlies modern technology and economics and explains why liberal democracy goes hand in hand with industrial and technological society. The goal of technology is to make us "the masters and owners of nature," in Descartes' words, which is driven by more than a desire to relieve suffering and increase material comforts. It is also rooted in an unwillingness to be subject to the forces of nature or to be at the mercy of a hostile and indifferent environment, a sense of pride in controlling human destiny through technology. Likewise, the driving force behind modern economics extends beyond the desire to overcome the pain and suffering of poverty and to enjoy creature comforts. A more fundamental motive is the desire for self-improvement, which means overcoming fatalism and resignation to one's lot in life and becoming instead the master of one's fate by hard work and rational planning.

Modern liberal democracy is thus composed of many strands—individual rights, republican self-government, technological mastery, and economic improvement—that together form a unified culture whose deepest, underlying premise is a notion of human dignity that equates dignity with autonomy and mastery of one's fate. Although this interpretation sounds grandiose, it accurately reflects the tendency of modern liberal democracy to raise politics to a metaphysical, cosmological, or quasi-religious level. It seeks to transcend narrow regime politics, in which one group rules over others, and aims at something that is truly universal—the good of all humanity, the inherent dignity of the human species. Modern liberal democracy, therefore, is more than a political system; it is a philosophy of freedom and a theoretical doctrine of human dignity translated into practical action.

CAN LIBERALISM VINDICATE HUMAN DIGNITY?

With the stakes of politics raised so high, it is only fair to ask if modern liberal democracy and its theoretical defenders have been able to deliver on their promise to uphold and to vindicate human dignity. The question may be answered on two levels. One is the practical level of daily living in which the characteristic way of life found in modern liberal democracies is evaluated, with special attention to the issue of whether it elevates or lowers the dignity of man. Here, I take the side of the theorists of "mass society," the great critics of modern democracy who have argued that the majority of people has been raised in certain material and psychological respects but the overall aim and tone of modern society have been lowered, resulting in a net diminution of human dignity. The second level of evaluation is theoretical; it means evaluating the arguments of the liberal philosophers from the seventeenth to the twentieth centuries. Here again, I take the side of the critics. I believe that the dominant schools of liberalism have followed a flawed strategy of trying to vindicate human dignity by denying the objective existence of a greatest good, thereby allowing each person or nation to determine its own identity. But this strategy is self-defeating, I shall argue, because it slides inevitably from liberalism to moral relativism and undermines all possible grounds for justice and respect. The critique of liberalism will prepare us for a fresh look at the need for a Christian foundation for liberal democracy.

Turning first to the practical level, I would argue that evaluating the characteristic way of life in modern liberal democracies requires us to examine a difficult trade-off. On the one hand, the modern democratic principle of equal respect for every individual has the inspiring effect of opening the world to individual talent by removing the advantages of hereditary privilege and overcoming the barriers of discrimination based on religion, race, and gender. On the other hand (and this is the point that usually goes unnoticed by enthusiasts for modern democracy), the same principle of equal justice has the unavoidable side effect and negative consequence of lowering the ultimate goals and aspirations of society. The simplest description of this change is the replacement of 'high culture' with 'popular culture'— the replacement of a culture that aspires to spiritual, philosophical, artistic, and heroic greatness with one dedicated to mundane pursuits and the tastes of ordinary people. While one might argue that the change in goals is not connected to a political revolution, I believe that the new goals are deeply intertwined with liberal democracy's cherished ideals of equality and freedom and have had a profound effect in lowering the aspirations of the human soul.

In a democratic age, the great monuments of high culture lose their appeal, except as objects in a museum. The noblest achievements of Western civilization—such as classical philosophy and poetry as well as classical art and architecture; the culture of the High Middle Ages, including Gothic architecture and Latin scholasticism; great modern literature from Shakespeare to Tolstoy and great modern music from Bach to Wagner; as well as the whole tradition of liberal arts education—seem too aristocratic or too 'high-brow,' too judgmental and demanding, for most people in a democratic society. Not only do the masses of people feel justified in ignoring them, but the educated elites themselves lose confidence in their enduring value and treat them with irony and contempt, becoming corrupt elites with a mission to subvert or deconstruct high culture. The strongest pressures in a democratic age are always downward from high culture toward popular entertainment, which originally meant replacing aristocratic and religious culture with middle-class and working-class culture but now means sinking to the lowest common denominator of the rebellious avant-garde and raucous youth culture, often of the crudest kind. When, for example, Mozart is replaced by the Beatles as the standard for music, or when Gregorian chant and Bach are replaced by folk music and guitars in Christian liturgy, a dramatic cultural revolution has occurred. The net result is to lower the overall spiritual and moral tone of society and thereby to diminish human dignity by discrediting the highest aspirations of the human soul. This trend has been accurately described as the 'leveling' effect of modern democracy.

In addition to the leveling of culture, modern democratic societies tend to promote a new and rather limited conception of the good life: the one-dimensional materialism of middle-class society, otherwise known as 'bourgeois' civilization or industrial and technological civilization. In evaluating this way of life, we once again face a difficult trade-off. On the one hand, bourgeois civilization increases the material standard of living and economic opportunities to unprecedented heights for the vast majority of people, overcoming the misery and degradation of poverty that most people have endured for centuries. But the negative consequence is a society dominated by the prosaic activities of material production and consumption, usually in the sterile atmosphere of an urban office building and impersonal suburb, where the chief concerns of people are economic security and status, bourgeois creature comforts, and physical health. These concerns are so obsessive that they begin to redefine reality and create a new metaphysical consciousness which turns the bodily/ material world into an absolute horizon. In some cases, the human body is worshiped in rituals that take on the aspect of a religious cult and that seek to deny bodily mortality—as in the jogging and fitness crazes of health fanatics, the elevation of antismoking and vegetarianism to the level of religious crusades, the pantheistic worship of the natural environment as a divine being (called Gaia), and the growing tendency to deny the awesome mystery of death by treating aging and mortality as technical problems to be solved by genetic engineering and pharmaceutical science. With only slight exaggeration, one may say that the work, play, and worship of modern democratic societies tends to deify material existence.

A crucial point to recognize is that such trends are not primarily imposed by the coercive state (though some are aided by it); nor do they triumph by insisting that other more noble activities are forbidden (one is always free to choose). Rather, they triumph because of widespread doubts about the real existence of a transcendent order of Being and Goodness beyond the material world and uncertainty about any higher purpose to life than middle-class careerism and popular entertainment. In most modern democratic societies, these are the only activities that call forth energy and commitment; all others are excluded by skeptical indifference and by demands for immediate sensations that seem harmless because they rarely lead to outright persecution. Instead, the dominant culture is imposed by the social tyranny of public opinion that, in principle, may be rejected but rarely is because the higher alternatives are treated with contempt or are simply forgotten. Thus, as Ernest Fortin has observed, "contrary to its stated aim, modern liberal democracy breeds a specific type of human being—one that is defined by unprecedented openness to all human possibilities. What this leads to most of the time [however] is neither . . . a noble dedication to some pre-given ideal, nor a deeper religious life, nor a rich and diversified society, but easygoing indifference and mindless conformism."[20]

The present problem of modern liberal democracy, then, is not the danger of imminent collapse, as Marx predicted, nor even the visible decline that eventually led to the fall of the Roman Empire. Everything may remain stable and prosperous for a long time to come. The fundamental problem is not the obvious one of physical decay or social disorder but the subtle and elusive one of moral degradation: the proclamation of a lofty commitment to respecting and cherishing the dignity of everyone, especially by eliminating historic barriers to human potential, combined with a culture of skepticism and materialism that drains the soul of all higher longings and encourages slavish conformity to mass society. Stated succinctly, modern liberal democracy proclaims in principle but subverts in practice the dignity of man.

This criticism may sound familiar to many people. It is, after all, a variation on the "theory of mass society" that has been developed by the greatest social critics of the modern democratic age—whom I would identify as Alexis de Tocqueville, Friedrich Nietzsche, and José Ortega y Gasset. In their analysis, the rise of modern democracy (along with modern science, industry, and technology) has unleashed the power and dynamism of the people while turning them into the anonymous "masses"—an undifferentiated collection of rootless, traditionless, and isolated individuals, each claiming to be unique and special but in reality identical to each other in their mundane pursuits, seemingly free but in reality slavishly conformist and ripe for exploitation by new kinds of tyrants, both violent and banal. With the empowering of the masses comes the prospect of a new kind of democratic tyranny.

As Tocqueville warns in *Democracy in America*, "the species of oppression by which democratic nations are menaced is unlike anything that ever existed in the world." He calls this new species of oppression "soft despotism" and describes it in terms that sound like the modern welfare state: It inhibits greatness and responsible freedom not by outright persecution but by imposing a multitude of minute rules on everyone in the name of equality and security; "it does not break men's will, but softens, bends, and guides it . . . so that in the end each nation is no more than a flock of timid and hardworking animals and the government its shepherd."[21] In more alarming terms, Friedrich Nietzsche spoke about the coming of "the last man," a new type of individual who was utterly indifferent to noble tasks or eternal longings but felt no sense of shame about his imperfections, a human being who was indistinguishable from a contented herd animal.[22] Similarly, the twentieth-century Spanish philosopher, Ortega y Gasset, described modern democracy as a "revolt of the masses" in which the self-satisfied people utterly rejected the challenge of heroic struggles yet assumed that the triumph of the masses constituted progress over all previous ages, an attitude he likened to that of a "spoiled child."[23] Warnings such as these have also been sounded by Leo Strauss, Eric Voegelin, Alexander Solzhenitsyn, Alasdair MacIntyre, Christopher Lasch, Walker Percy, Pope John Paul II, and other critics of the debased spirit of modern mass society.

What is important to see about these critics is that the new kind of human degradation that they describe is not an accidental by-product of liberalism but is caused by the theoretical project of liberalism itself. From the seventeenth to the twentieth centuries, liberalism—the modern philosophy of human liberty—has developed a persistent strategy of defending the rights and dignity of man by appealing to a notion of skeptical reason which denies the possibility of knowing objectively the highest good or the ultimate purpose of life. Although this strategy comes in several varieties, all share the common aim of defending dignity with doubt—claiming that the less certain we are about the highest ends of life the more all people gain in dignity by seeking to determine their own identities and becoming the masters of their fate. The liberal paradigm thus consists of two fundamental movements: (1) skepticism or doubt about knowing the greatest good when it is handed down as higher wisdom; and (2) confidence in individuals and nations to determine their fate by thinking on their own.

This paradigm reveals the source of liberalism's strength. It emancipates the human mind and will from the seemingly oppressive burdens of traditional authority (religious, political, and paternal) which have allegedly stultified the ambitions and dreams of people in the name of higher wisdom. The freedom and dignity of individuals and of whole nations are recognized for the first time and allowed to flourish. But the same formula also contains the fatal flaw of liberalism, for the skepticism or doubt which brings emancipation from traditional authority and the recognition of universal human dignity eventually leaves that dignity with no grounding at all in reality and with few resources to resist the pressures of modern mass society. To illustrate this fatal flaw more clearly, I will sketch briefly the high points of liberalism over the past several centuries as it has evolved through four schools of thought: (1) the natural rights school developed by Thomas Hobbes, John Locke, and Jean-Jacques Rousseau; (2) the idealist school developed by Immanuel Kant and the German Idealists; (3) the utilitarian-pragmatist school led by John Stuart Mill and John Dewey; and (4) the contemporary nonfoundationalist school associated with Richard Rorty, John Rawls, Bruce Ackerman, and Ronald Dworkin. The overall pattern that we find in the evolution of liberalism is growing doubt about the power of reason to know the greatest good combined with heightened moral demands to respect the equal dignity of every human being in a world of ever-increasing democratic conformity.

THE LIBERAL PHILOSOPHERS

If we go back to the beginning of liberalism in the seventeenth and eighteenth centuries, we can see clearly that its first and most powerful move is skeptical and subversive. There we find the natural rights school of Hobbes, Locke, and Rousseau who expressed their skepticism in the striking image of the state of nature—a description of human beings without political authority living in a chaotic and isolated condition. The state of nature is meant to show that political authority is not natural or ordained by God because no clear signs have been given from above that establish indisputable titles to rule. The traditional claims to rule—wisdom, virtue, holiness, or nobility— seem so intangible and so easily exploited by ambitious leaders seeking power over others that the natural condition of mankind is anarchy or warfare. The implication is that God and nature are so uncaring and so stingy that men must construct political authority on their own through an artificial social contract and create wealth by conquering and transforming nature though their own labor. This is the original reasoning behind natural rights: Providence does not give sufficient guidance or adequate support for human life, so men must provide for themselves and are naturally free and equal. The premise "men are born free" underlies natural rights because it means that we are born without obligations to higher authority and have the "right" to follow our own inclinations, primarily for self-preservation and property. In this way, skepticism about Providence leads to natural rights.

The problem with this school of liberalism is that it uncovers the rights of man as an autonomous being, but it also takes away the grounds of human dignity. The difficulty is most obvious in Hobbes, who views man as naturally free and as a machine without soul or freedom of the will, thereby abolishing the distinctiveness of human beings in comparison to other animals. While Locke and Rousseau are more reluctant to use mechanistic psychology to explain human behavior, they are not able to provide an alternative grounding for freedom and human dignity. Locke admits as much when he says there is no essential trait, such as the possession of a rational soul, that clearly distinguishes human beings from the other animals and directs them to rational perfection as a natural end.[24] The problem is even more acute for Rousseau. He is forced into the inconsistent position of waxing poetically about the dignity of man as a moral being, while seeking the ultimate human experiences in irrational sentiments (such as the sentiment of existence) that abolish our humanity and reduce us to the level of contented animals. The natural rights school is obviously at cross-purposes with itself, exalting and debasing man from one moment to the next.

In response to this dilemma about human dignity, a more idealistic school of liberalism arose in the eighteenth century, founded by Immanuel Kant. While Kant was certainly a philosophic genius, we should not be blinded by his stature from seeing that he was following the same flawed strategy as his predecessors. He tried to combine philosophical skepticism (which he learned from Hume) with a moral theory of human dignity (which he learned from Rousseau). Kant's hope was that by taking skepticism to a deeper level than his predecessors, freedom and human dignity could be taken outside of empirical and biological processes and put on a secure foundation as pure rational ideas. With this move, Kant restored the crucial distinction between human beings and the rest of nature: Human beings are higher than animals and dumb matter because they have rational wills which give them freedom or autonomy outside of nature. In Kant's eyes, this gives humans infinite worth or dignity; it makes them "persons," rather than "things," who have rights that must be recognized and respected by others.

Kant's contribution lies in making human dignity *the* theme of philosophy and the centerpiece of liberalism. With so much at stake, Kant realizes that a rational justification for human dignity must be provided and acknowledges that his whole case comes down to one crucial question: Is freedom of the will, which gives us our dignity as responsible moral agents, an illusion or a reality? The problem for Kant is that his commitment to skeptical reason makes positive proofs for the existence of freedom impossible; only 'negative' proofs are possible. Kant actually made three attempts at the negative proof for freedom; and the gist of all of them was the same: The existence of freedom can never be *disproven* because reason cannot grasp the ultimate nature of reality. Hence, free will and moral responsibility are not contrary to reason and may be assumed in moral action. The only positive support for freedom that Kant could offer was a glimpse into a mysterious "noumenal" world beyond the physical world in which freedom is assumed to operate as the intangible cause of unselfish acts that we often see in human affairs.

Despite Kant's best efforts, his negative proofs for freedom and dignity are deeply unsatisfying. They are more like wishful thinking than rational proofs because all they show is that we may act *"as if"* we were free, without knowing if it were really the case. Kant is unable to say for sure because his skepticism requires him to suspend judgment about the real existence of intangible things, such as the human soul or the mysterious noumenal world of intangible causes. Nor can Kant say if reason, which makes us free, is anything more than a cosmic accident: Does nature care for the human mind, or is nature basically indifferent to man? Kant's skepticism prevents him from deciding one way or the other, so human dignity is left as an ardent but ungrounded wish of all moral beings. Once again, liberalism comes up short.

Because of dissatisfaction with the natural rights and Kantian schools of liberalism, a third school arose in the nineteenth and twentieth centuries—the school of utilitarianism and pragmatism led by John Stuart Mill and John Dewey. Like every attempt to save liberalism from within, this version reacts to earlier failures by driving the wedge of skepticism even deeper. Utilitarians and pragmatists are more skeptical than their predecessors in rejecting not only permanent laws of nature (such as natural rights) but also static structures of the mind (such as Kant's moral law and mental categories). Utilitarianism and pragmatism are deeply suspicious of any kind of unchanging metaphysics. Instead of appealing to permanent laws or unchanging entities, they attempt to justify freedom and dignity with historicism—the belief in open-ended historical change, sometimes called progress or merely the endless flux of existence.

From the notion of open-ended change, Mill and Dewey developed the alluring idea of "individuality"—the belief that everyone possesses a unique personal identity that must be allowed to grow freely in a society of diverse personalities. Yet, like most liberal philosophers, they offer arguments for individuality that are primarily negative in character. Mill's main thrust is to attack the stultifying effects of middle-class conformity which he found in the materialism and diluted Christianity of Victorian England. Mill defends the maximum diversity of opinions and lifestyles within a stable order, including willful "nonconformity" and eccentricity, in order to reinvigorate modern societies. While Dewey is more accepting than Mill of modern industrial society, Dewey shares Mill's antipathy to any fixed structures that would inhibit individual self-expression. Dewey's alternative is the experimental method, which promotes the continuous growth of personality as an end-in-itself or change without reference to a predetermined end. It would be hard to underestimate the attraction of this idea of open-ended change for many modern people.

If we examine Mill's and Dewey's justifications for the growth of individual personality, however, we encounter the characteristic weak-

ness of philosophic liberalism. An appealing notion of individual dignity coexists with the denial of any ultimate purpose to life, which
leaves little more than the process of change itself as the reason for
living. This is apparent in Mill's principle of utility which he insists is
not merely a calculation of pleasures but a conception of man as "progressive being"—a being that continuously strives for higher levels of
culture and morality as measured on an open-ended scale of general
happiness. Dewey appeals to a pragmatic notion of "experience,"
which he tries to explain in metaphysical terms that depend on the
primacy of the human will: Through conscious interaction with the
dynamic flux of existence, the pragmatic will connects the thinking
subject with the reality of being.

The problem with these arguments is that they are too subjective
to provide adequate grounds for human dignity. Mill admits as much
when he says that the ultimate sanction for the principle of utility is "a
subjective feeling in our minds."[25] And Dewey puts the practical assertions of the will before thinking and being. Thus, there is no real
reason why individuals with strong subjective feelings or with strong
wills should not harm others by exploiting and dominating them instead of acting justly toward them or treating them with respect. The
fact that the theories of utility and pragmatism have generally supported liberal democracy rather than tyranny or anarchy is purely
accidental—a consequence of limitations imposed by the much ma-
ligned social conventions of the Victorian age and of moral virtues
still alive in the cultural heritage of the nineteenth and early twentieth
centuries (in Mill's case by the influence of a residual Aristotelianism
and in Dewey's by a residual Christianity). It thus appears that Mill
and Dewey, like earlier liberal philosophers, have fatal flaws because
they are committed to an approach that equates reason with skepticism and defines dignity as open-ended autonomy, leaving human
dignity standing on little more than wishful thinking and unfounded
faith in progress.[26]

Despite the problems, there is no rush to disavow the self-defeating
strategy of liberalism. The most recent school—the nonfoundationalist
or postmodern school led by Rorty, Dworkin, Ackerman, and Rawls—
is content to rework the strategies of the great liberal philosophers
of the past without recognizing the inherent flaw. In fact, the latest

philosophers are even more skeptical then their predecessors. They claim that the whole search for foundations is futile and harmful, a relic of metaphysical and theological prejudices preserved in earlier schools of liberalism that foster social division and uphold arbitrary patterns of domination. Without presenting a detailed critique here of postmodern liberalism, I simply would like to point out the staggering contradiction that lies at the heart of its teaching: On the one hand, it is deeply skeptical about knowing the greatest good or any foundation for justice; on the other hand, it insists on an absolute moral imperative to treat all people with equal concern and respect. This amounts to saying that there is no basis whatsoever for morality but, of course, we must still be decent to other people and treat them with respect!

My favorite example of this stunning contradiction is Richard Rorty's comments about defending human dignity in his influential article, "Postmodern Bourgeois Liberalism." There, Rorty frankly refers to postmodern liberals like himself as "freeloading atheists"— people who do not believe in God or any metaphysical grounds for morality, yet who absolutely affirm the duty of treating people with dignity and respect. He says, it is "part of our tradition . . . that [a] stranger from whom all dignity has been stripped [should] be taken in and re-clothed with dignity. This Jewish and Christian element in our tradition is gratefully invoked by *freeloading atheists like myself*" who think that metaphysical debates are futile. He even says that these debates have as little relevance to our treatment of each other as "the question of the existence of God."[27] What Rorty is admitting by calling himself a "freeloading atheist" is that he cherishes the Judeo-Christian inheritance of defending human dignity, but he thinks that it can be disconnected from belief in God. In the words of Friedrich Nietzsche, he adheres to Christian morality without believing in the Christian God—a strange mixture of nihilism and moralism that Nietzsche believed followed from the death of God in modern times.[28]

From this brief account of the evolution of liberalism or, more precisely, of the descent of liberalism into nihilism, we are led to a momentous conclusion: Liberalism lacks the intellectual courage and moral 'fire power' to vindicate the belief in human dignity that it assumes in all its activities and institutions. Hence, liberalism cannot stand without help from outside the liberal tradition. Above all, it cannot stand without faith in God—though I hasten to add that the need for God does not mean that any old god will do! The moral assumptions underlying modern liberal democracy cry out for religious and metaphysical assistance, but not every idea of the supreme being or of ultimate reality are suitable to its conception of human dignity.

This difficulty is abundantly clear from the recent writings of Vàclav Havel, the distinguished president of the new Czech republic. After fighting courageously for human rights and human dignity against communist tyranny, Havel has spent a considerable amount of time agonizing over the question of how to justify his cherished principles. He refers to his quest in religious or poetic language as Cosmic Anchoring—the search for a cosmic support for justice that has led him to invoke such ideas as the "Gaia hypothesis" (belief in the mother earth goddess of environmentalists) or Heidegger's Being (belief in the sheer existence of things by fateful dispensation). Havel is aware that he is trying to replace Christian faith, which he admires but is unable to embrace for reasons he never makes clear, with a post-Christian god or new spirituality that provides grounds for ultimate meaning. His hope is that the new gods will justify the moral code he so highly esteems. Yet, there is something whimsical and almost desperate about his invocation of new gods, as if any kind of fuzzy New Age religion is believable or provides support for man's inherent rights and dignity. At best, we find in Havel a search for principles that resemble natural law—a common minimum morality that, in his words, must come from somewhere: "from heaven, or from nature, or from our hearts: a belief that our deeds will live after us; respect for our neighbors, for our families, [and] for certain natural authorities; respect for human dignity and for nature . . . and benevolence towards guests who come with good intentions."29

What Havel yearns for in his quest for Cosmic Anchoring (but avoids without adequate explanation) is the biblical God who gives man a special place and dignity in this vast cosmos that might otherwise seem empty and inhospitable to human concerns. Havel especially needs to reconsider Christianity, which raises the claim of human dignity to the highest level by viewing man as a creature made in the image of God and redeemed by the Incarnation of God in the person of Jesus Christ. Following this suggestion, we may ask if it is possible for Christianity to come to the aid of liberal democracy and vindicate its assumptions about human dignity: Can liberalism be saved by grounding or regrounding its principles in the proposition that man is made in the image and likeness of God?

CHRISTIAN APOLOGETICS

Here we face two momentous issues. One is the truth of Christianity, which is the domain of theology traditionally called 'apologetics'— rational arguments for the truth of the Christian faith. The second issue is the politics of Christianity, which is the domain of 'political theology'—the implications of the Christian faith for political and social order. I will turn first to Christian apologetics with the awareness that it is a challenge of staggering proportions, though it is one that cannot be avoided in the present context. After all, skepticism may be the only honest position to hold, even if it is a disaster for modern democracy and leaves one in varying degrees of doubt about how to live. Another reason why we need to turn our attention to Christian apologetics is that philosophical alternatives to the self-defeating skepticism of modern liberalism do exist, namely, classical Greek philosophy as developed by Socrates, Plato, and Aristotle. Classical Greek philosophy has an advantage over modern liberalism by holding a more robust view of the human good than open-ended autonomy, and classical philosophy recognizes the need for groundings in a teleological view of nature.

But I would like to challenge the skeptical view of liberalism as well as the naturalism of classical Greek philosophy on the grounds that the supernatural claims of Christianity actually provide the most plausible account of the universe and man, even though they cannot be demonstrated with absolute certainty and therefore require faith in addition to reason. As I see it, the claims of the Christian religion can be reduced to three doctrines: the Creation, the Fall, and the Redemption through Christ. Though I will offer no more than a brief apologetic for each of these doctrines, I believe the rational arguments that I will make are sufficient to shake the complacent skepticism of modern intellectuals and to show the Christian doctrines are more plausible than alternative accounts of the universe and man.

First, let us consider Creation. According to Christian doctrine, the universe is created from nothing by an omnipotent God whose will is mysterious but benevolent. If we think broadly about the origin and existence of the universe, it is possible to argue that this doctrine provides the most likely account. It is certainly more plausible than the view of Aristotle, who apparently thought that the world is un-created or eternal in its present form (implying that the universe has always been here, pretty much as we see it today). This is implausible because modern 'Big Bang' cosmology has offered some compelling arguments about the expanding universe that indicate it has evolved to its present state from a unique beginning point. Yet, modern cosmologists are mistaken if they think that the unique beginning point is merely an accident, just as Eastern religions and existential philosophy are misguided in suggesting that the universe is simply 'given' and that awe at the sheer existence of things is our deepest response to the world. The claim that the universe is accidental or simply 'given' is unlikely, even though our universe does not have to exist at all, nor does it have to exist in the way that it does. The existence and present form of the universe are radically contingent, though it does not make sense to say it is accidental.

That is because the universe does not simply exist as a brute fact. It exists in a way that is highly rational and remarkably stable, even though the infinite vastness and littleness of its extremes will always be mysterious, as Pascal said. These characteristics of the natural universe—its rational order and remarkable stability combined with its radical contingency and deep mystery at the extremes—are more amazing than the sheer existence of the universe. The obvious inference is that something necessary must lie behind the contingent order and stability of the universe in order to keep them on track. Only a God who is a Necessary Being has the power to create a radically contingent universe from nothing and to make it operate by stable rational laws for a definite amount of time without collapsing or reversing itself. This is the miracle of Christian Creation. Though a miracle, it is more plausible than an accidental Big Bang which provides no explanation for the stability and intelligibility of the laws of nature. And it is more plausible than the universe of Eastern religion whose 'givenness' without rhyme or reason turns the stable and rational laws of nature into passing illusions to be succeeded by other illusions, like the images of a kaleidoscope. Contingent Being upheld by Necessary Being is a more plausible way to think about our rational and stable but mysterious universe than views which reduce it to accident or illusion. This implies a God who is infinite and unchanging, yet who changed without compromising Himself in creating the finite world—the Christian God.

The second essential Christian doctrine is the Fall, the corruption of the world by the rebellious will of man. The Fall provides the most plausible account of evil, suffering, and death. It is far more plausible than modern liberalism, which holds the Rousseauian idea that man is good by nature but society makes him bad through its unjust and oppressive institutions. The Rousseauian view is refuted by the fact that all social experiments in utopia inevitably fail, due to something deeply perverse in human nature. The view of Plato, that evil lies in ignorance (in irrationality due to our finite bodies), is better than Rousseau's explanation; but it is still not satisfying. Plato always looks foolish when he treats evil as irrationality, as an apparent good that can be cured by the complete rationality of philosophy. The tyrants Plato invents to embody evil and to challenge Socrates always look too benign, like misguided hedonists or 'erotic' men who somehow missed their calling. Plato is not naive about tyrants or the power of evil; but he is forced by the logic of his position to sound naive—to claim that evil is no more perverse than the apparent good of an irrational person who has been misled by passion or temporary insanity.

A better explanation is given by Paul, who states the Christian view of evil in Rom. 7:15–20: "I do not understand my own actions. For I do not do the good that I want, but I do the very thing I hate . . . I agree that the law is good . . . [yet] the evil I do not want is what I do." The meaning of Paul's deceptively simple statement is that evil is not an apparent good as Plato suggests. Paul is not deluded or confused about right and wrong; he knows the true good is obedience to God's law, and he is even aware that his "innermost self" delights in goodness. But he does the evil deed anyway. The implication is that evil is not simply ignorance or irrationality but pure perversity: willful rebellion for no other reason than to be equal to God or to be self-sufficient without God. This is best captured in the Christian doctrine of the Fall and its corollary, original sin—the idea that man was originally good but lost that goodness in a primary act of rebellion that has been transmitted by the first human beings to everyone afterwards. As a result of original sin, all people have rebellious wills that tempt them to do evil and that cause their sinful actions.

By combining the notion of original goodness with inherited rebelliousness, Christian anthropology offers the best account of man—an account of our dual nature, both divine and sinful, containing elements of greatness and elements of wretchedness that cannot be overcome merely by changing unjust social institutions or by philosophizing about the good. As many proponents of Christian anthropology have observed, the continuing power of evil and suffering in the world provides empirical support for the doctrine of the Fall and its theological elaboration as original sin which no philosophical doctrine is able to match.

The third basic Christian doctrine is the Redemption through Christ. How can this doctrine be made rationally plausible? The central point of Christian redemption is that evil and suffering are not inevitable because God in His divine mercy became man in order to redeem the fallen world. Admittedly, the doctrine of Redemption through the Incarnation of God in Christ is impossible to prove rationally or even to comprehend rationally. How could the infinite and unchanging God enter the finite world and still remain divine? Why would God do so? To these questions, I would reply, in the first place, that Creation from nothing also implies that the infinite God entered the finite world without compromising Himself for reasons we cannot comprehend. Hence, if the Creation is possible, then so is the Incarnation. At both unique moments, the eternal and infinite God entered time and space to display His gracious goodness.

Though a mystery, the doctrine of Redemption through Christ is the only way to make sense of the good deeds that human beings do in a world that often appears tragic or indifferent. Why bother to be good if the world is not a moral order? The Redemption shows that the world is a moral order, despite the existence of natural disasters, disease, poverty, war, and tyrannies that often ruin the most innocent of victims. The Redemption reaffirms the essential goodness of Creation and reminds us that suffering and evil are not simply 'given' as facts of life. The Creation of the universe is radically contingent, but it is also "good," even "very good" as the Bible says, which implies that the world is not inherently tragic, perverse, or indifferent. Yet, the evil and suffering that we witness in the world cannot be overcome by the efforts of mortal men. This is the illusion of modern humanism and progress—the illusion that human beings can redeem themselves through politics, technology, therapy, or social engineering. This is a false hope for redemption because sin is too deep to be overcome by self-help methods; and death cannot be conquered by anything but an omnipotent God. Instead, we need God's grace to restore original goodness, requiring the miracle of the Incarnation and divine atonement for sin.

Without redemption by divine atonement, we have no guarantee that goodness of the world can be affirmed against the enormous power of evil and suffering, no guarantee of moral order, no guarantee that good deeds are not folly or waste. The response of the Greek philosophers and Eastern sages to this challenge is detachment from the world through contemplation or meditation. But are not philosophy and meditation merely ways of escaping from the world and avoiding the problem of moral order? Every act of goodness is an implicit denial of the tragic and indifferent character of the universe; but such acts have no ultimate justification except faith in divine redemption that will set aright the wrongs of the world and bring about the cessation of evil. To embrace this crucial doctrine of the Christian religion is an act of faith; yet it makes more rational sense than pretending that man can redeem the world through human efforts alone or that one can deny the need for moral order.

To summarize my brief attempt at apologetics: I think that the most plausible way to defend the truth of Christianity is to begin with observations that few could deny—the existence of an intelligible and stable but contingent universe, the existence of evil and suffering, and the existence of good deeds—and then infer that the Christian doctrines of Creation, Fall, and Redemption provide the best possible explanations for the phenomena. The implication is that reason itself leads to Christian faith when we are able to see the supernatural mysteries behind the observable realities—when we see that behind the creation is the Creator, behind evil is the Fall, behind every act of goodness is the Redemption. None of this implies, of course, that other philosophies and religions lack elements of beauty and truth. It merely implies that other philosophies and religions, insofar as they approximate these doctrines, contain partial truths and need to be brought to fulfillment and completion.[30]

POLITICAL THEOLOGY

Having ventured briefly into apologetics and hopefully challenged the complacency of modern skeptics and classical naturalists, we are now ready for 'political theology' and the second half of the dilemma posed at the beginning: Liberalism needs Christianity, and Christianity is arguably the best account of the universe and man; but does the Christian religion necessarily support democracy and human rights? A growing number of serious scholars think that it does—that Christianity is especially well suited to provide a religious foundation for liberal democracy.

In the first place, they suggest, Christianity makes claims about the dignity of man that resemble the claims of liberalism in being both universal and personal. But instead of grounding those claims on skeptical reason, Christianity grounds them on the biblical claim that there is a God who created the universe and made every human being in His image and likeness and sent a Redeemer to save them by God's grace. Such claims about the moral order of the universe and the divine spark in everyone seem to be ideally suited for the defense of human dignity that liberalism needs but palpably lacks.

Second, Christianity has a deep reservoir of doctrinal resources that may be adapted to politics—including notions of Christian freedom and equality, prophetic traditions of denouncing oppression and injustice, as well as theological conceptions of conscience and covenant in the Protestant tradition and of natural law in the Catholic tradition. From these resources, one ought to be able to derive a principled argument for liberal democracy that is superior to secular theories of individual rights and democratic consent.

Third, Christianity has been associated historically with the origins and progress of liberal democracy in the modern world, from the Pilgrim settlement of early America to the antislavery and civil rights movements to the heroic struggles for religious freedom against tyrannical governments around the globe.

Fourth, Christianity in the twentieth century evolved internally toward more liberal democratic views, as occurred, for example, in the writings of Jacques Maritain, John Courtney Murray, Reinhold Niebuhr, and Dietrich Bonhoeffer, as well as in Christian movements from neoconservatism to liberation theology. Similar developments can be seen in the documents of the Second Vatican Council of the Catholic Church and in statements by Protestant and even Eastern Orthodox churches. All of these signs point to the essentially harmonious relations between modern liberal democracy and Christianity.

Accordingly, one might hope for a refounding of liberal democracy on Christian principles that rescues liberalism from its descent into nihilism and breathes into it moral and spiritual vitality. Surely, this is a noble endeavor. But I do not think that it is as easy to accomplish as it sounds. There is a major problem, frequently cited by the enemies of religion but insufficiently acknowledged by its friends: Christianity is not necessarily connected in principle to any form of government and may even be incompatible in crucial respects with liberal democracy, despite the hopeful signs mentioned above. In the chapters that follow, I shall explore this issue in depth while trying to avoid the wishful thinking of liberalism and of much of contemporary Christian theology.

CHAPTER TWO

THE ILLIBERAL
AND UNDEMOCRATIC
CHRISTIAN TRADITION

One of the disturbing implications of the preceding analysis is that modern liberals as well as many modern Christians are in a state of denial about the predicament of liberal democracy. On the one side, liberals tend to deny that their cherished principles of human rights and human dignity need a grounding in an objective moral order. They seem to think that skepticism about the good life is sufficient to justify the treatment of others with equal concern and respect. Some, like Richard Rorty, even boast that they are "freeloading atheists" whose respect for the dignity of individuals rests on nothing more than the residual moral sentiments of a religious and philosophical tradition that they have repudiated. But this leaves the entire liberal project unsupported, like a table without legs suspended in midair.

On the other side, religious believers often proclaim that the emptiness of liberalism can be overcome by religious revival—by a return to God—while ignoring the incompatibilities that might exist between their faith and their politics. Simply because the present political order needs a reinvigoration of spiritual beliefs, it does not automatically follow that Christianity, or any other religion, supports liberal democratic principles or is tied to a specific political regime. Can we really say with confidence, as a recent scholar claims, that an inner affinity exists between Christian faith and liberal democracy, that "just as Christianity is in some fundamental sense the truth of the liberal conception, so the liberal order can be considered the political

45

truth of Christianity"?[1] Before we affirm such a statement, we need to consider a serious objection: Neither the Bible nor the greatest theologians and church leaders of the past (for at least the first sixteen hundred years of the Christian tradition) were particularly sympathetic to democracy or to the various conceptions of personal and political freedom that arose from time to time. Instead, the Bible was understood to support kingship, theocracy, and other hierarchical institutions, and Christian theologians invariably defended such regimes. Was this a mistake or even a terrible misunderstanding of the Christian message? It is possible, of course, that the Christian message was misinterpreted for many centuries and that the will of God was distorted by prejudice and lust for power. But before we leap to such conclusions, we need to reconsider in honest fashion the reasons for the illiberal and undemocratic features of the Bible and the Christian tradition. Only then can we fairly assess the present consensus among Christians favoring liberal democracy.

THE POLITICS OF THE BIBLE

The simplest beginning is an overview of the Bible. What does it teach about politics and the best political order? The first point to note is that the Bible does not speak explicitly about democracy or human rights. Instead, the Old Testament or Hebrew Bible speaks about the covenant that God made with Israel and the divine law revealed to Moses. While some modern scholars, such as Daniel Elazar, have found in the Hebrew covenant (*brit*) a prototype of democratic consent or social contract, this claim is at best a partial truth.[2] The biblical covenant is a promise from God to show steadfast love and mercy to His people in their sufferings and sins, regardless of how badly they behave; but it is also a contract with the chosen people that is accompanied with rewards for obedience and punishments for disobedience. In both dimensions (as a promise based on love and as a contract backed by sanctions), the biblical covenant is undemocratic: God is not bound by the covenant and keeps His promises solely out of His own divine self-limitation. By contrast, man is bound to obey God and to obey the prophets that God has appointed to deliver His message, even under penalty of death and destruction. The element of voluntary consent is missing from the covenant with Israel, both for the prophets, who are often unwilling and reluctant servants of God, and for the people, who frequently resist the prophets and rebel against the divine law but are no less obliged to follow it. There is nothing voluntary or consensual about the biblical covenant; and the most severe punishments are threatened by God for disobedience, culminating in the Babylonian captivity and exile of the Jewish people from their homeland.

It should also be noted that, insofar as the covenant with Israel sanctions specific forms of government, the main ones are illiberal and undemocratic: God establishes the tribes of Abraham which are patriarchal, the regime of Moses which is theocratic, and the king-ships of Saul, David, Solomon, and their successors which are estab-lished by divine right and only afterward affirmed by the people. A brief description of each of these political structures will support this interpretation.

The oldest form of government sanctioned by God's covenant is the patriarchal family from the time of Noah to Abraham and his des-cendants (they are legitimized by the first and second covenants). One could also say that the patriarchal family, headed by the father but with a place of high honor given to mother, is the cornerstone of ancient Hebrew society and the primary means by which God works His will in the early stages of the world. God's selection of a chosen people to worship Him alone begins with father Abraham and con-tinues with Isaac, Jacob, and the sons of Jacob who sire the twelve tribes of Israel. But by the time the patriarchal family reaches the sons of Jacob, it has been exposed as an inadequate mode of rule because the sibling rivalries have become too contentious and self-destructive to maintain stable rule. So, the patriarchal tribes are superceded but not abolished by the rule of law—by the divine law revealed to Moses that is ratified by the third covenant, the covenant on Mount Sinai.[3]

The precise power structure created by the covenant on Sinai is dif-ficult to describe, though it is hardly liberal or democratic. Sovereignty is unified in one man, Moses, who combines spiritual authority (as the chief prophet) with civil power (as the chief lawgiver and nation builder) and military power (as the chief strategist and battlefield commander). Although power is unified in one man, Moses does not deserve the label that Paul Johnson gives him, "totalitarian of the spirit."[4] For power is not only unified in Moses, it is also delegated and divided—to Aaron the high priest, to Joshua the top general, and to judges in a judicial system. In addition, the twelve tribes of Israel retain their clan leaders, the seventy elders, who constitute a confederacy of tribes beneath Moses' unified nation of divine laws. And the people have a role in what are loosely called congregations or assemblies that mete out punishments to violators of the law. These additional bases of power make Moses relatively weak in practice, as evidenced by the frequent rebellions against him. Yet, the whole arrangement is much too jumbled to fit the neat classification of a constitutionally balanced mixed monarchy, as Thomas Aquinas describes it.[5] And it is certainly not a type of protosocial democracy, as some modern scholars have argued.[6] The best description I can suggest for the polity of Moses is a weakly ruled theocracy—"a kingdom of priests and a holy nation," as God calls it in Exod. 19:6, that Moses establishes but never manages to unify or to control.

Though the polity of Moses is not a liberal or social democracy, many still argue that its mission of liberating the people from oppression makes political freedom or national self-determination the ultimate teaching of the Hebrew Bible. For this reason, Exodus has inspired many oppressed peoples throughout history to seek freedom from slavery, even though this interpretation captures only half of the message.[7] For the Bible shows that God delivers the people from slavery in Egypt and supports national liberation, not for the purpose of enjoying their political and economic rights, but for the purpose of putting on the yoke of the law in the polity of Moses. And even though the Mosaic law teaches the people moral and political responsibility, it does so for the sake of performing sacred duties according to the divine law rather than for exercising human rights. The emancipation from slavery is fulfilled, in other words, by theocracy rather than by liberal democracy.

Moreover, the content of the divine law revealed to Moses consists, in the first place, of the Ten Commandments rather than the Ten Bill of Rights, commanding duties to God, family, and neighbors rather than establishing protections for personal freedom. The Ten

Commandments are followed by a complex set of judicial laws—a series of concrete "case" laws that apply the general principles of the Decalogue to the practical problems of the household and civil society. These civil laws command strict sexual ethics, the utmost respect for parental authority, fair and responsible dealings with fellow citizens, and compassionate treatment of the poor, slaves, and strangers. They are followed by a host of ceremonial and dietary laws that, when taken together with the household and civil code, regulate all aspects of religious, personal, and social life. The illiberalism of the Mosaic code is most evident in the large number of actions punishable by the death penalty—including murder, striking, and even cursing, one's parents, incest, homosexuality, bestiality, adultery, practicing magic or human sacrifice, oppressing a stranger, kidnapping, violating the Sabbath, blasphemy, and, of course, idolatry. As the Lord says, the objective of the Mosaic law is to make the Israelites a holy people like their holy God—"You shall be holy, for I am holy" (Lev. 11:45)—rather than to promote self-government like a modern constitution; and holiness demands severe punishments. Though Deuteronomy teaches that obeying the law out of love is better than obeying out of fear, it is clear that loving obedience to a highly exacting legal code does not leave much room for political or personal freedom.

To this observation, one might add that those Jews who take the law most seriously today—the Orthodox Jews—are the farthest from liberal democracy. Even conservative Jews who are frank about the tensions between Judaism and modern democratic life admit this point. As Adam Garfinkel argues in a provocative article published recently in *Conservative Judaism*, the notions of authority in Judaism and in American democracy are incompatible: "The principle of individualist equality that flows from American sacred texts . . . cannot be reconciled with the hierarchical, communal principle that flows from *halakah*, Jewish law . . . [where] authority rests in a line of revelation through time from God to Moses to the Judges and Prophets, to the talmudic *tana'im*, to the sages after them to the rabbis of our own day." In firm language, Garfinkle states that even though "Judaism is spiritually egalitarian, nothing about Judaism implies social or political egalitarianism as we understand it today"—above all, in the special covenant that God makes with one nation among others.[8] It is thus difficult to find in the Hebrew covenant and Mosaic law a theory of rights and democracy.

A more promising avenue might be the teaching on kingship in the Hebrew Bible. The books of Samuel, Kings, and the latter prophets offer rich possibilities for democratic theorists, who have mined them for lessons about the evils of kingship and the pursuit of righteousness or justice in terms resembling the modern idea of 'social justice.' Though tantalizing prospects appear here, I would caution against indulging in wishful thinking that dilutes the original message of the latter prophets, which is far more mysterious and radical than modern theologians admit. A few illustrations will indicate why.

In the first book of Samuel, kingship is established by God in the Promised Land against the wish of Samuel and even against God's own wish in order to satisfy the Hebrew people's desire to have a king like other nations (to lead them in battle and to judge them). As Martin Buber points out, God opposes the idea because He thinks that the demand for human kingship is a rejection of His kingship— "the kingship of God"—but gives in as a concession to human weakness and to teach the people a lesson.[9] Samuel is instructed to warn the people in graphic terms how kings will become corrupt and tyrannical; then, Samuel is told to "anoint" Saul as the first king. Thus, the Bible teaches a strange lesson: God does not favor human kingship because it is a type of idolatry that will lead to misery, but God nevertheless endorses kingship and then specifically chooses the men who would be kings. This paradox helps to explain why the Bible combines a theory of divine right kingship with popular consent. Kings come directly from God as the Lord's "anointed" but the people must ratify them afterwards, which they do by public acclamation for Saul and David. The people must be part of God's plan—accomplices, as it were, in His harsh methods of instruction. One suspects that God gives the people their wish so they will eventually repent of it and come back to the kingship of God (rather like a parent who lets his children try cigarettes in order to discourage them from smoking).

The latter Hebrew prophets, as critics of both kings and people, amplify this message with their powerful social criticism. Isaiah, Amos, and the other latter prophets employ the stinging rhetoric of righteous indignation against a "sinful nation" that resembles modern democratic calls for social justice. The prophets condemn corrupt rulers, complacent affluence, and the oppression of the weak by the powerful; they advocate the "righteousness" (*tsedaqah*) of caring for the poor, the widows, and orphans as the true spirit of the law rather than empty ritualism. Modern Christians have frequently turned here for theories of rights and liberation: liberation theologians, civil rights leaders, and democratic ideologists rely heavily on the latter prophets for their message of social justice.[10] And, they are right insofar as God's love for the poor and oppressed and the duty to treat them justly are strongly proclaimed by the latter prophets. Yet, there are two critical problems for the modern democratic theorists.

First, the latter Hebrew prophets place the sin of idolatry above the sin of oppression on the scale of sins committed by the people. Offenses against the sovereignty of the one true God are more serious than offenses against fellow citizens. In addition, the latter prophets combine their social criticism with visions of a messianic age in which perfect harmony and peace will reign; and they envision ideal kingship as the means to universal harmony and peace. In so doing, they stand the original view of biblical kingship on its head, turning something negative into a positive ideal—turning God's begrudging concession to a weak and sinful people into the messianic ideal of Davidic kingship that God has selected for the future salvation and redemption of the world. Seen in this light, the latter prophets are *visionary monarchists* rather than social democrats. They passionately proclaim, in the words of Isaiah (32:1), "Behold a king shall reign in righteousness" and in the words of Ezekiel (34:23), "My servant David shall be king and . . . they shall have one shepherd." As Max Weber states in *Ancient Judaism*, "no prophet was a champion of 'democratic' ideals; in their eyes, the people need guidance, hence, everything depends on the qualities of the leaders."[11]

The conclusion I draw from this survey of the Hebrew Bible is that the theory of kingship and righteousness proclaimed in ancient Israel overlaps partly with modern concepts of social justice (struggling against oppression on behalf of the oppressed). But God's larger plan is the spiritual education of the people and the redemption of the world through kingship rather than through democracy. Thus, the Old Testament offers several models of divinely sanctioned political regimes; but the leading ones are patriarchy, theocracy, and messianic kingship rather than democratic human rights.

If these are some of the political lessons of the Old Testament, what are the political teachings of the New Testament? My first observation is that God is less political in the New than in the Old Testament: God no longer works through a covenant with a chosen people or through prophets who deliver the law and anoint kings but through the Incarnation of God in the person of Jesus Christ. The result is a religion, Christianity, that does not view the divine law in political terms as a legal and civil code, like the *halakah* of Judaism or the *sharia* of Islam. Instead, Christianity is a religion of faith in Jesus Christ as the Messiah and Son of God who has come "not to destroy the law and the prophets but to fulfill them"—to simplify and purify the teaching of the Mosaic law and the Hebrew prophets by reducing their many specific commandments to the two great commands of charity or love: to love God with all one's heart, mind, and soul and to love one's neighbor as oneself (Matt. 5:17 and 22:37–40). The replacement of the detailed legal and civil code of the Jewish state with the duties of charity is one reason why Christ is able to distinguish duties to God from duties to Caesar and why Christ endorses no specific form of government as the best regime: The charity or love commanded by Christian divine law transcends political justice and cannot be codified directly into civil law or translated into a specific political order.

Instead of speaking about an earthly regime, Christ speaks about the "kingdom of God" which exists partially in this world but transcends institutional embodiment and is fully present only in the world-to-come. Though these teachings about charity and the kingdom of God clearly favor the poor and the humble over the rich and the powerful, they do not constitute a political ideology or point to a clear political agenda. Almost all the great questions of political, economic, social, and military organization are left blank in the Gospels because they are no longer specified by divine law. The message of the Gospels is paradoxical because it is revolutionary in one sense, exalting the lowly and challenging the natural basis of existing hierarchies and stripping away the sacred auras of rulers and nations; at the same time, it leaves many existing institutions in place and commands obedience to Caesar in his realm and God in His realm. The Gospel's message is therefore spiritually radical but politically conservative. Though Christ says that the meek shall inherit the earth and Mary sings that the Lord "has put down the mighty from their thrones and exalted those of low degree" (Luke 1:52), neither leads a political revolution. Even Christ's association with humble people and social outcasts (fishermen, carpenters, ordinary soldiers, tax collectors, Samaritan women, lepers, and prostitutes) never causes Him to say that the common people should rule politically or that democracy should replace Caesar's monarchy. Nor does Christ's distinction between rulers who use power to serve others and those who merely dominate others indicate if 'service rule' is best realized in a republic or a monarchy. His statement, "Whoever would be great among you must be your servant" (Matt. 20:26), leaves open the question of the best form of government.

In the Epistles and Book of Acts, Christ's distinction between duties to God and duties to Caesar provides support for most earthly governments, regardless of their structure. According to Paul and Peter, the Roman emperor is a human authority instituted by God to restrain man's sinful nature, requiring conscientious obedience, though the Book of Acts adds the qualification that when human authority conflicts with God's law "we must obey God rather than men" (Acts 5:29). A further refinement of the Christian attitude to political authority is Paul's notion of Christian freedom. Yet, as Paul indicates, Christian freedom and political obedience to Caesar are compatible with each other because true freedom is inner freedom—the mastery of one's sinful desires by having the spirit triumph over the flesh and the emancipation of Christians from the obligations of the Mosaic law in favor of Christ's free gift of grace. Christian freedom in these senses is a moral and spiritual concept, and it is compatible with obedience to external political authority, even with political oppression. Nor does Paul's statement about spiritual equality—that "there is neither Jew nor Greek, slave nor free, male nor female, for all are one in Christ Jesus" (Gal. 3:28)—mean that the burdens of slavery are automatically negated.

To see this point, every modern Christian should reread Paul's Letter to Philemon. In that letter, Paul addresses a Roman master converted to Christianity, Philemon, and instructs him in the proper way to treat his runaway slave Onesimus. Paul tells the master to take Onesimus back and to treat him as a brother in love; but Paul never mentions emancipation and even tells the slave to return to his master. The assumption is that Christian charity or brotherly love transcends the social order and does not immediately affect the status of slaves because it affects the heart first and foremost; and it makes salvation more important than political freedom. Nevertheless, Paul does not reject political freedom outright. Instead, he refers to it conditionally as an opportunity for proper use rather than as a right to be claimed: "Were you a slave when you were called? Do not be concerned, but if you can gain your freedom, use it more [in Greek: *mallon chresai*, or more use]" (1 Cor. 7:21). The implication is that the value of political freedom is measured by its proper use for spiritual things which are the things of primary importance.

From these observations, I would draw the simple but momentous conclusion that the Christian message in the New Testament is transpolitical, though not entirely apolitical. That is, it puts spiritual duties above political duties and may or may not support democratic human rights depending on how one draws out the indirect political implications of an essentially spiritual teaching. And this is precisely the crux of the matter. A Christian argument for liberal democracy cannot be found in the Bible, in either the Old or the New Testaments, because it is not there in so many words. Neither the biblical covenant, nor the divine law, nor the witness of the prophets, nor the kingdom of God, nor charity and universal love for all classes of people automatically translates into a political teaching in favor of democracy. If an argument for democracy is to be found at all, it must be inferred indirectly, mainly from the Bible's conception of a common humanity or a common human dignity.

This conception, in turn, rests on two fundamental claims: (1) that every human being is made in the image and likeness of God (the *Imago Dei*) and (2) that God became man in the person of Jesus Christ, whose redemptive suffering enables human beings to become "partakers of the divine nature" (2 Pet. 1:4). Do these statements about the divine image, the divine redemption, and even the divinization of human nature contain the seeds of a democratic creed of innate dignity and human rights? Many modern Christian theologians believe they do, but the Bible itself does not point in this direction. Why not?

THE BIBLICAL *IMAGO DEI*

The biblical ideas of the divine image and the divine redemption make powerful claims about human dignity, perhaps the most powerful of any philosophy or religion in the world. They give human beings a lofty and special place in the cosmos by placing the human species at the peak of the created universe (or just below the angels). They even single out the human body as worthy of the godhead, challenging polytheistic religions that have viewed birds, reptiles, and other animals as divine images or divinities. By exalting man above the animals as an image of divinity, the Bible 'divinizes' humanity in some sense. Yet, the biblical conception of human dignity, based on the *Imago Dei,* is not the same as the liberal democratic conception of human dignity based on autonomous self-determination; and it does not necessarily support human rights. Instead of pointing directly to such political notions, the Bible locates human dignity in spiritual notions, such as the *immortality* that man possessed before the Fall and the capacity for *holiness.* The political implications of these notions are not clear immediately or, when clarified, often turn out to be undemocratic.

To illustrate the essentially spiritual conception of the *Imago Dei* in the Bible, I will begin by citing two passages. One is from the Book of Wisdom (2:23), where it says, "God created man for *incorruption, and made him in the image of His eternity,* but through the devil's envy, death entered the world" (emphasis added). This statement explicitly equates the divine image in man with lost immortality. A second passage is from Leviticus (11:44–45), where God justifies obedience to the divine law by saying, "You shall be holy, for I am holy," which implies that man is most like God in the holy activity of obeying the divine law. The first meaning of the *Imago Dei,* lost immortality, is supported by Genesis and Paul's letters and may be regarded as the specifically Christian one. The second meaning, holiness, is emphasized by Moses and the Hebrew prophets, though it is also central to

Christianity. Together, the two meanings indicate that the divine image in man is the original immortality that was lost in the Fall and that may be recoverable by holiness. The biblical conception of human dignity is therefore defined in terms of relations with God and the capacity for eternal life rather than in political terms of equality and freedom.

Let me elaborate this interpretation by discussing the three references to the *Imago Dei* in the book of Genesis. In the first and most familiar one (Gen. 1:26–28), God creates human beings in His image and likeness, distinguishing male and female and telling them to "be fruitful and multiply" and to have dominion over the earth. This reference places human beings at the peak of creation as the only creatures made in the divine image; but it does not specify in what respect they resemble God, though the context emphasizes the ability to procreate, as if procreation through male-female sexual differentiation were an image of God's power to create. The problem here is that animals also have the ability to procreate, but they are not said to be made in the image and likeness of God.

The second reference to the divine image in the book of Genesis (5:1–3) draws a further parallel between God's power to create and man's power to procreate: "When God created man, He made him in the likeness of God. Male and female He created them, . . . and named them man [*adam*] . . . When Adam had lived a hundred and thirty years, he became the father of a son in his own likeness, after his image, and named him Seth." The obvious problem in both passages of Genesis is that procreation may be an image of God's creative power, but it is not peculiar to man: The animals also are told to be fruitful and to reproduce "after their kind" (though animals may not be as conscious as human beings about passing on a personal likeness to their children, as Adam was about imparting his likeness to Seth).

The puzzle is deepened by the third reference to the divine image in Genesis, which also refers to something common to man and animals. In the story of Noah, God blesses Noah and his family and then tells them to be fruitful and to multiply and to respect human life: "For your lifeblood I will surely require a reckoning . . . Whoever sheds the blood of man, by man shall his blood be shed; for God made man in His own image" (Gen. 9:5–7). Opponents of capital punishment hate this passage, because it so clearly links respect for human life as something made in the image of God with the command to put murderers to death. The point seems to be that putting murderers to death vindicates the lifeblood or divine image of their victims and that murderers are subject to capital punishment because they have forfeited their own lifeblood or divine image.[12]

In these three passages, we have the only explicit references to the *Imago Dei* in Genesis and (astonishingly) in the entire Hebrew Bible. All three make procreation and lifeblood the Godlike image in man; yet these are things that man shares with other animals. This is a real puzzle, one that is fraught with important moral implications. Many of the great commentators pass over the textual problems too hastily, usually because they have a preconceived notion of the attributes that reflect the divine image in man (the most common view is that reason and free will are the distinguishing features, although they are not mentioned explicitly in the passages on the divine image). What, then, is the Bible saying about the *Imago Dei*?

The only sense that I can make of this puzzle is that procreation and lifeblood, while common to man and animals, must have a deeper meaning for humans than for animals. Procreation and lifeblood must be pale reflections of the original vitality and life-giving power that man alone possessed before the Fall when he possessed immortal life. The image of God in man would thus refer to man's original immortality—an immortality that animals never possessed and that is different from God's immortality in the crucial respect that man's original immortality could be lost (it is an *image* of immortality, after all, not the real thing). In the biblical view, then, man stands between the animals and God as a creature with special dignity because he once possessed the Godlike attribute of immortality but lost it and became mortal, without, however, losing the hope of recovering it and gaining true eternal life.

This interpretation is supported by the whole account of the Fall, which is about the loss of immortality and innocence. Through disobedience, Adam and Eve become mortal and sinful; but a kind of afterglow of immortality remains in the longevity of Adam and the early patriarchs (some of whom live over 900 years) with the pattern of longevity continuing until God sets an arbitrary limit to human life at 120 years. As a compensation, the surrogate immortality that Adam found in his son Seth continues through procreation in families that endure for generations, as Abram soon learns when God makes him Abraham, the father of his people.

Thus, we see that the divine image in man, in the sense of his original immortality, is partly inalienable and partly alienable; the potential is retained by everyone, but the actuality is subject to loss and recovery. The moral implication is that the Bible teaches a basic spiritual equality of all human beings as a pale reflection of their original perfection. But the Bible also permits inequalities among people, depending on the degrees of corruption or incorruption that take them farther away or closer to eternal life. This makes human dignity in the Bible comparative rather than absolute, an idea capable of sustaining hierarchies rather than requiring democratic notions of equality and freedom: Everyone has an image of original immortality—an original divine spark—but not everyone will recover its full power and attain eternal life.

After the Book of Genesis, there are no more references to the *Imago Dei* in the entire Hebrew Bible. Beginning with Exodus and continuing in subsequent books, man is compared with God in the capacity for holiness (*kadosh*). The command of God, "You shall be holy, for I am holy" (Lev. 11:45), is forcefully stated as the reason for obeying the divine law. The implication seems to be that God no longer draws humans toward divinity through the surrogate immortality of the family of Abraham but through the divine law revealed to Moses which requires holiness. Indeed, the express purpose of the Mosaic law is to make a "holy nation" (Exod. 19:6) through a myriad of laws that requires the utmost devotion. To be "holy" in this sense has many connotations which are hard to define precisely. In a formal and almost tautological sense, holiness means being set apart from the profane. But it also implies separation from the profane in specific ways—by superior purity in sexual and dietary matters, by transcendence of the mundane through the mysterious presence of the invisible God, and by a high degree of righteousness in the execution of justice and social responsibilities. The divine image in man found almost exclusively in the Book of Genesis is thus superceded but not abolished by the imitation of God's holiness in observing the divine law—making people more Godlike in their purity, transcendence, and righteousness. Perhaps the Hebrew Bible is saying that the lost image of God from Genesis (the lost immortality of Adam and Eve) may be recovered through the extended family and the divine law— partly by continuing forever the generations descended from Abraham but above all by keeping the eternal covenant and obeying the law of Moses which makes people holy like the Holy One of Israel.

It is not until we arrive at the New Testament that the original language of Genesis about the *Imago Dei* reappears in the Bible. Here we find about a dozen references to the image, likeness, figure, and form of God as well as a variety of references to similar notions such as the children of God, the sons of God, and "partakers of the divine nature." Some of these terms are reserved especially for Jesus Christ, who is called "the image (*eikon*) of the invisible God, the first-born of all creation" (Col. 1:15; Heb. 1:3). These descriptions are clearly intended to connect the *Imago Dei* of Genesis with the central article of the Christian faith—namely, the Incarnation, in which the invisible God becomes a visible man in Jesus Christ. As Paul says of Christ, "though He was in the form of God, He . . . emptied himself, taking the form of a servant, being born in the likeness of men" (Phil. 2:5–7). The point of using the language of image and likeness from Genesis to explain the birth of Christ may be inferred from Paul's theology: While God originally created man in the divine image, that image has been obscured or lost; hence, it needs to be restored by Christ, who is the real image of God and the image of man. Christ combines in His person the image of God (immortality) and the likeness of fallen men (mortality) and therefore is able to restore the lost image of God to man (to restore lost immortality).

Although Paul tends to reserve the *Imago Dei* for Christ, he also applies it in a different manner to ordinary mortals. In one of his most controversial statements, he sees a further, if dimmer, reflection of the image of God in males as the head of the household: For "the head of every man is Christ, the head of a woman is her husband, and the head of Christ is God . . . [hence] a man ought not to cover his head, since he is the image and glory of God; but the woman is the glory of man . . . [and] ought to have a veil on her head." The reason Paul gives is that "man was not made from woman, but woman from man," meaning that Eve was created from Adam's rib; but he cautions that man's authority over woman is also a kind of reciprocity, for "man is now born of woman; and all things are from God" (1 Cor. 11:3–16). The significance of Paul's statement is that he uses the image of God, as it was used in the Old Testament, to establish a hierarchy according to the order of divine creation. Here the hierarchy extends from God to Christ to man to woman and is justified not in terms of natural superiority but by the supernatural creation of God. Nevertheless, Paul indicates that the created order may be thought of as natural and even ought to be reflected in social conventions, such as women covering their heads as a sign of modesty. A continuum thereby emerges from created hierarchies to natural hierarchies to social hierarchies.

Herein lies the fundamental difference between the biblical and the contemporary understanding of human dignity. In the biblical view, dignity is hierarchical and comparative; in the modern, it is democratic and absolute. The Bible (both Old and New Testaments) promotes hierarchies because it understands reality in terms of the "image of God" which is a type of reflected glory—a reflection of something more perfect in something less perfect. Hence, dignity exists in degrees of perfection rather than in abstract equalities. The dignity or glory possessed by something made in the image of a more perfect being carries moral claims of deference, reciprocal obligation, and duty rather than equality, freedom, and rights.

Following the logic of reciprocal obligations, there is no contradiction between the statements of the New Testament that require obedience to hierarchies—whether they be divinely created, natural, or conventional—and passages that speak of the spiritual dignity of all human beings. This point needs emphasizing because nothing is more confusing for modern Christians than to read passages in the Gospels and Epistles commanding obedience to the Roman emperor and acceptance of the patriarchal household and of social inequalities and then to read other passages asserting that all people have a divine spark within them and are one in Christ. For example, we find, on the one side, passages implying that all people have spiritual dignity and may even become divinized—a kind of spiritual democracy. The most well-known passages are: "There is neither Jew nor Greek, slave nor freeman, male nor female, for you are all one in Christ"

(Gal. 3:28); and through Christ's "divine power . . . you may . . . become partakers of the divine nature" (2 Pet. 1:3–4). Yet, in apparent contradiction, we also hear harsh, undemocratic statements such as "Render to Caesar the things that are Caesar's" (Mat. 22:21); "Let every soul be subject to the governing authorities" (Rom. 13:1; also 1 Pet. 2:13); "Wives, be subject to your husbands, as to the Lord" (Eph. 5:22; also 1 Cor. 11:3, 1 Pet. 3:1); "Slaves, be obedient to your earthly masters" (Eph. 6:5–7; also Col. 3:18–25, Titus 2:1–10); "I permit not woman to teach or to have authority over men" (1 Tim. 2:12); and "Go into all the world and preach the Gospel . . . He who believes and is baptized will be saved; but he who does not believe will be condemned" (Mark 16:15). Are these statements a denial of the universal spiritual dignity implied in the previous passages?

The apparent contradiction is resolved by recognizing that human dignity in the Bible is both universal and selective: It proclaims the spiritual dignity of every person in light of their original perfection, but it permits and even requires different degrees of dignity in the created and fallen world based on God's election of special people and the institution of human authorities. The Bible also seems to imply that while dignity in some sense is given and therefore 'inalienable' (as we would say today), it is also something to be won or lost, merited or forfeited, augmented or diminished. And it implies that obedience to emperors and masters, who are a part of the fallen world and largely conventional in status, does not violate the dignity of the Christian believer because true dignity lies in the possession of an immortal soul and interior freedom.

Some of these points may be inferred from passages which allude to human beings as children of God possessing a divine spark within themselves. When Peter says that we may become partakers of divinity through Christ, he adds the qualification that divinization is attained through virtue: Christ's "divine power has granted to us all things . . . that through these you may escape from the corruption that is in the world from passion, and become partakers of the divine nature. For this very reason make every effort to supplement your faith with virtue, and virtue with knowledge, and knowledge with self-control, and self-control with steadfastness, and steadfastness with godliness, and godliness with brotherly affection, and . . . love" (2 Pet. 1:3–8). The words of Peter are spiritually *un-democratic* because they link divinization with virtue—with moral virtue, such as self-control, and intellectual virtue, such as knowledge, and spiritual virtue, such as charity or love—which are not attained by everyone in the same degree because they require personal effort and a personal "call and election" (ibid., 1:10). Partaking in divinity, then, enhances the glory, excellence, or dignity of some but not all, creating a spiritual elite of those who "will be richly provided for . . . [in] the eternal kingdom" (ibid., 1:10–11).

Likewise, when Paul speaks of the children or sons of God, he makes distinctions of rank based on spiritual virtue. The primary distinction is between those who live by the flesh and those who live by the spirit: "If you live according to the flesh you will die, but if by the spirit . . . you will live. For all who are led by the Spirit of God are . . . sons of God . . . [and] children of God" (Rom. 8:13–16). But who are the sons or children of God? Paul indicates that they are the few predestined saints: "For the creation waits with eager longing for the revealing of the sons of God . . . [when] the Spirit intercedes for the saints according to the will of God. . . . For those whom He foreknew He also predestined to be conformed to the image of His Son . . . [and to be] glorified" (ibid., 8:19, 27–30). A more mystical view of the children of God can be found in the Epistle of 1 John 3:1–10 where they are distinguished from the children of the devil by their moral purity and are rewarded with the vision of God: "Beloved, we are God's children now; it does not yet appear what we shall be, but we know that when He appears we shall be like Him, for we shall see Him as He is. And everyone who thus hopes in Him purifies himself. . . . By this it may be seen who are the children of God and who are the children of the devil."

The spiritual inequalities described in these passages may be summarized in two general points about biblical Christianity. First, dignity is expressed in the language of image, likeness, sonship, and children of God because dignity is a type of reflected glory from a more perfect to a less perfect being. This is the very meaning of the word "glory," which is abundantly used in the New Testament (usually a translation of the Greek *doxa* meaning reputation, honor, glory and also appearance, seeming, opinion). Glory is the closest word to "dignity" in the

New Testament, and it is almost always used to express a hierarchical relation among more or less perfect beings: In the Transfiguration, Christ, Moses, and Elijah "appeared in glory" (Luke 9:30–32); resurrected bodies are "raised in glory" (1 Cor. 15:43); and in the cosmos "there are celestial bodies and terrestrial bodies; but the glory of the celestial is one, and the glory of the terrestrial is another . . . [every] star differs from star in glory" (1 Cor. 15:40). Thus, there are different glories or degrees of dignity for the whole universe as well as for human beings, usually measured by degrees of corruptibility and incorruptibility or mortality and immortality.

The second point is that biblical Christianity distinguishes created and natural hierarchies from political and social hierarchies. The created and natural hierarchies are upheld as expressions of the divine will, while the political and social hierarchies are conventions and matters of prudence which inculcate good habits. The created hierarchy is stated most strongly, extending from the invisible God to His image in the visible Son of God, to the children of God who through personal effort and election attain virtue. The natural hierarchy includes the image of God in the male head of the household and both male and female human beings in their dominion over the lower species of animals. In addition to these hierarchies, there is the social and political order which is largely conventional because Christ distinguished the duties to God from duties to Caesar. This means that the state and social classes are not determined by created or natural hierarchies but are to be accepted "for the Lord's sake"—not because they are inherently just, but because God willed these institutions to restrain sinful human nature and to teach lessons of reciprocal obligation between master and servant and rich and poor. The strangeness of this teaching is that it requires Christians to accept most social conventions as mere conventions, even while recognizing that the poor and the powerless are closer to God in their faithfulness and charity.

In the last analysis, the New Testament teaches obedience to created, natural, and conventional hierarchies because the dignity of every person is a matter of inner freedom that is independent of external authority. Unconditional submission to Christ as Lord and King is the only absolute demand; all other obligations (to one's nation, emperor, social class, the whole natural world, and even to one's family) are conditional. A new realm is opened up in everyone— the "innermost self" (Rom. 7:22), the "hidden person of the heart" (1 Pet. 3:4)—which concerns the intimate question of the soul's relation to God. The inner realm is the real source of dignity in all persons because it means that something infinite is at stake in their life's choices: Everyone has an immortal soul with an eternal destiny which has at risk its eternal salvation or damnation. Compared to this question, the various forms of external obedience are of secondary importance. Thus, it is possible for the Bible to uphold the dignity of every human person as a creature made in the image of God and redeemed by Christ while supporting created, natural, and conventional hierarchies.

If this interpretation is correct, then the main conclusion we should draw is that both liberalism and the Bible seek to defend human dignity, but they define human dignity in different ways and draw different political conclusions. Liberalism equates dignity with autonomy of personality and mastery of one's destiny—political ideas that are inherently tied to democratic human rights. By contrast, the Bible equates the dignity of human beings with their relations with God, especially in their original immortality and their capacity for holiness—spiritual notions that permit spiritual hierarchies as well as undemocratic and illiberal politics. These different conceptions of dignity leave us with the dilemma that I posed at the beginning of the book: Modern liberal democracy needs God, but the biblical God is not inherently liberal or democratic in His political teachings. Faced with this difficulty, we need to turn to the Christian theological tradition in order to see if it is more compatible with liberal democracy than the Bible.

THE CHRISTIAN THEOLOGICAL TRADITION

Once again we face disturbing news. Many of the greatest Christian theologians and church leaders were as illiberal and undemocratic as the Bible is. In a recent book entitled *Christianity and Democracy in Global Context*, prominent scholars speak regretfully of "the church's long road to political democracy" and "the late friendship between Christianity and democracy."[13] One might go further and observe that Christianity for much of its two-thousand-year history has been rather illiberal and undemocratic—not only in its shameful excesses, such as the Spanish Inquisition and the wars of religion, but also in many of its core teachings about spirituality, church organization, and political structures.

For contemporary Christians, however, this is *not* a serious problem. When confronted with unpleasant facts about the tradition, they respond initially with embarrassment and then with the firm conviction that one can disregard the tradition. With a sigh of relief they comfort themselves: Thank God we have gotten over the tradition! But such dismissals leave a very awkward implication. They imply that Christianity is not defensible or authentic until it catches up with modern liberalism. They also tend to imply that the Bible and the Christian tradition are little more than rationalizations for unequal power structures written by the victors and that liberalism is the new 'revelation' because it connects the Christian belief in universal love and the infinite worth of every human being with a political imperative to respect individual rights in a democratic society.

Although such views are popular today, they need to be challenged because they usually rest on little more than unexamined assumptions about the superiority of the modern age to the past. The first step in a critical examination is simply to describe the illiberal and undemocratic views of the great theologians and church leaders of the past—views that sound so shocking to us if we take them seriously instead of dismissing them immediately as outmoded or biased. Some of these views were mentioned briefly in the Introduction; but they are worth repeating along with numerous other examples in order to remind ourselves how recent and, in a way, how unusual is the present situation where most Christians favor liberal democracy.

In the first place, we should remember that Paul and Peter were taken as the authoritative guides to politics for early Christians and for many generations afterwards. While Paul and Peter both affirmed a common humanity in Christ, they also laid down sweeping admonitions about obeying human authorities that taught Christians to accept kingship, Roman citizenship, and the hierarchical institutions of the day. Many of the early church fathers said similar things. Only a few, such as Tertullian, counseled separation from Roman society on the grounds of irreconcilable differences between classical and Christian culture. The majority tried to find a place for themselves as citizens of the Roman Empire. Although they emphatically rejected the cult of the emperor and his claims of divinity (and even accepted martyrdom as the price of their faith), they viewed the state as divinely ordained for the purpose of keeping order. And even though they sought *libertas ecclesiae*, the freedom of the church to evangelize without repression, they were loyal Roman citizens even during the periods of persecution. Their behavior, in the words of Hugo Rahner, was a curious mixture of "no" and "yes" to state power: They insisted on the supremacy of the church to the state; and bishops, such as St. Ambrose, did not hesitate to rebuke emperors for their unjust or immoral behavior; but they honored the emperor as a power instituted by God.[14]

As for the ethical teachings of the early Christians, they had some effect in changing pagan culture on practices that conflicted with Christian morality. Attempts were made to diminish the harshness of slavery by encouraging manumission, as John Chrysostom did with some success, and some former slaves became bishops of the church. Infanticide was opposed by Christian teachings against abortion and the exposure of unwanted infants. Polygamy and homosexuality were challenged by insisting on sex only within monogamous marriage. Suicide was criticized by opposing Stoic notions of honorable escape from life and by rejecting euthanasia. And warrior virtues were softened by elevating milder virtues over martial glory. Despite these direct challenges to pagan ethics, the early Christians developed no real political theory and demanded no revolutionary changes in the politics or social structure of the Roman Empire.

The first comprehensive statement on politics by the church fathers was St. Augustine's *The City of God*. In this classic work, St. Augustine is neutral about which form of government is best, sometimes praising the early Roman republic for its heroic virtues and sometimes defending Christian emperors such as Constantine and Theodosius, while regarding coercive political authority as a necessary restraint on man's sinful nature. He justifies obedience to established rulers as long as certain limits are not exceeded: "As for this mortal life, . . . what does it matter under whose rule a man lives . . . provided the rulers do not force him to do impious and wicked acts?"[15] Augustine's political theory is thus a type of limited or benevolent authoritarianism.

After Augustine, most theologians and church leaders were monarchists of one sort or another. John of Salisbury, St. Thomas Aquinas, Dante, John of Paris, and Nicholas of Cusa spanned the High Middle Ages and defended the rule of national kings or the Holy Roman Emperor. In the ideal, they argued for kingship limited by law and dedicated to the common good within a corporate hierarchy of social and ecclesiastical orders. The most influential medieval Scholastic, St. Thomas Aquinas, defended mixed monarchy that combined elements of monarchy, aristocracy, and democracy.

Among the Protestant reformers, views on authority varied, but none of the leading figures of the first generations embraced democracy or liberalism. Martin Luther followed St. Augustine in his politics, with a stronger emphasis than Augustine himself on obedience to established princes and opposition to rebellion. John Calvin was distrustful of kings but still thought they should be obeyed; his idea of the best form of government was an aristocracy that served the theocratic ends of a "Christian polity." Richard Hooker was an Anglican conservative, a defender of the Elizabethan settlement and an upholder of monarchy and national episcopacy against Puritan insurgents. Even the American Puritans were quite illiberal and undemocratic in their early phases. As John Cotton said (in 1636): "Democracy, I do not conceive that ever God did ordain as a fit government for either church or state. . . . As for monarchy and aristocracy, they are both of them clearly approved and directed in Scripture . . . [which] setteth up theocracy in both."[16] John Winthrop's ideal was a corporate hierarchy held together by Christian charity and headed by gentlemen rulers bound by their covenants with God and the people; he dismissed democracy with the observation that "among civilized nations, it is accounted the meanest and worst of all forms of government."[17]

One might add that even the more progressive Protestant reformers were still far from embracing liberal democracy. In 1717, John Wise defended self-governing churches but favored mixed monarchy in the political realm: "the fairest in the world is that which has a regular monarchy settled upon a noble democracy . . . the British Empire . . . is such a monarchy."[18] Nor should it be forgotten that Jonathan Edwards, the leader of the Great Awakening of the mid-1700s, favored a model of Christian community that resembled Winthrop's corporate hierarchy in which everyone is bound together by charity with magistrates acting as "fathers of the commonwealth"; he pointedly said that Christians should "know it is best that some should be above others and should be honored and submitted to as such."[19] John Wesley, the founder of Methodism in the eighteenth century, is a spiritual reformer whose religious teachings had democratic implications but whose politics were those of an Anglican Tory; indeed, Wesley said of himself and his movement, "We are no republicans and never intend to be."[20] Even the nineteenth-century Danish Protestant, Søren Kierkegaard, known for his religious individualism, wrote against the leveling tendencies of democracy and criticized women's emancipation; he sardonically notes in one of his journals, "The hatred for the monarchical principle has gone so far that people want to have four-part solos."[21]

If we turn from the theologians to the practices of the churches, we see a similar pattern for much of the two-thousand-year history of Christendom. The Roman Catholic Church, for example, has only recently come to embrace liberal democratic politics. Its views on the best organization of the state evolved through four historical periods: (1) During the first three centuries of Christianity, the Church accepted the authority of the Roman emperor as a human authority without developing a doctrine of the state; (2) From the fourth century when Emperors Constantine and Theodosius embraced Christianity to the late nineteenth century, the Church sought official state establishment for Catholic Christianity and supported Christian kingship of one sort or another (either a Christianized Roman emperor or Christian national kingship) while often resisting emperors and excommunicating specific kings; (3) Beginning with Pope Leo XIII at the end of the nineteenth century and continuing through the 1950s with Pope Pius XII, the Church reevaluated its stance on kingship and Catholic establishment, permitting some flexibility in accepting democracy and religious liberty; (4) Finally, the Second

Vatican Council of 1962–65 put the Catholic Church on the side of constitutional democracy and religious liberty and explicitly endorsed democratic human rights (with qualifications about how rights should be properly used). Thus, the Catholic Church supported emperors and kings for most of its history and embraced liberal or constitutional democracy as a matter of principle only in the past thirty-five years.

In the Eastern Orthodox tradition (an important tradition that is often unjustifiably neglected in the Western world), the connection between the church and the state has been more intimate than in the Latin West. From the time of Emperor Constantine, the Eastern churches sought a close collaboration between the emperor and the church or between monarch and patriarch in predominantly Orthodox nations. Though some refer to this relation as "Caesaro-Papism," many Orthodox theologians reject the label because it implies subordination of the church to the state. A more accurate view, according to the distinguished Orthodox theologians Alexander Schmemann and Timothy Ware, is that Orthodoxy regards church and state— priesthood (*sacerdotium*) and kingship (*imperium*)—as distinct but equal powers working together to achieve the Byzantine ideal of "harmony." In other words, the divinity of the emperor must be rejected as a pagan heresy; but the emperor and the empire (especially the original Byzantine Empire emanating from Constantinople) have a special religious significance beyond the defense of Orthodox doctrine: The state is a reflection or "icon" on earth of the divine governance of God in Heaven.[22] Needless to say, the ideal of Byzantine harmony was rarely attained and usually meant the subservience of the church to the monarch. Yet, the ideal lasted well into the twentieth century in Orthodox nations such as Russia, Greece, Romania, Bulgaria, and Serbia; and it is not clear if the autocratic ideal has been entirely rejected or merely put on indefinite hold in the present democratic age.

Among Protestant churches, the patterns are extremely varied, with many currents flowing between church and state. If one may generalize at all about Protestant views of the state, one should emphasize the crucial dividing line between two groups: On the one side, Anglicans and Lutherans have consistently supported monarchy, established princes, and national churches; on the other side, the churches growing out of the more radical reformation in Switzerland, begun by John Calvin and Huldrych Zwingli, promoted a more congregational model of church organization that eventually led to democratic practices in state and society. In the former cases, Anglicans obviously have been tied to the English monarchy, both at home and throughout the British Empire or Commonwealth. Lutherans have favored national churches and established authorities, which in Germany made them distrustful of democracy as late as the 1920s, when many Lutherans opposed the Weimar Republic, following the slogan, "Yes, to the state, no to democracy!" Such distrust was not entirely overcome until the 1985 proclamation of German Lutherans on "The Evangelical Church and Democracy."[23] Even Methodists, as noted above, were initially Anglican Tories despite the long-term democratizing effects of their evangelical methods.

In a view that captures the conventional wisdom of many church historians, James H. Nichols said in *Democracy and the Churches* (1951) that most Roman Catholic, Eastern Orthodox, Anglican, and Lutheran churches have been distrustful of democracy and that only radical offshoots of Calvinism—"left-wing Puritans," as he calls them—such as Congregationalists, Baptists and Anabaptists, Presbyterians, Unitarians, Quakers, Disciples of Christ, Salvation Army, and later Methodists were reliable carriers of the democratic faith among Christians. This is similar to what Ernst Troeltsch said in 1911: "At the present day, Calvinism feels itself to be the only Christian ecclesiastical body which is in agreement with the modern democratic and capitalistic development, and, *moreover, the only one which is suited to it.*"[24]

None of these observations is intended to deny the fact that, outside the dominant patterns favoring kingship and hierarchical structures, there have been democratic or egalitarian movements inspired by Christianity. In the New Testament, the Book of Acts records the first Christians living in societies that practiced communal sharing of property. Though the experiment is shown to unwind due to hoarding of property, it has inspired radical sects and apocalyptic visionaries to seek a new social order in which power and wealth would be equalized—sects such as the Lollards and Waldensians of the Middle Ages, the "free-church" Anabaptists (some committed to peaceful change, others to violent revolution), and millenarian movements of different kinds (Levellers and Diggers). The point that I am making is that the radical sects have been a small minority compared to overwhelming numbers of theologians and church leaders who have supported corporate hierarchies, usually with monarchical or aristocratic forms at the top mixed with elements of participation and consent at other levels. This pattern predominated until at least the seventeenth century in the major denominations and only gradually changed over the last three hundred years, eventually producing a new democratic consensus among Christians at the end of the twentieth century.

WHY WERE THEY ILLIBERAL AND UNDEMOCRATIC?

The obvious question raised by this overview is: Why were so many of the greatest Christian theologians, from the early church to the early Reformation and beyond, illiberal and undemocratic? Why has the dominant model of a Christian polity been a corporate hierarchy rather than a liberal or social democracy? Is such a tradition inconsistent with Christian ethical teachings which favor the poor and humble over the rich and powerful and which recognize the equal dignity of all human beings in the eyes of God?

One possible explanation for the dominant pattern is that Christianity is essentially indifferent to politics. It is often argued, for example, that many early Christians believed that the end of the world was imminent and the kingdom of God would begin in their lifetime, making ordinary politics irrelevant and inclining them to accept the politics of their times without protest. This explanation is not convincing, however, because it is not clear how many of the early Christians believed the end was near; some did, but others may have been guided by Christ's explicit statement that no one but the heavenly Father knows the day and hour when the world will end (Matt. 24:36). Whatever is the case, the beliefs of early Christians do not explain the persistence of monarchical and hierarchical views for the next seventeen to twenty centuries when expectations about the end of the world were (for the most part) indefinitely postponed.

Another possible explanation is the otherworldliness of the Christian religion—the belief in salvation in the world to come where "the last shall be first" accompanied by the belief that the conditions of this world are not subject to fundamental progress or improvement. The implication is that one should be satisfied with the powers that be, even though they are matters of historical contingency. Formulating this view more precisely in *A History of Medieval Political Thought, 300–1450,* Joseph Canning says, "In itself Christianity advocated no particular form of government, but because the church was confronted with monarchy as the only form of rule existing in late antiquity and the early Middle Ages, Christian political thought emerged as monarchical."[25] In my view, this thesis is only partly true. The element of truth lies in the observation that Christianity advocates no particular form of government as a requirement of divine law. In this respect, Christianity is more transpolitical than Judaism, whose divine law or *halakah* includes a civil and legal code as well as political notions such as God's covenant with a chosen people and the designation of a sacred territory as the Promised Land. Christianity is also more apolitical than Islam, whose divine law or *sharia* includes a comprehensive legal and civil code and whose founder, Mohammed, combined the roles of prophet, lawgiver, and military leader.

While Christianity recognizes a greater distinction between the spiritual and political realms than Judaism and Islam, one may still argue that the preference shown for kingship and hierarchical structures throughout much of the Christian tradition is not simply a matter of historical accident. Indeed, I think it is possible to argue that the great Christian theologians and church leaders arrived at their views of authority by recognizing that there is something *inherently hierarchical* in the Christian religion. In my judgment, there are several powerful reasons for the predominance of hierarchical patterns of authority in the Christian tradition that cannot be easily dismissed as prejudice or historical accident.

One is the doctrine of the Two Cities, according to which the universe has been divided into two great realms as a consequence of the Fall—the city of God or spiritual realm and the earthly city or temporal realm. While this doctrine does not automatically set the pattern of authority for each realm, it does establish a hierarchy of ends that theologians developed into a rationale for corporate hierarchies in each realm. In the spiritual realm, the end to be served was eternal salvation which God advances through the "divine election" of holy people—prophets, saints, apostles and their successors. This notion justified the divinely ordained hierarchy of the church as well as an ascending order of spiritual perfection from sinners to saints and the holy angels. In the temporal realm, the ends to be served were civil peace, moral virtue, and the defense of Christian orthodoxy. Political authority was understood as instituted by God for these temporal ends, which most theologians thought were best achieved through kingship or mixed regimes given the fallen nature of man. An important influence on both realms of authority was Greek philosophy and its conception of the natural universe as a hierarchy of beings, ascending from lower to higher substances in an order of rational perfection. When brought together in theological systems, these powerful doctrines—the Two Cities, the advancement of salvation through divine election, the attainment of temporal ends in the fallen world of politics, the ascending order of beings and substances— favored corporate hierarchies in each of the realms or in a unified Christian commonwealth. In general, traditional Christians were illiberal and undemocratic because they conceived of God's created universe as a hierarchy of being and thought that institutions should promote rational and spiritual perfection—ideas that cannot be easily dismissed as prejudice or accident.

THE TWO CITIES AND SPIRITUAL HIERARCHIES

For much of its two-thousand-year history, Christianity derived its views on authority from the doctrine of the Two Cities, variously stated as the Two Kingdoms, Two Powers, Two Swords, or Two Realms. It was developed quite logically from the New Testament where Christ distinguished the duties to God from duties to Caesar and said that His kingship is not of this world. While setting God above Caesar, Jesus insisted that earthly kings hold legitimate power because God ordains or permits them to rule, implying political authority is divinely sanctioned and should be obeyed in its sphere. In the centuries after Christ, influential figures such as St. Ambrose, St. Augustine, and Pope Gelasius elaborated the distinction into a formal doctrine of two realms, the spiritual and the temporal, both authorized and ordained by God for the relatively distinct ends of heavenly and earthly happiness. This doctrine was accepted by most Christian theologians and canon lawyers at least until the seventeenth century, when it began to be challenged by unified views of church-state relations, such as the divine right of kings and certain brands of Calvinist theocracy. While the Two Cities doctrine does not directly determine the internal organization of the realms, both were developed in a hierarchical direction for important reasons.

In the spiritual realm, the Catholic Church, the Eastern Orthodox Church, and the Anglican Church interpreted the Bible to mean that Christ founded the institutional church through the Apostolic Succession—that Christ gave the Apostles authority over dogma, sacraments, and morals which was then passed on to the bishops of the church and to their successors who also ordained priests and deacons. Some of the influential passages of Scripture cited over the centuries to support the Apostolic Succession are the following: Christ's statement that Peter is the rock on which the institutional church will be built and His grant to Peter of spiritual authority as represented by the keys to the kingdom of Heaven (Matt. 16:18–19); Christ's grant of authority to all the Apostles to settle disputes in the church in the Father's name (Matt. 18:18); Christ's grant of sacramental powers to all the Apostles, specifically the powers to receive the Holy Spirit in order to forgive or to retain sins (John 20:23), to institute the Eucharist, understood as His own body and blood (Luke 22:19–20; John 6:48–59), and to baptize disciples in all nations (Matt. 28:19). Building on Christ's grant of spiritual authority and sacramental powers, the Apostles, especially Peter and Paul, then passed on His authority by the laying on of hands or other outward signs to special persons, as in the apostolic designation of Stephen by laying on of hands (Acts 6:5), Peter's laying of hands on certain Samaritans (Acts 8:14–18), Paul appointing elders in every church in Antioch (Acts 14:23), and Paul designating Titus to appoint bishops and presbyters in every town of Crete (1 Titus 1:5–7). In this way, the Apostles designated as their successors those who became bishops (*episkopoi*, a title that originally meant overseers or stewards and was not always clearly distinguished from *presbyteroi* or elders in the Book of Acts), giving them spiritual authority by divine institution.

While the historical record beyond the New Testament is sketchy, it indicates that the Apostolic Succession was developed formally into the fixed office of bishop or episcopal authority by the end of the first century. According to the Eastern Orthodox tradition, the bishops were direct successors to the Apostles who first established the Christian church in five great cities (Rome, Constantinople, Alexandria, Antioch, and Jerusalem); those bishops eventually received the title Patriarch in recognition of their authority over a major ecclesiastical realm. Among the church fathers, the office of bishop was described and defended by important figures in the first and second centuries, such as Clement of Rome, Irenaeus, and Tertullian. Of these early authors, Irenaeus is most explicit about the succession, saying, "we can enumerate those who were appointed bishops in the churches by the Apostles, and their successors, down to our own day"; he then proceeds to name the succession in Rome established by Peter and Paul through twelve bishops and claims that the same may be done for the church in Asia minor (*Against the Heresies*, III, 3.1–3.4). In the third and fourth centuries, Cyprian and Eusebius also affirmed the doctrine and practice of episcopal authority derived from the Apostolic Succession.[26] As both defenders and critics have shown, episcopal authority led to a hierarchical church governed by bishops with recognition of the primacy of Peter, the bishop of Rome, and his successors, the popes—a church structure known as the 'monarchical episcopate.'

While the claims of episcopal authority predominated, they were always contested in some fashion by models of church authority that were more 'congregational.' For the Gospels, Book of Acts, and Epistles show not only the Apostolic Succession, but also the council of Jerusalem presided over by Peter and the Apostles that included the whole congregation in some decisions and other Christian communities outside of Jerusalem converted by Paul that made consensual decisions as congregations. In addition, all Christians were charged with the apostolic mission of spreading the faith and were included in Paul's description of the church as the "body of Christ," whose various parts are motivated by the same spirit to work together like the organic parts of the body. One might also note that appointing bishops in the early church occurred not only by the designation of the Apostles and by fellow bishops but sometimes through the input of priests and local rulers. Some Roman emperors even sought to control councils of bishops and claimed episcopal power for themselves (creating jurisdictional disputes that continued through the Middle Ages over the 'investiture' of bishops by kings).

Despite the ongoing disputes between proponents of hierarchical and congregational authority, the hierarchical model predominated for reasons that are more than statements about power. One reason is that Christianity is a religion based on divine revelation that claims to be binding on all mankind. Such a claim presupposes the unity of revealed truth and ultimately requires judgments about revealed doctrines from an authority that stands above rational disputation and possesses universal binding power—an authority that attains the greatest legitimacy when its origins are traceable by unbroken succession to Jesus Christ and when its jurisdiction (and visible presence) are not merely local or national or regional but universal. In other words, the unity of revealed truth proclaimed by the Christian faith necessitates an authoritative hierarchy that speaks to the whole world with one voice. Through a complex evolution, this requirement led to a church speaking through general councils that were approved by the pope.

A second reason for the necessary emergence of the hierarchical model is the sacramental character of Christianity, which requires a priesthood that lays claims to supernatural or mystical powers—powers that transform profane things like bread and wine into sacred things or that use outward signs like water and ritually spoken words to transform the inner state of the soul from sinfulness to purity. Sacramental powers are extensions of the incarnational reality of God in Christ because they bring the presence of the divine into the physical world. Hence, they attain their greatest authenticity when derived from an unbroken succession of ordained bishops and priests whose authority and even whose physical designation and form are traceable to Christ. No congregation acting on its own through consensual choice or majority decision, without assurance of higher authority, could confer the spiritual powers to celebrate sacred mysteries (which explains why the denial of the Apostolic Succession eventually led to the demotion of the sacraments from sacred mysteries to mere symbols).

A third reason for the predominance of the hierarchical model is Paul's description of the church as "the body of Christ." The point of this term is to compare the church to a human body whose various parts all play an indispensable role and are motivated by the same Holy Spirit to work for the common good, but whose organic structure resembles a corporate hierarchy in which head and eyes guide hands and feet (1 Cor. 12:4–31).

These reasons help to explain why the belief in a divinely instituted church hierarchy, headed by bishops who are seen as successors to the Apostles and who are capable of determining doctrines and ministering sacraments, prevailed in the Roman Catholic Church, the Eastern Orthodox Church, and the Anglican Church. Even the Conciliar movement of the fourteenth century, which elevated ecumenical councils above the pope and developed a representative theory of church authority, accepted the Apostolic Succession and viewed the church as a corporate hierarchy.[27] Later papal critics such as Martin Luther also retained something of the Apostolic Succession in accepting episcopal ordination in the visible church, while proclaiming the priesthood of all believers in the invisible church and settling for local selection of pastors and ministers. A clean break with the doctrine of the Apostolic Succession was made by Calvin, who rejected the apostolic authority of bishops and episcopal ordination in favor of church governance by presbyters, now understood as the representatives of the church chosen by congregations under the guidance of the Holy Spirit.[28]

Thus, the two basic choices for the organization of the Christian church over the centuries have been: (1) the episcopal model based on the Apostolic Succession and (2) the congregational model based on the Holy Spirit working through the people or gathered bodies of Christians (the former developed in various ways by Catholics, Eastern Orthodox, Anglicans, and Lutherans; the latter by Calvinists, Presbyterians, Baptists, Quakers, and other free-church denominations). Throughout the first sixteen hundred years of the Christian tradition, the episcopal model prevailed overwhelmingly for reasons stated above and continues today in the nonreformed churches for the same reasons. This fact explains why the spiritual part of the Two Cities, at least as it is embodied in the visible church, has been ordered in predominantly hierarchical fashion—led by popes, bishops, patriarchs, and priests while permitting some consent through the influence of councils, political rulers, and popular participation.

One must hasten to add that the visible church does not encompass the entire spiritual realm. In its full sense, the spiritual realm consists of the entire kingdom or city of God—an elusive concept that refers to God's supernatural order operating here and now in this world and even more fully in the world-to-come. Thus, the spiritual realm in the full sense is the divine order of charity and grace that is manifested not only in the holy church but also in all holy people and holy beings—in the communion of saints and angels, as it is traditionally called. Though informal and often intangible, this dimension of the city of God is also hierarchical because it is an order of spiritual perfection, sometimes overlapping with the hierarchy of the visible church and often at odds with the hierarchies of the world based on talent, birth, wealth, and power.

In the Christian understanding of spiritual perfection, Greek philosophy has played a crucial role. This does not mean that Scripture lacks its own hierarchies of spiritual perfection. On the contrary, the idea of 'divine election' pervades the Bible and results in many kinds of spiritual inequalities whose basis is sometimes unfathomable (the mysterious elections of an inscrutable God) and sometimes reasonable. The biblical accounts of Noah, Abraham, Moses, the latter prophets, Jesus Christ, the Apostles, the holy men and women of the early church, and the saints described in the Epistles and the Apocalypse are based on rankings of beings in terms of lower and higher levels of holiness. And more abstractly, the Bible frequently refers to degrees of "glory" or degrees of incorruptibility among earthly and heavenly beings, indicating degrees of perfection in their closeness to God. The crucial point is that Christian theology started with these scriptural ideas and developed them into theological doctrines with the aid of Greek philosophy, producing doctrines of spiritual perfection that combined in complex fashion divine election and free will. Platonism and Neoplatonism influenced the early church, and

Aristotelianism shaped the Scholastic theology of the Middle Ages, culminating in the metaphysical doctrine of the hierarchy of being—a ladder of different substances, essences, forms, or souls that ascend from lower to higher levels of perfection.

This conception of reality had enormous importance for the Christian understanding of human dignity. Building on the account of creation in Genesis, theologians employed Greek philosophy to interpret the *Imago Dei*—the divine image in man—as one part of a hierarchical "great chain of being" extending from rocks, to plants, to animals, to human beings, to angels, to God. In this scheme, man was described as a rational substance with an eternal destiny or as a composite of body and soul possessing intellect, free will, and passions that is innately directed (despite tendencies to sin) to the perfection of mind and character—that is, to the moral, intellectual, and theological virtues. The dignity of man could thus be identified with a rational soul that was an image of God's intellect and will, a view that gave man a high dignity in the universe, although not the highest because the angels were seen as a more perfect kind of rational substance. And within the human species, all persons could be seen as possessing a common human dignity because of their reason and free will; yet, they could also be ranked unequally according to a hierarchy of perfection or degrees of virtue. Many statements of this view can be found in patristic, medieval, and even in early Reformation theology.

For the Eastern Orthodox and Catholic traditions, Gregory of Nyssa was an influential church father of the fourth century who developed a mystical theology of spiritual perfection based on Neoplatonic and Scriptural sources. In his commentary on Genesis, titled *On the Making of Man*, Gregory describes the divine image in man as the possession of a rational soul with intellect and free will, attributes that give him a "royal dignity" and justify his dominion over lower animals. The rational soul of human beings serves "no lord and is self-governed, swayed autocratically by its own will; . . . to whom [else] does this belong than to a king? . . . Thus, human nature, made to rule over the rest [of creation] was made by its likeness to the King of all [the universe.]"[29] In exalting the human intellect, Gregory extends rational activities beyond the acquisition of empirical knowledge or technical skill. The mind moves by loving ascent toward God in mystical contemplation—transcending the senses and the passions in ascetical detachment from the world, driven by a passionate desire to know God that Gregory describes as a combination of Platonic *eros* and Christian *agape*, a longing for immortality through sacrificial love. While affirming the exalted status of every human being, Gregory's view of rational and spiritual perfection leads to a ranking of souls according to their capacity for the highest states of mystical union—a doctrine of spiritual inequality.

Like Gregory of Nyssa, St. Augustine also combined Neoplatonic and Christian ideas in a metaphysical and theological doctrine of the hierarchy of being. According to Augustine, the biblical name for God in Exodus is properly rendered "I am He Who Is" because it identifies God as the supreme being: "God is existence in a supreme degree—He supremely *is*—and He is therefore immutable." When God created the world, God gave existence in varying degrees to creatures that He made out of nothing. But none was given the fullness of God's immutable and eternal being: "To some He gave existence in a higher degree, to some lower, and thus He arranged a scale of existences of various natures."[30] Sometimes Augustine says the angels have the highest place in the created order, on the assumption that the intangible "light" that God made on the first day of creation refers to the pure minds of the angels who exist at the peak of intellectual being. Sometimes Augustine suggests that man is at the peak because one can recognize in humanity "an image of God, that is of the Supreme Trinity . . . [so] there is nothing in the whole of God's creation as near to Him in nature" as man. Whichever is the highest, the universe as a whole is arranged as a hierarchy of being that is also a hierarchy of rational substances: "Living things are ranked above inanimate objects; those which have the power of reproduction . . . are superior to those who lack that impulse. Among living things, the sentient rank above the insensitive, and animals over trees. Among the sentient, the intelligent take precedence over the unthinking, men over cattle. Among the intelligent, immortal beings are higher than mortals, angels higher than men. . . . This is the scale according to the order of nature." The ambiguity about which created being is highest is resolved by Augustine's observation that in "the order of rational beings, such weight is attached to the qualities of freedom and love that, although angels are superior to men in the order of nature, good men rank above evil angels in the criterion of righteousness." In sum, Augustine holds that "there is a scale of value stretching from earthly to heavenly realities, from the visible to the invisible; and the inequality of these goods makes possible the existence of them all."[31] What Augustine means is that the creation of the universe by God is a reflection of His goodness, and a good creation requires an ordered hierarchy of unequal parts—an order that is further differentiated after the Fall by the distinction of the heavenly and earthly cities.

Following in the same tradition, St. Thomas Aquinas says that man is "made to God's image, in so far as the image implies an intelligent being endowed with free-will and self-movement."[32] While this description may sound like the rational individual of Kantian liberalism who has dignity by virtue of his reason, freedom, and power of self-determination, the Thomistic conception of man is not that of an autonomous being whose rational will is an end-in-itself. For Thomas, reason has an end beyond itself—the knowledge and love of God and of God's creation. As Thomas says, since man resembles God "by reason of his intellectual nature, he is most perfectly like God . . . in this, that God understands and loves Himself. Whereof we see the image of God in man in three ways. First, inasmuch as man possesses a natural aptitude for understanding and loving God . . . Second, inasmuch as man actually or habitually knows and loves God, though imperfectly, and this image consists in the conformity of grace. Third, inasmuch as man knows and loves God perfectly, and this image consists in the likeness of glory . . . The first is found in all men, the second only in the just, the third only in the blessed" (*S. Th.,* I, 93.4). In other words, Thomas sees reason and free will as capacities directed to knowing and loving God as well as to contemplating the likeness of God in the whole created universe. This sets up an unequal ranking of human beings. The first level includes everyone because all rational creatures have a certain natural desire to the know the Creator. The second level includes only those who have received the faith through grace and therefore have actually come to know and love God as much as they can in this life. The third level includes only those blessed with glory who will know and love God perfectly in the world-to-come—a reference to the saints in heaven (who will also be ranked according to greater or lesser proximity to God).

In Thomas's hierarchy, grace works together with free will, which means people are responsible in part for enhancing or diminishing the image of God in themselves. This has important consequences not only for salvation, but also for law and criminal justice. While Thomas says it is always wrong to take the life of an innocent human being, he thinks it is just to punish murderers with the death penalty. One reason is the priority of the common good to the individual: The execution of a murderer by lawful public authority is like cutting off an infected limb to save the whole body. But the deeper reason has to do with human dignity and depravity: "By sinning, a man departs from the order of reason and consequently falls away from the dignity of his humanity, in so far as he is naturally free and exists for himself, and he falls to the slavish state of the beasts, [and may be] disposed of according as he is useful to others. . . . Hence, although it be evil itself to kill a man so long as he preserves his dignity, yet it may be good to kill a man who has sinned, even as it is to kill a beast. For a bad man is worse than a beast" (*S. Th.*, II-II, 64.2, ad. 3; 64.6). In other words, the criminal alienates his human dignity by murder, falls to the level of an animal (or lower) and deserves to be treated as something useful or harmful, justifying the death penalty. This teaching shows that the dignity of the rational soul may be lowered as well as raised on the scale of being and perfection which God has established in the whole hierarchical order of the universe.[33]

The crucial point to remember about Christian theologians like Thomas, who viewed man as a rational creature made in the image of God and the universe as a rational order made in God's likeness, is that they appealed to a different notion of "reason" than the one prevalent today. Modern philosophers see reason as an autonomous power that reflects on itself or legislates for itself. But the patristic and Scholastic theologians viewed reason in Platonic and Aristotelian fashion as a kind of *eros* or as potentiality directed toward actuality that seeks unification with the First Cause, which is God, and with the eternal ideas that exist in God's mind as the rational patterns after which the universe is created. Using the classical conception of reason, human dignity and cosmic order appear on a comparative scale of rational substances. The human species stands near the top of the hierarchy that makes up the created and uncreated order of being—the hierarchy ascending from rocks, to plants, to animals, to humans, to angels, to God. And dignity within the human species depends on one's fullness of being as a rational substance whose mind and soul are drawn upward to God.

While this conception establishes a connection between rational and spiritual perfection, it does not imply that the smartest people are the ones closest to God. Since reason in the traditional view is not simply 'brain-power' but 'metaphysical-power' or even 'love-power,' reason merges together with purity and holiness: It is an activity of the soul that abstracts from sensation and transcends the here and now, that loves the eternal good and stands with humble awe before the Creator and the sacred realm of mysterious being. In this sense, rational activity is quite different from calculation, problem solving, imagination, creativity, or other contemporary measures of intelligence. Though it involves practical judgment as well as contemplative thought, it is captured by phrases such as the "intellectual apprehension of the good" or the longing for the everlasting vision of God (where the soul hopes to see God face-to-face, and the mind's eye seeks to see the invisible Creator behind the visible creation). The implication is that someone with a low IQ in conventional terms—a simple but pious believer—may be operating at the highest level of the intellect by meditating on the eternal God and His governance of the created world. By contrast, the modern specialist with a high IQ is operating with a degraded intellect by thinking only about technical means while remaining utterly indifferent to the highest ends.

This insight exalts the humble people who meditate on eternity while humbling the smart people who think only of the here and now. Yet, it is still not democratic or egalitarian; nor does it mean that everyone has a right to be accepted as they are. It means that a comparative hierarchy of perfection exists, with souls that have been purified of sense images, earthly attachments, and sin ranked near the top as the most holy, blessed, saintly, and Godlike beings—a spiritual hierarchy ascending upward from sinners to saints and mystics to the holy angels whose minds are illuminated directly by light from above. Such an order differs as much from a democracy of autonomous wills as it does from a hierarchy of worldly success, neither of which shows much interest in the ladder of rational and spiritual perfection.

To see this point most clearly, we need to remind ourselves how seriously the traditional Christian theologians took the existence of the most perfect spiritual beings, the holy angels, which they understood as minds separated from bodies or minds only accidentally attached to bodies that serve as messengers of God or as supernatural agents that uplift creation toward God. While the doctrine of angels—"angelology," as some call it—may be hard for people to take seriously today, one cannot deny its importance for the traditional understanding of spiritual hierarchy (though belief in angels is making a comeback today in folk religion as well as in scientific searches for intelligent life beyond our planet). The existence of angels is significant because it humbles as well as exalts human beings. It humbles them, as Aquinas says, because "the dignity of angels surpasses that of men," lowering the rank of humans in the cosmos by one grade (*S. Th.*, I, 59.3). Yet, angels also elevate man because they perfect the universe by enabling spiritual substances to predominate over material ones and draw lower beings upward to God.

According to the most influential work on angels, *The Celestial Hierarchy* by the unknown Pseudo-Dionysius of the fifth century A.D., such movement is the very purpose of heavenly hierarchies: "A hierarchy is a sacred order . . . approximating as closely as possible to the divine. . . . For every member of the hierarchy, perfection consists in [being] uplifted to imitate God as far as possible . . . it ensures that when its members have received this full and divine splendor they can then pass on this light generously . . . to beings further down the scale."[34] In the Neoplatonic Christianity of the author, the angels are necessary beings because God is utterly transcendent and hidden, beyond all created being; yet the unknown God also enters the known world, which requires the angels as intermediary agents. Hence, God "first emerges from secrecy to revelation by way of mediation by these first powers." The highest order of angels (seraphim and cherubim) are the first to know God and lovingly "raise their inferiors," while the "lower ranks . . . look upward to those intelligent beings of the first rank through by whom they . . . will be uplifted to the possible likeness of God" (ibid., ch. 13.3–4). But the capacities for divine imitation vary, like the capacities for absorbing and reflecting light, so each intellectual substance will be elevated according to its measure.

Whatever one may think about the existence of angels (a possibility that cannot be dismissed as long as the mind's relation to matter remains mysterious), one must acknowledge the power of believing in them: They have inspired some of the greatest works of 'heavenly' beauty in Christian civilization, such as the soaring luminosity of Gothic cathedrals, the celestial choir music of Palestrina and the *Panis Angelicus* (a hymn to the Eucharist as the bread of angels), and the lofty rhetoric of Lincoln's appeal to the "better angels of our nature." Such monuments to human dignity would not exist without the Scholastic theory of rational substances. They persist in our age as reminders of the hierarchy of being, according to which creatures gain their dignity, not as a matter of right, but by being drawn upward to something higher and more beautiful than themselves in proportion to their varying capacities for divine illumination.

Thus, it may be said that there is something inherently hierarchical about the spiritual realm in traditional Christianity because it includes the hierarchical church derived from the Apostolic Succession as well as the Platonic-Aristotelian and Scholastic conception of a hierarchy of being and substances. This upward thrust is so powerful that even when the Scholastic doctrines were called into question at the beginning of the Protestant Reformation by Luther and Calvin, the spiritual realm was still viewed in hierarchical terms—as the predestination of the elect who, as a tiny minority, constitute a spiritual aristocracy of saints. In addition to emphasizing the divine election of saints, the reformers preserved the hierarchy of angels while rejecting the Scholastic underpinnings. On the subject of angels, Calvin explicitly opposes the Neoplatonism of Pseudo-Dionysius's *Celestial Hierarchy*, calling it "nothing but talk" and bidding "farewell to that Platonic philosophy of seeking access to God through angels."[35] Nevertheless, Calvin strongly affirms a belief in angels in their lesser capacities as messengers of God and bearers of gifts because their existence is supported by many passages of Scripture. The conclusion I draw is that a scriptural version of the hierarchy of being persists in the Reformation, progressively detached from Greek philosophy and from the ascending and descending scales of being but no less hierarchical in distinguishing sinners and reprobates from angels and saints.

THE TWO CITIES AND TEMPORAL HIERARCHIES

In turning from the spiritual to the temporal realm, we seem to encounter little more than an extension of principles from one sphere into another: The kind of corporate hierarchy favored by traditional Christian theologians in the church—monarchy or aristocracy mixed with elements of participation and consent by lower orders—is also favored in the state. Moreover, the foundational argument for both structures often seems to overlap. Many theologians of the medieval period argued by analogy that the governance of the cosmos by one God implies a single head of church and a single ruler in the state. The implication is that the doctrine of the Two Cities may differentiate the institutions of church and state, but the principles of both realms are derived from the same doctrine: The hierarchy of being in the cosmic order justifies hierarchies in church and state.

Now it is certainly true that many traditional theologians employed the argument by analogy that the existence of one God goes together with one pope and one king (reaching an extreme in Dante's *De Monarchia* where the belief in one God is said to support one world government under a universal monarch, the Holy Roman Emperor).[36] In my view, however, the notion that traditional Christian theologians simply deduced their politics from metaphysics and cosmology is misleading and actually obscures an important feature of Christian political thought in the premodern era. In point of fact, the organization of the temporal realm was often determined by using prudence or practical wisdom, a different kind of reasoning than that employed in the spiritual realm.

The evidence for this thesis is that many traditional theologians from St. Augustine to the early Reformation clearly recognized the revolutionary contribution of Christianity to politics—namely, the doctrine of the Two Cities, which implied that the political order is not simply an application of divine law or an extension of the spiritual realm but a semi-independent authority derived from natural law and human law. The Two Cities clearly indicated, for example, that sacred kingship and the divinity of emperors, as found in polytheistic cultures such as Egypt and Rome, were no longer tenable. The belief that kings were high priests or divine intermediaries between Heaven and earth could no longer be accepted in Christian politics because Jesus Christ was the sole mediator between God and man and the sole source of priestly powers. Christian theologians also understood that Christianity differed from the other monotheistic religions, Judaism and Islam, because the New Testament did not contain a divinely revealed legal code for governing the state. The Two Cities doctrine even made it difficult to advocate theocracy in the sense of direct governance by priests, prophets, saints, or messianic figures with pretensions to redeem the world through politics. Expressed in more familiar terms, the Christian doctrine of the Two Cities desacralized the temporal sphere by recognizing a spiritual realm above the state and a spiritual Savior who transcended all political power, thereby giving the state a certain independence from the influence of churches and priests as well as from metaphysics and cosmology.

At the same time (and here was the tricky part), the Two Cities doctrine did not mean that the state was entirely secular or independent of the will of God. As every theologian knew well, Paul said in Rom. 13:1 that "there is no authority except from God, and those that exist have been instituted by God." For most traditional Christian theologians, this implied that government in general was sanctioned by God; but God did not specify the best form of government, nor did God send prophets to select specific political rulers anymore (as He once did in choosing Saul and David as kings for the Hebrew people). Paradoxically, the state was recognized as divinely ordained yet it was not a sacred institution. What did this mean?

In some cases, it meant that the state was treated as little more than an instrument of the church, a secular tool of a sacred authority. In other cases, it meant that divine cosmology was still employed in political tracts to justify kingship, that hopes for a Christian empire or Holy Roman Empire never evaporated, that the idea of a unified Christendom or *res publica Christiana* flourished, that the pope's "plenitude of power" was seen as the direct source of temporal power, that Eastern Orthodox nations like Russia routinely referred to the tsar as "the Lord's anointed," and that belief in the king's sacred body or magical powers (reminiscent of paganism) persisted in the Christian era.

Nevertheless, traditional Christians felt obliged to distinguish the spiritual and temporal realms in some fashion while recognizing that there was no clear guideline for doing so. A range of options was possible for delineating the boundaries of the state, from a fairly unified or integrated version of the two powers in a Christian commonwealth to a fairly separated or dualistic version of the two powers. It all depended on how one defined the legitimate ends of the state in a religion that lacked a clear-cut doctrine of the state. As I interpret the great Christian theologians from Augustine to the early Reformation, they tended to define the legitimate ends of the state in terms of a hierarchy of goods that could be divided into three broad categories: (1) civil peace or tranquillity of order, meaning the basic good of preservation or security in a stable political regime; (2) moral virtue or moral order, meaning the higher good of justice, understood as the common good in which all parts of society receive their due, along with other moral virtues, such as courage, moderation, and prudence as well as civic friendship and some degree of political participation; and (3) Christian piety, meaning the highest good of recognizing God as the source of all earthly authority and more specifically the promotion of Christian faith by defending orthodoxy and punishing heresy as the church defined them.

Since these three basic goods made up the legitimate ends of the temporal realm, the critical question for politics was how to combine them in a coherent view that could be implemented in the practical world. While some theologians argued for a minimalist approach—limiting the state mainly to civil peace and tranquil order—others argued for a more expansive approach that balanced the demands of civil peace with the inculcation of moral virtues and the promotion of Christian orthodoxy. The choice of the best political regime was therefore a matter of prudence—of determining the best 'means' for attaining the 'ends' of temporal happiness defined as a hierarchy of goods in a world shaped by the fallen but rational nature of man.

Despite the variety of possible choices, none of the traditional Christian theologians argued for liberal democracy as the best means for attaining temporal happiness. The doctrine of the Fall and original sin, which highlighted the selfish and rebellious nature of man, meant that even the minimal goal of maintaining order was difficult to achieve and required a strong dose of coercive authority that only hierarchical regimes could provide. Insofar as reason was not entirely corrupted by the Fall, the inculcation of moral and intellectual virtues was also possible. This, too, pointed toward hierarchical institutions—especially, the establishment of virtuous rulers above the people who could direct their souls upward to rational perfection. And the need for spiritual perfection meant popes, bishops, and priests could interfere in the political order to define Christian orthodoxy. On prudential grounds, most Christian theologians thought that the best means for realizing these ends were mixed regimes— corporate hierarchies in which the higher orders were embodied in a king or an aristocracy who would govern lower orders in accordance with virtue and all elements would play a role for the sake of the common good. Prudence also dictated that less perfect regimes could be legitimate, including fairly authoritarian or corrupt ones, as long as the primary good of civil peace was realized and temporal rulers did not unduly usurp spiritual powers. And even tyrannical regimes had some claims to obedience, with varying degrees of resistance permitted. Within the framework of the Two Cities, the compatibility of Christianity with a variety of political systems could be justified without succumbing to cultural or moral relativism, though a mixed regime combining elements of monarchy and/or aristocracy with democracy was considered best in most circumstances.[37]

The Politics of the Great Theologians

To clarify this view of the temporal realm, I will conclude by discussing the politics of the four leading Christian theologians of the premodern era—St. Augustine, St. Thomas Aquinas, Martin Luther, and John Calvin. While presenting them in chronological order, I do not mean to imply that they show progressive development toward modern principles, either toward greater sympathy for liberal democracy or toward secularism. Instead, my aim is to show that all four shared a common approach to politics based on the Two Cities and that their differences are attributable to judgments of prudence, meaning practical disagreements about how far the state should go in trying to realize the hierarchy of ends proper to the temporal realm.

St. Augustine set the course for traditional Christian politics by articulating the doctrine of the Two Cities. As he says in *The City of God*, the two cities refer to two kinds of love which, in turn, produce different associations. The city of God is the spiritual association of all those who love God more than the world. They are members of the heavenly city, otherwise known as the communion of angels and saints, because they have been predestined to attain salvation in the world to come where they will enjoy forever the vision of God. The city of God also refers to the "shadowy representations" of Heaven on earth, meaning all the holy and righteous people in the Bible from Able and Noah to Abraham, Moses, and David to Christ and the Apostles. Occasionally, Augustine uses the term to refer to the institutional church, including the visible Catholic Church as well as the invisible church whose members (including some non-Christians) are known only to God.[38] Formulated in Neoplatonic terms as a hierarchy of being, the city of God applies to all levels of spiritual perfection in the visible and invisible worlds, from the pilgrim church on earth to the angels and saints in Heaven.

While the city of God is inspired by divine love, the earthly city is driven by love of the world. The earthly city continuously intermingles with its heavenly counterpart, but the course of the earthly city is sufficiently distinct that one can trace its historical course. It begins with the biblical Cain, the murderous brother who founded the first city, and continues through all the nations and civilizations of the world from the ancient Egyptians and Assyrians to the Roman Empire (except for the nation of Israel, which is part of the heavenly city). The earthly city exists as a consequence of the Fall and uses coercive political authority to restrain man's sinful nature, which means it is motivated by something far less exalted than charity and grace. It does not even attain political justice most of the time. The noblest pagan philosophers claim that it aims at justice, but even the best nations behave like gangs of robbers. They usually begin by seizing the territory of some settled people, they expand by violence and conquest, and they live with factions and class conflicts that verge on civil war. 'Justice,' understood as the common good in which all parts of society receive their due, is rare or impossible in the earthly city.

Arguing from this brutal realism, Augustine lowers the goal of the earthly city from charity and justice to the "tranquillity of order" (*tranquillitas ordinis*)—a somewhat elusive concept that emphasizes peace and stability but includes more than Hobbesian security. At a minimum, the tranquillity of order refers to the suppression of conflict by the coercive state; yet Augustine also says that it means arranging things "in a pattern which assigns to each its proper position" according to "the law by which the natural order is governed." This expansive concept of order almost sounds like a natural moral order in politics because it implies a harmony of parts within a whole, as in the harmony of a well-ordered family or the harmony of ruler and ruled that serves higher ends than self-preservation. Nevertheless, Augustine usually refers to the tranquillity of order as a type of "peace" rather than as a type of "justice" in order to lower expectations about politics. The implication, I believe, is that Augustine regards civil peace as the only realistic goal of the state in most cases, because charity and justice are so hard to achieve in the fallen world of politics; at the same time, Augustine does not want to rule out higher aims—such as inculcating moral virtue or seeking a harmony of parts—if auspicious circumstances make them possible to attain.[39]

To determine which ends are possible, one must use political prudence, which Augustine outlines in his teaching on law. He indicates that political judgments should be made by balancing the demands of two kinds of law: (1) eternal law, meaning the divinely revealed law of God, such as the Ten Commandments; and (2) temporal law, meaning human law or the civil law and customs of nations. In a passage of the *Confessions* where Augustine discusses the two types of law, he says, "the law of Almighty God . . . is the law *by which each age and place forms rules of conduct best suited to itself,* although the [divine] law itself is always and everywhere the same." The sense of fitness by which the unchanging divine law is applied to particular times and places to form human law is the main feature of Augustinian prudence. Often, it indicates that local customs should be respected. Yet, Augustine adds, "If God commands a nation to do something contrary to its customs or constitutions, it must be done . . . [and] if it were not a law before, it must be enacted." The two specific examples that he mentions to illustrate the priority of God's law are "sins against nature" and "sins of violence"—meaning unnatural sexual practices and violent acts of cruelty or revenge. Augustine's prudence thus teaches that divine law allows human law to remain intact, except when egregious violations of the Ten Commandments or practices contrary to natural moral virtue occur in the areas of sex and violence.[40]

To see how much latitude this actually permits, one may cite Augustine's views on the best political regime and the relation of church and state. Regarding the best regime, Augustine is neutral between different forms of government because he believes that God did not indicate a preference for one form over another, even though God sanctioned political authority in general as a remedy for the Fall. The choice is a prudential judgment about which form is best for maintaining tranquil order—understood minimally as civil peace and maximally to include higher ends, such as moral virtue and piety, if they can be achieved. This helps to explain why Augustine praises three regimes in *The City of God* without choosing one over the other. He praises the early Roman republic because it inspired heroic self-sacrifice and austere civic virtue in its citizens, even though the motive was earthly glory (5.12–18). He praises the Christian Emperors Constantine and Theodosius and treats them as models of how a "Christian Prince" should rule—not for earthly glory but out of a sense of duty to establish strong authority in a sinful world (tempered by mercy and forgiveness) and to advance Christian worship (5.24–26). In addition, Augustine says that a confederation of small kingdoms might be "a happier state" than a great republic or an imperial monarchy because it would maximize harmony and concord (4.15). While praising three different regimes, Augustine makes no definitive choice in *The City of God.*

This means the choice is neutral from the point of view of divine law, but it is not neutral from the perspective of prudence and temporal law which require rulers to do the best they can in an imperfect world. In an early dialogue, *On Free Choice*, Augustine offers some advice for making such judgments. Speaking in his own name, he says a republican government is best if the people possess the moral and civic virtue to rule themselves; but if the people are corrupt, then government by one or a few virtuous rulers (monarchy or aristocracy) is a better choice. The lesson is that temporal law "although it is just, can nevertheless be changed in the course of time."[41] Thus, the choice of the best political regime is secondary compared to the attainment of eternal happiness; but it is not arbitrary in relation to the ends of the temporal realm. It is a judgment of momentous practical importance that requires statesmen to weigh the goods of order and moral virtue in order to make a wise decision, depending on the moral level of the people and other historical circumstances.

Similarly, the relation between church and state is not a strict deduction from divine law but depends on circumstances. Augustine even changed his mind on this question—on whether the state had a duty to promote Christian orthodoxy or to permit religious liberty. In his early period, he argued that the New Testament did not allow state coercion of those who held heretical beliefs; but he later changed his mind after violent attacks by the Donatist sect in North Africa endangered the lives of Catholics and the unity of the church. He then argued for the use of state power to protect Catholics and to compel by imperial edict the members of the heretical sect to come back to the church, although he never thought that coercion could make anyone believe the truth or that heretics should be put to death.

In *The City of God,* he is also of two minds about using the state to impose the faith. When praising Christian princes, he speaks in favor of state imposition of religion: "We Christians call rulers happy . . . if they put their power at the service of God's majesty [and] extend his worship far and wide" (5.24). Yet, his broadest statement on the relation of the spiritual and temporal powers advocates greater separation: "The Earthly City, *whose life is not based on faith,* aims at earthly peace and limits the harmonious agreement of citizens . . . to the establishment of a kind of compromise between human wills about the things relevant to mortal life. In contrast, the Heavenly City . . . *which lives on the basis of faith* . . . must make use of this peace . . . and does not hesitate to obey the laws of the earthly city . . . provided that *no hindrance* is presented to the religion which teaches that the one supreme and true God is to be worshiped" (19.17, emphasis added). What I infer from these passages is that the Two Cities doctrine permits flexibility on this question: Augustine recognizes a minimal position of "no hindrance" by the state to the worship of the One True God and a maximal position of state support for Christian orthodoxy. Like the question of the best political regime, the relation of church and state is a prudential judgment that has minimum and maximum conditions that must be judged according to historical circumstances. In most cases, the minimal conditions are all that can be achieved and may well reflect the most stable balance of the Two Cities (implying that the freestanding church of the early Roman Empire is the norm, while the maximum position of state support for Christianity in the Constantinian era is the exception).

As these examples attest, St. Augustine cannot be charged with relativism or indifference simply because he offers no definitive answer to the question of the best regime or church-state relations. His main lesson is to work within the limited horizon of the earthly city that is set by God's created hierarchy of being and man's fallen condition. As long as a political regime provides stable order and punishes the wicked, promotes a modicum of civic virtue and social harmony, and does not hinder the free exercise of Christian faith, it has a basic legitimacy. If it also comes to the defense of the true faith when violently attacked or is able to extend the faith without undue persecution and hypocrisy, then so much the better. The political regime can therefore take different forms. It could be a monarchy, aristocracy, or republic depending on the morals of the people; and the relations between church and state could vary considerably. In general, though, a political regime is legitimate if it sticks to the comparatively modest ends of tranquil order through strong coercive authority and does not allow Caesar to usurp God's power by commanding immorality or impiety. While flexible, such prudential wisdom is not indiscriminate and would require condemnation of tyrannies that we today call totalitarian because they flagrantly violate the Two Cities minimal rule of "no hindrance" to faith by demanding state-imposed atheism and state idolatry. St. Augustine's political teaching is thus a kind of moderate authoritarianism that respects the limited boundaries of the earthly city—a teaching that cannot be called liberal or democratic but one that is also antitotalitarian and consistent with constitutional limitations on governmental power.

If we turn to St. Thomas Aquinas, it seems at first glance that Thomas departs significantly from Augustine's politics because Thomas embraces the Aristotelian notion that political community has a natural basis in man's rational and social nature. Thomas also seems more doctrinaire than Augustine in arguing that one form of government—mixed monarchy or limited kingship—is clearly the best and in using cosmological analogies with God's rule over the natural universe to justify kingship (see *S. Th.*, I, 103.3). Despite these features, Thomas follows Augustine by adopting the framework of the Two Cities and the prudential approach to politics.

In fact, Thomas develops the Two Cities doctrine by articulating precisely the different kinds of laws for the spiritual and temporal realms: Divine law is the basis of the spiritual realm, and human law guided by natural law is the basis of the temporal realm. As Thomas says, "human law is ordained for one kind of community, and the divine law for another kind, because human law is ordained for the civil community, implying mutual duties of man and his fellows. . . . But the community for which the divine law is ordained is that of man in relation to God, either in this life or in the life to come" (*S. Th.*, I-II, 100.2). In other words, divine law directs man to his supernatural end, eternal happiness, through the ecclesiastical community or church, which Thomas derives in orthodox fashion from the Apostolic Succession. Divine law also guides the entire spiritual realm which Thomas articulates in Neoplatonic terms as a ladder of spiritual perfection ascending to the saints and holy angels who enjoy the everlasting vision of God or beatific vision in Heaven.

By contrast, human law aims at the common good of the temporal realm whose end is earthly happiness. Human law is embodied in the civil law or positive right of the political community which statesmen and legislators lay down as the fundamental law of the land in written constitutions or in customs and traditions. But human law is not merely conventional or arbitrary. As Thomas says, "it belongs to the notion of human law to be derived from the law of nature," which means that human law must be in accordance with natural law to be authentic (*S. Th.*, I-II, 95.4). And natural law directs man to his perfection as a rational creature—to the virtues of a creature made in the image of God with reason and free will. Thus, Thomas says, "all virtuous acts belong to the natural law" (*S. Th.,* I-II, 94.3). This would seem to give politics a higher end than Augustine's tranquillity of order by setting the bar above civil peace and aiming directly at moral virtue.

And, of course, Thomas follows Aristotle by saying forthrightly: "In order that man might have peace and virtue, it was necessary for laws to be framed, for, as the Philosopher says, 'a man is the most noble of animals if he be perfect in virtue, so he is the lowest of all if he be severed from law and justice' " (*S. Th.,* I-II, 95.1). Yet, it is also true that Thomas has a keen sense of man's fallen and sinful nature and insists that it must be taken into account when human laws are framed. The challenge of prudence is precisely to determine how the lofty teachings of natural law should be applied to the imperfect realm of politics. Since the natural inclinations to higher ends are often thwarted by irrational and sinful desire (concupiscence), one must lower the goals of politics from rational perfection to something more realistic. One must make compromises with man's fallen but rational nature in many ways, which means the state should have fairly modest ambitions and limited ends.[42]

For example, Thomas says, the vast majority of people are weak and fallible, so it would be imprudent for the state to try to legislate all of the virtues. It cannot even suppress most vices, "only the more grievous vices from which it is impossible for the majority to abstain . . . [and] without which human society could not be maintained . . . [meaning] murder, theft, and suchlike." Hence, Thomas lays down as a general maxim that "the purpose of human law is to lead men to virtue, *not suddenly but gradually*" (*S. Th.,* I-II, 96.2, emphasis added). Respecting this advice, the framers of human law should concentrate primarily on external actions rather than inner intentions of citizens. They may also allow lesser evils to go unpunished, including some heretical beliefs, because the cost of punishing every evil act would be continuous persecution and civil conflict. Prudence also recognizes the natural tendency of humans to love their own possessions, which Thomas takes as a legitimate basis for private property and for "moderate gain" in trade and commerce. In a further concession to human frailty, Thomas admits that unjust practices such as usury may sometimes be tolerated, even though usury is against natural law. At the same time, Thomas upholds the priority of the common good over the private good, acknowledging that certain inequalities of wealth and power are just but also demanding that the rich share their wealth with the poor when disparities are too great (and even permitting the poor to steal from the rich in cases of extreme necessity).[43] The aim of political prudence, in short, is to achieve the best approximation of the temporal common good that is possible by balancing the competing demands of civil peace and moral virtue in an imperfect world.

On the question of the best regime, Thomas also argues in prudential fashion. He follows Aristotle's sixfold classification of regimes from best to worst—from monarchy, aristocracy, and polity to democracy, oligarchy, and tyranny—and allows statesmen to make the most suitable choice in the given circumstances. Though flexible, Thomas makes the case more definitely than Aristotle or Augustine ever did for the superiority of one regime, namely, mixed or constitutional monarchy. In describing this regime in the *Summa Theologiae*, Thomas argues for a mixture of three elements—monarchy, aristocracy, and democracy (I-II, 105.1). The monarchical element is embodied in a king who is "given the power to preside over all according to his virtue." Under him is an aristocratic body composed of wise and virtuous elders, such as the Roman Senate or the seventy elders chosen from the tribes of Israel to assist Moses. And the democratic element is found in the people who should have a role in choosing their rulers because "all are eligible to govern." The advantage of this regime is that it combines the strengths of each form in a hierarchical order that not only promotes virtue but also balances each against the others so that none can act in tyrannical fashion (especially the king). It ensures peace and stability by giving all parts of society a share in the government and all the people a stake in their nation.

On relations of state and church, Thomas argues that mixed monarchy should be accompanied by an independent class of priests who preside over divine worship and set the requirements for salvation. But their precise relation to the political rulers is left unresolved. Sometimes Thomas sounds like he favors a high degree of unity between the spiritual and temporal realms, as in the assertion that "human government is derived from divine government and should imitate it" (*S. Th.*, II-II, 10.11). But imitating divine government does not abolish the distinction between the Two Cities because the human realm can never attain spiritual perfection and the state has an independent natural basis. The divine law acts as a backup for natural law, obligating the interior motives of Christian citizens and providing sanctions for sins that could not be punished by external punishments. And even though divine law gives the church the right in principle to overthrow non-Christian princes, Thomas does not think the right should be exercised in practice (*S. Th.*, II-II, 10.10). In general, he shies away from defending an integral Christendom of pope and emperor and does not endorse the medieval claim of "plenitude of power" which derives all temporal authority from the pope's spiritual authority (though Thomas does make an exception for the papal states where the pope exercises temporal power).[44] Drawing upon Aristotle, the polity of Moses, Roman history, and the New Testament, Thomas develops an argument for a corporate hierarchy consisting of the common people, aristocrats, kings, and an independent priesthood.

In the eyes of some modern scholars, Thomas prepares the way for the mixed monarchy of the English constitution where king, lords, and commons share power along with the bishops of the established Church of England. This interpretation, popularized by Lord Acton, treats Thomas as the first 'Catholic Whig' whose teaching has been progressively developed into the Anglo-American constitutional system of ordered liberty.[45] Though intriguing, Acton's interpretation is misleading because Thomas defends power sharing and political participation, not as a right of the people to parliamentary consent nor as a means for protecting personal rights and liberties, but as the prudent application of natural law whose ends are best realized in a stable constitutional order dedicated to peace, virtue, and Christian piety. This is medieval corporatism applied within the doctrine of the Two Cities rather than the first stirring of modern liberty.

When we turn from Catholic theology to the great Protestant reformers, we see something curious happening to Christian political thought. Both Martin Luther and John Calvin were Augustinians in spirit who emphasized man's fallen nature and the need to obey the established authorities according to Paul's admonitions in Romans 13. Yet, each reformer takes a part of Augustine and pushes him in one direction. Luther takes Augustine's "tranquillity of order" and pares it down to the coercive security state that is radically separated from morality and religion, while Calvin turns Augustine's praise of Christian princes into a "Christian polity" that virtually joins state and church into a theocracy. Despite divergent tendencies, however, both retain the framework of the Two Cities and a prudential approach to politics that favors corporate hierarchies in the temporal realm.

In Luther's case, politics often seems like a tactical exercise in which political rulers who favor his reformist views are supported and those who reject his views are opposed. Behind the tactical maneuvers, however, Luther possesses a coherent and systematic political doctrine: the "Zwei-Reiche" or "Zwei-Regimente-Lehre," usually translated as the Two Kingdoms—the kingdom of God and the kingdom of the world (or the kingdom of the devil). Obviously a variation on the classic Two Cities, Luther's doctrine holds that God instituted two orders for man's existence, the spiritual and temporal, corresponding to his two natures, the spirit and the flesh.

The spiritual realm is the order of salvation in which man exists solely in relation to God, mediated only by the Word and grace of God. The connection to the institutional church is ambiguous because the church's external structure bears little resemblance to the true church, which is spiritual or mystical. For Luther, the true Church exists wherever the Word is preached and the sacraments are properly ministered and includes all faithful followers of Christ on earth and in Heaven—the community of saints or *communio sanctorum*. Nevertheless, Luther is not indifferent to external church structures. He propounds the "priesthood of all believers" rather than the sacramental priesthood of the Catholic Church, yet he does not advocate democratic congregationalism as the alternative. He sometimes favors General Councils influenced by German princes and does not reject episcopal ordination as long as it is understood that no form of church authority is divinely instituted, a position that eventually led most Lutherans to settle on national churches headed by national synods which elected bishops and approved local ministers.

In the temporal realm, Luther favored no particular form of government, though in practice he dealt with princes or kings and strongly supported their authority and denounced rebellion against them. In his most systematic work, "On Secular Authority: To What

Extent It Must Be Obeyed" (1523), Luther argues for a separation of the kingdom of God and the kingdom of the world. His reasoning bears little resemblance to modern liberalism, however, because it derives from Christian dualism rather than from private rights. The kingdom of God is the spiritual realm, consisting of the society of true Christians (a tiny population) that requires no laws or coercion because it is sustained by freely given love that produces perfect righteousness. By contrast, the kingdom of the world is the secular authority consisting of the coercive state, which true Christians do not need but must obey because they are commanded by God to do so and because Christian charity includes the duty to care for the safety of one's neighbor in a dangerous and sinful world. Following this minimal role, the state should make no pretense of promoting morality or religion, even if it means tolerating errors in religion. The main purpose of the state is to punish the wicked, for which wicked princes are often most suitable, prompting Luther's famous statement that "frogs must have storks," meaning wicked princes are necessary as a sort of population control over evil men.[46] For Luther, Christian rulers should rely on the power of the Word alone to protect true religion (a principle that Luther did not always follow in practice, as in the case of the militant Anabaptists, whose suppression Luther supported because he felt their revolutionary and millenarian doctrines upset true religion as well as stable order).

Obviously, Luther is a practitioner of Christian prudence in the temporal realm, insisting that the divine law has almost nothing to say about politics except to obey the established powers as authorities ordained by God and rejecting almost entirely natural law or natural moral perfection. His version of Christian prudence is therefore more pessimistic than that of Augustine and Aquinas. Even the language he uses in discussing secular authority is unusually cynical: "Princes are the greatest fools or worst criminals on earth . . . [but they] are God's jailers and hangmen . . . it is His divine will that we should call His hangmen 'gracious lords' . . . and be subject to them in all humility, so long as they do not overreach themselves by wanting to become pastors instead of hangmen" (ibid.). Naturally, Luther says, it would be better if rulers were not simply hangmen but "Christian Princes" who governed out of a sense of Christian duty to serve others. And he even appeals to rulers to respect morality as expressed in the "law of love" and "natural law"—both of which teach the Golden Rule (ibid., p. 42). But the Golden Rule does not spell out precise political and social institutions, which leaves Luther with a fairly stark contrast between the loftiness and inwardness of the Christian spiritual life and the brutality of politics—a nearly unbridgeable gap between the city of God and the earthly city. Perhaps the reason why Luther distinguishes the two realms so sharply is that he sees no continuum of lower and higher goods, no ascending scale of ends from preservation to natural moral perfection to knowledge of God, that earlier Christians derived from Neoplatonic or Scholastic doctrines of the hierarchy of being. This doctrine, as we saw, enabled St. Augustine, despite his considerable pessimism about politics, to expand the state's goal of "tranquillity of order" beyond preservation to include classical moral virtues and some concern for religion; and it allowed Thomas Aquinas to elaborate a natural law teaching about the ends of the temporal realm with some precision. Lacking a clear hierarchy of ends from which to choose, Luther's prudence is confined to judgments about Hobbesian security that can easily lead to contempt for politics (an attitude that later confused many Lutherans when totalitarianism came to Germany and distinctions between tolerable and intolerable regimes needed to be made).[47]

For John Calvin, the political implications of the Reformation went in an entirely different direction. Whereas Luther tended to separate the spiritual and temporal realms, Calvin tended to unite them in a theocratic vision of activist government that he explicitly calls a "Christian polity" (a term which none of the previously mentioned theologians ever employed and which cannot be found in the New Testament). One of the great puzzles is to understand how Luther and Calvin, starting with many of the same theological assumptions—about justification by faith alone, reliance on Scripture alone, the predestination of the elect, and the total depravity of man—could arrive at such different views of the state. I tend to agree with scholars who argue that Calvin's belief in the possibility of knowing with certainty that one is a predestined saint enables Calvin to defend positive government in the name of Christianity. The inner certainty of salvation links Calvinist predestination with confident activism rather than with pessimism and withdrawal from politics. In addition, Calvin's classical training undoubtedly made him more open than Luther to the idea of using the state as a means for educating citizens in virtue.[48]

However he came to his political views, Calvin concludes the *Institutes of the Christian Religion* with a chapter "On Civil Government" (Bk. IV, ch. 20) that outlines a Christian polity in which civil magistrates act as "representatives of God" on earth. The magistrates are responsible for the complete hierarchy of temporal ends: maintaining peace and tranquillity, protecting property and administering justice, promoting "upright conduct and decency," providing social welfare for the poor, the widows, and the orphans, and, above all, establishing correct worship in religion by punishing blasphemy, idolatry, and heresy (IV, 20.2–3, 20.9). This is a maximalist vision of active government—a sort of theocratic welfare state—which Calvin himself worked to achieve in Geneva through the city council for about twenty-five years (from 1536–60, with mixed results).

Calvin's theory of the state is sometimes portrayed as an extension of his views on church government—as a call for a spiritual aristocracy of predestined saints to govern both realms, in violation of the distinction between the Two Cities. This description is not accurate, however, although it fits some of the offshoots of Calvinism, such as the early American Puritans, who incorporated Old Testament ideas of a political covenant with a chosen people into their Christian faith. Calvin himself has a more sober view of politics than later Calvinists. He begins his discussion of civil government in the *Institutes* with the traditional distinction between the spiritual realm, which concerns the "inner man" and his eternal salvation, and the civil realm, which concerns the "external man" and justice in conduct. The civil magistrates are primarily concerned with the external man, though Calvin refers to them as an image of God's justice (in striking contrast to Luther's "hangman" view of princes). Nevertheless, Calvin does not say that rulers must be members of the predestined elect or saints. And he warns that the two realms should not be confused: "We are not to misapply to the political order the Gospel teaching on spiritual freedom" (III, 19.15).

Nor does Calvin think that civil law should be taken directly from the Old Testament or the law of Moses. He says, "it is a dangerous error . . . [to] deny that a commonwealth can be properly ordered if it is simply governed by the laws common to all nations without embracing the political laws of Moses" (IV, 20.14). In a more precise statement, he admits some of the Mosaic law may be used by dividing it into three parts—the moral, judicial, and ceremonial laws. Equating the moral law with the Ten Commandments, Calvin argues that they alone, and not the elaborate judicial and ceremonial laws, may serve as a model for civil law because the Ten Commandments correspond to the natural law: "The Law of God, which we call the moral law is acknowledged to be none other than the testimony of natural law . . . which is engraved in the souls of men by God, and so the whole content of equity is prescribed by it. Hence, equity alone must be the end and rule of all laws . . . even though they vary amongst themselves or differ from the Mosaic Law" (IV, 20.16). Equity is the universal standard for civil law, but its applications may vary because they are determined by prudence, which takes the prohibitions of the Ten Commandments against murder, theft, adultery, and false witness and applies them to specific cities and nations. The complex picture Calvin draws of civil law means that the spiritual and political realms share some common precepts, namely, the Ten Commandments as well as the defense of Calvinist orthodoxy; but the laws of the state aim mainly at equity and may resemble the civil laws of other nations.

On the question of the best form of government, Calvin acknowledges that divine law is silent, leaving prudence to decide what is best based on judgments about man's fallen but rational nature. Sounding more like Aristotle than either Moses or Jesus, Calvin discusses the best regime by evaluating the three common forms of government found in classical Greek philosophy—monarchy, aristocracy, and "polity" (the classical term used by Aristotle and Calvin for uncorrupted democracy). Calvin acknowledges that it is difficult to choose among the different forms because the advantages and disadvantages of each are fairly evenly balanced. Kingship is liable to turn into tyranny, aristocracy to produce factional strife among elites, and popular rule to degenerate into anarchy and sedition. After weighing the options and admitting that "the circumstances are crucial" in deciding, Calvin finally takes his stand. He asserts that "aristocracy, either pure or a mixed form compounded of aristocracy and polity" is best—not because the aristocratic or mixed forms are inherently better but because "it is very rare for kings to exercise . . . self-control . . . [or] to be equipped with such prudence . . . as to be able always to discern what is good and useful." The main advantage of aristocracy is that its several rulers can share their counsel and guard each other to avoid abuses of power. "It is therefore the vices or defects of mankind that make [aristocracy] safer and more tolerable" than other forms (IV, 20.8).

Calvin's argument for aristocracy or a mixed regime of aristocracy and polity is an appeal to the need for collective wisdom in rulers and for limitations on power through checks and balances. While this may sound like modern constitutionalism, it lacks the liberal notion of protecting individual rights or an inviolable private sphere. It is a kind of limited theocracy governed by a moral elite who are not identical to the predestined elect but who may cooperate with them in governing. Yet even with its theocratic tilt, the form of government itself has no inherent spiritual significance for Calvin: It is not modeled on the covenant with Moses or on Israelite kingship and does not pretend to be a New Jerusalem. It is more modest than the vision of many American Puritans or Scottish Presbyterians who expanded Calvin's thought to claim that the predestined saints should govern directly and that the state is a "covenant" like that of the Old Testament and they are the new Israelites.[49] Unlike his followers, Calvin derived his brand of moral authoritarianism from the New Testament distinction of the Two Cities and the prudent choice of the best means for attaining civil peace, moral virtue, and Christian piety.

DUAL HIERARCHIES

I began this chapter with the observation that the Christian tradition for much of its two-thousand-year history has been illiberal and undemocratic, not only in its shameful excesses, but also in many of its central teachings. Contemporary Christians view much of the Bible and the tradition as a regrettable mistake that has now been overcome by a deeper awareness of the Christian conception of human dignity that calls for a democratic political order in which the rights of everyone are respected. Hopefully, I have shown that such attitudes toward the Christian tradition are based on hasty judgments.

In the first place, I argued, the traditional theologians (from the early church to the early Reformation) had a keen appreciation of Christianity's new teaching that everyone is made in the image of God and redeemed by Christ, and many developed this teaching by incorporating insights from Greek philosophy. This produced the idea that men are fallen but rational creatures whose original immortality and goodness have been corrupted but not entirely lost, requiring higher authorities to draw them upward to rational and spiritual perfection. Thus, the loftiness of human dignity was acknowledged, but it was interpreted in the light of the Two Cities and the hierarchies of perfection appropriate to each realm. In the spiritual realm, the hierarchical church was developed either from the Apostolic Succession or from the predestination of the elect, along with a ladder of perfection ascending from sinners to saints and angels. In the temporal realm, kingship and mixed regimes were recommended on prudential grounds as the best means for realizing the common good—keeping civil peace while raising souls upward to moral virtue and Christian piety.

Within this common framework, many variations emerged in the first 1600 years of Christian political thought—Augustine's "tranquillity of order" and limited authoritarianism, Thomas Aquinas's natural law and mixed monarchy, Luther's Two Kingdoms and hangmen princes, Calvin's aristocratic Christian polity, as well as others that I mentioned but had little time upon which to elaborate. Despite the variations, the general model of the best political regime was a corporate hierarchy guided by higher law and mixed with elements of consent in order to achieve the temporal common good.

The overall picture of the tradition is less authoritarian than it is sometimes portrayed because the dual hierarchies of the spiritual and temporal realms limited each other's power. This arrangement may have guaranteed the disunity of Christendom that modern political philosophers such as Machiavelli, Hobbes, and Rousseau detested. But it made it difficult for the state to absorb the church and civil society as modern totalitarianism later did; and it prevented the church from definitively capturing the state (because kings and free cities could always claim some independence from the church according to the Two Cities doctrine, and lower orders could always insist on some participation as part of the corporate common good). Thus, the Christian tradition was not totalitarian because the two distinct orders resisted unified sovereignty and permitted corporate political freedom that was limited but often quite vibrant. Yet, the tradition was not liberal or democratic either, because the two orders were seen as instituted by God; they had a unitary spiritual foundation that resisted secularization, while making it impossible for the state to embark upon utopian experiments in transforming human nature. Neither totalitarian nor liberal, the Christian tradition for centuries produced dual hierarchies of different kinds—with popes, patriarchs, bishops, and predestined saints in rivalry with emperors, kings, princes, aristocratic bodies, and local councils.

Such a tradition cannot be dismissed as misguided prejudice, even if its hierarchies were sometimes imposed with excessive severity or un-Christian cruelty, for the foundational doctrines of the traditional view—the Two Cities, the hierarchy of being, the prudential approach to politics, the demand for moral and spiritual perfection as well as civil peace—capture something essential about the Christian religion. They are doctrinal formulations of Christ's distinction between the realms of God and Caesar, of Christ's admonition that His kingdom is not of this world, of divine election and spiritual perfectionism, and of the limits of justice in the imperfect world of politics that will not change fundamentally until Christ returns in glory at the Second Coming and inaugurates a New Heaven and a New Earth.

Our next task is to explain how the traditional vision began to change in the modern period by movements opposed to these foundational doctrines—gradually replacing the Two Cities with a more unified view of sovereignty, the hierarchy of being with a more homogenous conception of being, and prudential politics with a more ideological approach to politics. Ultimately, we will need to ask if it has been wise to dispense with the traditional doctrines and, if it is not wise, how they might be recovered and reapplied in the modern age.

CHAPTER THREE

THE OPENING OF
CHRISTIANITY
TO DEMOCRACY AND
HUMAN RIGHTS

Since the beginning of the book, we have wrestled with the dilemma that modern liberal democracy needs Christianity but Christianity is not necessarily a liberal or a democratic religion. To sharpen the dilemma, I explored the Bible and the Christian tradition. The Bible teaches that every human being is made in the image of God, which it associates with lost immortality and the capacity for holiness. Such notions, I argued, are spiritual rather than political. They make the highest priority the regaining of immortality through God's redemptive grace and obedience to divine law. Insofar as a connection is made between redemption and politics, it occurs in the Old Testament where God makes a covenant with Israel in order to establish a holy nation that will be a light to the world. The covenant with Israel provides a divine foundation for several political regimes, all of which are undemocratic: the patriarchal tribes of Abraham, the theocracy of Moses, the kingships of Saul, David, and their successors, and the messianic kingship envisioned by the latter prophets. By contrast, the New Testament distinguishes the spiritual from the political. God no longer works through a covenant with a chosen people but through His Incarnation in Christ, who preaches charity and the kingdom of God. Though addressed to all people and favoring the poor and the humble over the rich and the powerful, these teachings do not point to a specific political order. They are transpolitical. They recognize a common humanity but require obedience to Caesar unless Caesar's

107

commands violate the law of God. Thus, the Bible makes a powerful statement about human dignity but is silent about democracy; it teaches that all are worthy of charity or love, but it does not say if anyone is worthy of human rights.

Most of the great theologians of the Christian tradition (from Augustine to the early Reformation) also had a lofty view of human dignity but held political and ecclesiastical views that were illiberal and undemocratic. They developed Christ's distinction between God and Caesar into the doctrine of the Two Cities and conceived of authority in both realms as corporate hierarchies—the hierarchical church and ladders of perfection in the spiritual realm, along with kingship or mixed regimes in the temporal realm. This arrangement limited the power of the state and permitted a certain amount of political freedom, but only as part of the temporal common good not as a claim of popular sovereignty or human rights.

Such patterns of authority were dominant for the first sixteen centuries of Christendom. Though radical sects arose from time to time, no significant challenges occurred until the sixteenth and seventeenth centuries when several movements began to chip away at the traditional patterns. Gradually, over the next four hundred years, changes occurred that produced a whole new outlook. The result is a consensus at the end of the twentieth century in which almost all Christian churches and theologians (Protestant, Catholic, and, most recently, Eastern Orthodox) have embraced democracy and human rights as the core of their political teachings. From both a historical and a theological perspective, this development is quite remarkable.

The obvious question we must now ask is how and why the dramatic change occurred. A less obvious but more difficult question is whether the change has been a good idea. Needless to say, the full story is an immense and controversial topic—the story of the "democratization of Christianity."[1] Since it is impossible to tell the whole story in one chapter, I will select six movements or factors that are commonly cited as causes of change in Christian politics: (1) Medieval constitutional ideas, such as representation and higher law; (2) The Protestant Reformation and its notions of individual conscience and covenanting communities; (3) Neo-Scholastic ideas of popular sovereignty developed by sixteenth-century Jesuits and Dominicans; (4)

The role of the Enlightenment and liberalism in producing religions of reason and God-given natural rights; (5) The struggles of Christian churches against colonialism, slavery, and the industrial exploitation of workers; and (6) The Christian response to totalitarianism in the twentieth century. After surveying these six movements, I will advance a controversial thesis about the most important cause of change. I will argue that a specific strand of Enlightenment liberalism—namely, Immanuel Kant's philosophy of freedom and his notion of the human person as a possessor of inalienable rights—has been the decisive factor in changing Christian politics. The challenge will be to assess the impact of multiple causes in order to make the case that Kant's philosophy of freedom is the crucial one in reconciling Christianity with democracy and human rights.

MEDIEVAL CONSTITUTIONAL IDEAS

The first factor raises a serious objection to the whole thesis that I have sketched. According to a distinguished school of medieval historians, Christianity actually began to change in the direction of democracy and human rights in the Middle Ages rather than in the early modern period. In this view, the roots of modern democracy can be traced to various aspects of 'medieval constitutionalism'—to the canon law of the twelfth century, to the higher law theories of the thirteenth century, and to the theories of representation developed by the Conciliar movement of the fourteenth century. The argument comes in several varieties and has enjoyed varying degrees of influence.

One popular version was developed by Lord Acton at the end of the last century. He argued that Thomas Aquinas was a 'Catholic Whig' who provided the earliest version of the Whig theory of government—the theory of constitutional monarchy and progressive history that underlies the English constitution and its evolution toward the goal of ordered liberty. An updated version of Lord Acton's thesis that applies it to the American political tradition can be found in M. Stanton Evans's book, *The Theme Is Freedom: Religion, Politics, and the American Tradition*. Evans opposes the conventional historical wisdom that locates the sources of the United States Constitution in the

Enlightenment and traces them instead to medieval ideas of representation and consent, to Aquinas's higher law limits on the state, and to the common law tradition.[2] Other proponents of the 'medieval roots' thesis are Brian Tierney, who finds the first stirring of natural rights in the twelfth-century canon lawyers, and Richard Tuck, who emphasizes the contributions of Conciliar theorists to natural rights and representative democracy.[3] Taken together, these scholars form a very distinguished group which deserves much credit for revitalizing medieval studies; but, in my judgment, they have vastly overstated the progressive elements of earlier thought.

Consider the claims made on behalf of medieval Conciliarism—a movement that flourished from 1378 to the 1450s, during and after the Great Schism when the Catholic Church was split by two or three rivals for the title of pope. The Conciliar movement took its name from the General Councils, which were seen as the best means for healing the Great Schism. In this view, the councils stood above the pope as the highest authority because the councils represented the whole church (including the pope, cardinals, bishops, clergy, and laity) and expressed the consent of all its parts. Did such a theory contain the seeds of modern representative democracy? I doubt it. While appealing to the representation of the whole Church, the Conciliarists were not advocating the sovereignty of the people or representative democracy. As Paul Sigmund points out, the Conciliar concept of representation was hierarchical rather than democratic, despite the criticism of the pope's supremacy. Like other medieval theories, it envisioned authority in the Church as a corporate hierarchy, with legitimacy ordained from above by God through the Apostolic Succession and from below through consent in order to ensure the harmony of all parts of the Church.[4]

The theological foundation of this view of authority was the traditional Neoplatonic doctrine of the hierarchy of being—a notion that pervades the writings of Conciliarists Jean Gerson and Nicholas of Cusa—supplemented with a theory of consent. As Cusa argues, consent ties lower orders of being together with higher orders in a harmonious cosmic whole, creating "a continuous ordered relationship of concordance [that] is found throughout the whole hierarchy."[5] Cusa also follows traditional natural law in seeing superiors in wisdom and virtue as the natural rulers of inferiors; but he insists that superiors need the consent of all for maximum unity. In this scheme, *consent means consensus*—a sign of concord that indicates the Holy Spirit is at work guaranteeing infallible results. Since the ultimate aim of Conciliarism is the harmony of the whole rather than the sovereignty of a part, one can understand why Cusa switched at the end of his life from supporting councils to supporting the pope; at that point, the councils had helped to resolve the crisis and the pope seemed to offer the best hope for unity. Nor is it surprising that, after the 1450s when the schism was over, the Conciliar movement died out without making a lasting impact on the Catholic Church. And despite the influence of Conciliarism on Martin Luther, it had no historical connection with the rise of representation as an expression of popular will because it was essentially a variation on medieval corporatism.

A second problem with finding the medieval roots of modern democracy concerns higher law—specifically, natural rights. Brian Tierney has devoted much of his scholarly career to finding the origins of natural rights in the canon lawyers of the twelfth and thirteenth centuries. His quest takes him back to the medieval scholar, Gratian, who produced a summary of canon or church law in 1140 called *The Harmony of Discordant Canons* (or *Decretum*). Tierney's chief finding is that later commentators on Gratian—obscure canon lawyers named Huguccio, Rufinus, Godfrey of Fontaines—developed a new dimension of justice when referring to *jus naturale* (variously translated as natural right, natural justice, or natural law). According to the traditional understanding of *jus*, the term refers to an "objective right"—to what the moral order of the natural universe indicates is just, for example, that the wise should rule the unwise. The canon lawyers argued that the notion of *jus* also includes a "subjective right"—a power or faculty in the human soul that enables the agent to do what is right. Tierney and other scholars (such as Richard Tuck) call the latter subjective right because it inheres in the "subject" who performs the action rather than in the external world and seems to imply a right of personal choice or individual freedom.[6] The crucial question is whether the subjective right of canon lawyers implies the personal freedom or neutral zone of privacy that prepares the way for modern natural rights.

Despite the mountain of suggestive evidence supplied by Tierney, I do not think that he makes a convincing case. As Tierney admits, the subjective right of medieval canon lawyers is still required to follow right reason to its proper ends, which means it is guided by natural teleology rather than individual will. Thus, he quotes Rufinus saying in 1160, "'Natural right (*jus*) is a certain force (*vis*) instilled in every human creature by nature to do good and to avoid the opposite'" (ibid., 62). This is not a permissive right to do what one wants or what seems best for the sake of self-preservation (as in Hobbes and Locke); it does not recognize the autonomous reason of the moral agent as an end-in-itself (as in Kant); it is not a claim made against state authority or fellow citizens for an inviolable private sphere (as in modern constitutionalism), nor is it a claim of entitlements (as in the modern welfare state). Hence, it is not a forerunner of any of the important senses of modern natural rights. The most accurate label for it is a virtue—a power in the soul of a rational agent for attaining perfection—which leads me to conclude that Tierney has found virtuous powers rather than natural rights (ibid., 41, 62–63). Or, as Tierney admits, he has found "rights" (*jura*) as grants of power from higher authorities—for example, the lawful permission to do God's work, such as the "right" (*jus*) of a priest to preach the Gospel, to administer sacraments, or to receive tithes for the church's maintenance. Or, the right (*jus*) of a criminal to be punished. Or, the right (*jus*) of the sun to shine, as God has directed it (ibid., 218–27). The latter senses, of course, are almost the opposite of modern rights because they are grants or directives from higher authority rather than claims from below.

In assessing the work of Tierney and other medieval scholars, I would argue that their research has uncovered vast stores of buried treasure whose significance has been misinterpreted. What they show is that canon lawyers and Conciliar theorists were deeply concerned about gaining obedience to higher law and to church authority rather than giving new freedoms and power to the people; but out of respect for man's rational nature, they emphasized voluntary compliance rather than coercion or sheer assertion of authority. So Conciliarists put new emphasis on consensus in an age of schism; and canonists emphasized the subjective powers of individuals to do what is right according to divine and natural law in order to bring harmony to discordant traditions. This means that their intention was the conservative one of harmonizing a tradition or enforcing a moral order rather than the revolutionary one of emancipating the people. In other words, they were Burkeans rather than Rousseauians!

A third criticism of the 'medieval roots' thesis is the inherent flaw in looking for historical continuities when discontinuities were actually at work. The hope of finding continuity between medieval Christianity and modern democratic freedom is undoubtedly the reason why these impressive scholars have overlooked the crucial issue in opening Christianity to democracy and human rights. I would argue that the crucial change is not simply the "democratization" or "liberalizing" of a monarchical and hierarchical tradition, although that is the end result: *The crucial change is a breakdown in the doctrine of the Two Cities and a rejection of the prudential approach to politics.* By this observation, I mean that the distinction between the spiritual and temporal realms, which was preserved in some fashion from the early Church to the early Reformation (despite temptations to theocratic unification), began to give way to the view that God sanctions one and only one form of government—initially monarchy and eventually democracy.

This change helps to explain why the first steps in modernizing Christianity were not the progressive development of medieval ideas but doctrines diametrically opposed to medieval views of the Two Cities. The most important was "the divine right of kings"—a doctrine whose historical significance is often misunderstood because it appears to contain nothing new. As the influential church historian John Figgis has demonstrated, divine right kingship is a specifically modern doctrine that arose in the sixteenth and seventeenth centuries with King Henry VIII and King James I of England and King Louis XIV of France. Their notion of divine right kingship was distinguished from earlier Christian kingship by the unification of sovereignty under one ruler who claimed to be the head of state as well as the head of the church, meaning the king of the nation also claimed to be God's representative on earth (taking the place of popes and bishops).[7] Divine right kingship was thus a rejection of the Two Cities as well as a rejection of prudential politics in the insistence that God requires an absolute hereditary monarch to head state and church and even brings royal families to power by His particular providence.

This is a kind of 'Old Testament Christianity' that was used by modern kings against the popes, whose assertion of spiritual authority over the temporal realm was exploited to control the king's subjects and to diminish royal power by excommunication. As Figgis shows, the divine right of kings was essentially an ideology of modern nationalism led by monarchs of the Anglican and Gallican Churches that changed Christian politics by unifying the Two Cities under a political sovereign (ibid., pp. 137–45, 175–76). To support this conception of power, ideologists of divine right kingship had to go back to the Old Testament for models of political authority—in the case of Robert Filmer, author of *Patriarcha* (1650), to Adam's patriarchal dominion that was transmitted to kings as the fathers of their nations; and in the case of Bishop Bossuet, author of *Politics Drawn from Holy Scripture* (1680s), to Hebrew kingship that made an idealized version of King David the model for King Louis XIV of France.

The rise of divine right kingship indicates why the thesis of continuous evolution from medieval to modern constitutionalism is mistaken. Medieval constitutionalism limited the state by asserting the supremacy of the church and confining the state to the modest ends of the temporal realm. It was challenged in the early modern period by various forms of royal absolutism that unified church and state under the national king. Royal absolutism was challenged in turn by modern constitutionalism, which separates church and state and thereby looks like a restoration of the medieval view. But the modern separation of church and state is actually a continuation of political absolutism because it relegates the church to the private sphere along with other civic associations and thereby puts the state over the church while limiting the state by an inviolable sphere of private rights. Thus, there could be no progressive development from medieval to modern constitutional theories because the former recognize the supremacy of the spiritual realm while the latter deny it. My conclusion is that the real changes in the Christian tradition did not begin in the Middle Ages but in the early modern period when proponents of divine right kingship sought to unify sovereignty under the head of state, thereby repudiating the Two Cities doctrine, and

claimed that God sanctioned only one legitimate regime, thereby repudiating prudential politics. But these changes still favored monarchy, which means other factors must be admitted to explain the final
outcome favoring democracy.

THE PROTESTANT REFORMATION

A second movement that is commonly cited as playing a major role in
democratizing Christianity is the Protestant Reformation and its ideas
of individual conscience and covenanting communities. The account
usually runs as follows. Martin Luther began the Reformation by proclaiming "justification by faith alone," the "priesthood of all believers," and "Scripture alone" as the source of truth. These ideas were
the original sources of modern liberal democracy because they challenged the medieval church by dispensing with priests as mediators
between God and man, recognizing instead the unmediated conscience of every person as the highest authority. By freeing the individual to judge Scripture for himself and to receive God's grace
directly without a sacramental priesthood, Luther, it is said, brought
to fruition the Christian concept of the person as a free and infinitely valuable being. This promoted democracy within the church,
which then spilled over to the political realm as the Reformation
unfolded—leading to demands for the state to recognize freedom of
conscience and to be founded on a covenant or social contract. Such
demands encouraged the struggle for other rights, eventually leading
to the recognition of universal human rights in all spheres of life.[8]

In my judgment, this popular theory of the Protestant origins of
modern liberal democracy is misleading because it glosses over a critical question: Did the Protestant notion of spiritual freedom, understood as unmediated conscience, necessarily lead to parallel notions
of political freedom, understood as individual rights and popular sovereignty? This point, as we saw in chapter two, was specifically denied
by Luther and Calvin and, much earlier, by Paul, all of whom thought
that spiritual freedom did not necessarily translate into political freedom. If there is no such necessity, then one may doubt that the Reformation inevitably led to modern liberal democracy, even though it

had a democratizing effect on church structures and on broad cultural patterns (for example, by expanding literacy among ordinary people).

Another way of posing the question about the relation of spiritual and political freedom is to ask how one may determine the exact democratic or liberal moment in the unfolding of the Protestant Reformation when Luther was quite authoritarian in his politics and Calvin defended an aristocratic Christian polity. The same Luther who called for the spiritual "freedom of a Christian"—freeing people from the burden of earning salvation through works—also called for the violent suppression of peasants and Anabaptists. And Calvin may have distrusted kings, but he distrusted democracy even more, despite his oft-quoted remark about resistance to kings by lower magistrates. Thus, the democratic turn is not in Luther or Lutheranism (remember that German Lutherans were distrustful of democracy up to the time of the Weimar Republic in the 1920s). Nor is it in Calvin or in Calvinist Presbyterians whose vision of authority included a nationally established Presbyterian Church (which they achieved in Scotland but not in England). Though the Presbyterians were the original rebellious Puritans who sought to 'purify' the Anglican and Lutheran Churches of residual Catholicism, they held fairly conservative conceptions of corporate hierarchy in church and state.

Following the logic of this argument, one would have to locate the democratic turn at those moments when the spiritual freedom and equality proclaimed by the early Protestant reformers were extended to political doctrines of freedom and equality, against the will of the original reformers. When and why did this occur? Obviously, there is no simple answer to this question, given the complexity of the Reformation. All that I would like to propose here is that the turn to political democracy was not inevitable and that it went against the grain of Luther, Calvin, the Anglican Church, the Puritan rebellion against the Anglican Church, and the early American Puritans; moreover, even the most radical proponents of the Reformation did not arrive at full-fledged liberal democracy.

To see these points, one must investigate the radical reformation—meaning, the radical offshoots of Calvinism and the radical followers of the Swiss reformer Huldrych Zwingli, the so-called 'left-wing Puritans' and Anabaptists who rebelled against the original reformers and produced the separatist and free-church movements. The distinguishing feature of the radical reformers was the idea of the church as an independent congregation—a self-governing assembly of the people that is more or less independent of other churches—and the belief that the political community should also resemble a democratic assembly. Yet, even among congregationalists, one must be careful about overstating the progressive elements in earlier thought. Many of the Puritan congregationalists restricted their independent congregations to a few visible saints, creating a spiritual aristocracy who governed church and commonwealth. Though such residual undemocratic and illiberal features persisted, the radical reformers were developing a doctrine called "covenantal theology" that contained the seeds of democratic political community.

The great puzzle, as Perry Miller points out, is that covenantal theology does not have a clear origin historically or biblically, though it may well be the most influential political offshoot of the reformed Protestant tradition.[9] Covenantal theology is a theory of divine politics that Christians took from the Old Testament idea of God's covenant with a chosen people and applied to themselves, turning the reformers of various Puritan sects into the New Israelites charged with the mission of saving the Reformation in a new Promised Land. Though developed by Protestant Christians, the theory is neither in the New Testament nor in Luther and Calvin. It is another type of 'Old Testament Christianity' that was espoused in different versions by Puritan groups such as the French Huguenots, Swiss Zwinglians, English, Scottish, Dutch, and American Congregationalists, and Pilgrims. In much of covenantal theology, a democratic element coexists with an intense theocratic element because the covenant between God, rulers, and people requires the imposition of the true divine law (reformed Protestantism) and the people are given a large role in protecting the divine law.

One of the likely sources was the French Huguenot who wrote *Vindiciae, Contra Tyrannos* in 1579 (usually attributed to Philippe Mornay). He argues that a covenant exists between God and the king to establish the true law of God and a second covenant exists between rulers and people to uphold the divine law. If the king rejects the true law of God, then the people have a right of resistance against the tyrant because they, too, are defenders of the divine law. Obviously, there is a democratic element here (though not much liberalism); but the democratic element is imbedded in theocratic kingship and theocratic populism. Another likely source was Heinrich Bullinger, the Swiss reformer sometimes credited with the first statement of covenantal theology in *The One and Eternal Testament or Covenant of God* (1534). It argues for a sort of theocratic populism in which the people do not rule but act as checks on rulers in order to ensure that rulers impose the correct divine law—a view of biblical politics in which one continuous covenant exists, rather than a sharp distinction between "old" and "new" covenants, producing another variation of Old Testament Christianity.[10]

In America, Puritans such as Jonathan Winthrop and John Cotton saw the covenant as a theocracy organized as a corporate hierarchy, with rulers accountable to God as well as to the people. They were spiritual elitists who limited active citizenship in the commonwealth to church membership. When they spoke of liberty they meant, as Winthrop said, the moral liberty of self-mastery under proper authority and corporate consent to the true version of the divine law, rather than natural rights or popular sovereignty. And even though their self-governing churches or congregations had democratic impulses, they punished dissenters and heretics with exile and persecution. For these Puritans, the covenant with God sanctioned the corporate hierarchies of a righteous and holy people—a self-governing spiritual aristocracy.

As is well-known from New England history, it was not the Puritans of Massachusetts Bay but the separatists and persecuted dissenters who promoted versions of liberal-democratic practices. The most famous separatists were the Pilgrims under William Bradford who arrived on the shores of America before Winthrop and pledged in the Mayflower Compact of 1620 "for the glory of God and advancement of the Christian faith and honor of our king and country . . . [to] covenant and combine ourselves together into a civil body politic."[11] For the Pilgrims, the spiritual freedom to spread the Gospel was allied with a political covenant or social contract that promoted democratic self-government. Likewise, the persecuted dissenters from Winthrop's

Puritans extended spiritual freedom to the realm of politics. Roger Williams of Rhode Island and the persecuted Quakers and Baptists were the main spokesmen in the colonies for religious toleration on religious grounds—demanding freedom of conscience in order to protect the purity of faith from the corrupting entanglements of church and state. In another variation, Thomas Hooker founded Connecticut on democratic consent, asserting in 1638 that "the choice of public magistrates belongs unto the people, by God's own allowance"; but Hooker still insisted on an established church for Connecticut rather than the religious liberty of Rhode Island.[12]

Reflecting on these complex developments, we are reminded of the crucial question: Was it inevitable that the dissenting offshoots of the Protestant reformers—the radical reformers and 'left-wing Puritans'—would emerge as the most dynamic force and then be further secularized, producing a continuous line of development from Martin Luther and John Calvin, to John Winthrop and John Cotton, to Roger Williams and Thomas Hooker, to Thomas Jefferson and James Madison? When stated in this sweeping fashion, it sounds improbable. The chain of reactions is more contingent than necessary, arising from uncritical extensions of spiritual freedom to political freedom and unwarranted Christianized versions of Old Testament politics. Because such trends were unpredictable, the Protestant Reformation did not develop automatically on its own into modern liberal democracy nor could the early American Puritans have created all of the ideological fire of the American Revolution. They may have championed a covenantal or contractual view of church and state, but they still lacked the doctrine of God-given natural rights that is expressed in the Declaration of Independence. One should not be surprised that Lutherans, Calvinist Presbyterians, Anglicans, early Puritans, and many later evangelical revivalists defended corporate hierarchies or theocratic authoritarianism. And when the dissenters from Puritanism, such as the Anabaptists, carried their democratic church ideas into the political realm, most were not very liberal because their vision of politics was providential, prophetic, and theocratic. Thus, I conclude that the Protestant Reformation and its ideas of individual conscience and covenanting communities had important democratic impulses, especially in church government.

But, contrary to sweeping theories about the Protestant origins of modern politics, the Reformation did not contain the political theory of modern liberal democracy.[13]

NEO-SCHOLASTIC THEORIES OF POPULAR SOVEREIGNTY

A third movement that has contributed to the democratizing of Christianity is less well-known than radical Protestantism. It took place within Catholicism—among the Jesuits and Dominicans of the sixteenth and seventeenth centuries who developed St. Thomas Aquinas's teachings on natural law into theories of popular sovereignty. Later called neo-Scholastics, this group included Francisco Vitoria, Francisco Suarez, and Robert Bellarmine—impressive scholars who are often overlooked in the history of modern democracy because of their role in the Counter-Reformation and its reactionary efforts to roll back the tides of Protestantism. Yet their strong defenses of papal authority in the spiritual realm went together with a new political doctrine that traced the legitimate authority of the state to the consent of the people; and they even extended the consent of peoples to the native Americans of the New World, making the neo-Scholastics 'right-wing' churchmen and 'left-wing' politicians. Their writings are fascinating examples of theological development in which seemingly inconsistent doctrines were combined by adapting a living Thomism to the problems of a new age.

To illustrate these points, I will focus on the great Jesuit theologian Francisco Suarez (1548–1617). He has been called "the first modern democrat" by one of his biographers—a description that may be acceptable if it is understood in the right way.[14] For Suarez was not trying to be self-consciously modern when he wrote his political treatises, *On Laws and God the Lawgiver* (1612) and *A Defense of the Catholic and Apostolic Faith against the Errors of the Anglican Sect and King of England* (1613). Following Thomas, Suarez accepted the Aristotelian proposition that man is by nature a social animal, but he denied that man is a political animal with a natural distinction between ruler and ruled. According to Suarez, there are no natural hierarchies except for those in the family. The authority of parents over their children and that of husbands over wives are forms of natural rule; but the state is a human creation. Though God creates human beings with a need for political community, God does not specifically ordain political rulers by divine right and nature does not appoint political rulers by natural law. Because the form of government is not determined by higher powers, the choice is left to the people, which Suarez formulates in his "transfer" theory of power. The theory holds that political authority resides in the whole community of people who "transfer" their original power to specific rulers—by consent, custom, or acquiescence to conquest—which the people understand as a total alienation of their power, rather than a mere delegation to a representative. The justification for the transfer is Suarez's sweeping declaration that "in the nature of things, all men are born free . . . no person has political jurisdiction over another by nature."[15]

Herein lies one of the paradoxes of Suarez's political thought: God supports government in general but not a specific form, which leads to a principled argument for democracy or popular sovereignty based on natural freedom and consent. Suarez even goes so far as to ground natural political freedom in the *Imago Dei*—in the "natural dignity of man" as a creature made in the image of God—which he interprets to mean that human beings are born in the natural state without subjection to other men, both before and after the Fall.[16] Hence, there is no justification for natural slavery and no claim for natural superiors in wisdom and virtue to rule; nor is there justification for kings to claim immediate power from God, as in the divine right of kings (which Suarez attacks in *The Defense of the Catholic and Apostolic Faith*). In Suarez's transfer theory of power, the chain of command runs from God to the people and then to political rulers.

When applying these principles, Suarez preserves a role for prudence, but it has a secondary role compared to its role in the theories of Thomas or Aristotle because democracy is the original form of government: "The perfect civil community by the law of nature is free and subject to no person . . . which if it were not changed would be a democracy" (*Defense*, III, 2.9). Yet, Suarez argues that it is most prudent for the people to transfer their power to a king for the sake of unity and efficiency and least prudent to keep it in a democratic assembly. Monarchies rarely exist in pure forms, however; and given the "frailty, ignorance, and wickedness of mankind, it is expedient to add some element of common government which is executed by a number of persons" (*Laws,* III. 4.1). Surprisingly, Suarez winds up close to Thomas in his practical recommendation of mixed monarchy, but Suarez separates prudence from Thomas's hierarchy of perfection and puts it in the service of a contractual view of the state.

This move implies a new relation between natural law and positive law. Unlike Thomas, Suarez derives natural law primarily from intrinsic good and evil (the conformity of actions to man's "rational nature") rather than from a hierarchy of natural inclinations and natural ends. This makes Suarez's natural law more uniform and egalitarian and more of a challenge to the inequalities of existing positive law than Thomistic natural law. For Suarez, natural law makes three radical demands: (1) natural freedom from hierarchies (except in the family and, of course, in the Church, which is a divinely ordained hierarchy); (2) natural democracy, in which the whole community holds original power; and (3) a natural community of goods, prior to any private ownership. For Suarez, the state and property relations have little or no natural basis; they are human creations arising from transfers of power, existing by positive right alone and upheld as a matter of obligation rather than natural inclination. While Suarez insists that such obligations are justified, his natural law doctrine has more revolutionary potential than Thomas's; even Suarez's rhetoric is less cautious in endorsing tyrannicide and in permitting expropriation of the "superfluous" wealth of the rich for the poor.[17]

Moreover, Suarez, like other neo-Scholastics, had a version of natural rights, even though it is embedded in the social nature of man and does not contradict the primacy of the common good or the people's transfer of power to the political rulers. In his famous definition of *jus naturale,* Suarez says, "It is customary to call *jus* properly a certain moral faculty that anyone has either regarding his own thing or something due to him; and so the owner of a thing is said to have a right in the thing (*jus in rei*) and a workman is said to have a right to his wage (*jus ad rem*) (*Laws,* I, 2.5 and 2.24). Suarez also speaks of "an intrinsic right of liberty" and "a natural dominion over one's own actions" and a natural right of self-defense against unjust aggressors, including tyrants (ibid., II, 14.16). While it is difficult to say what kind of rights these are, they are clearly stronger than the grants of power that one finds in Thomas, where every rightful action must be found "licit" according to natural law—implying that one must first ask the law for permission to act and then proceed by meeting a list of qualifying conditions (e.g., self-defense is permitted by natural law, if the intention is to stop the aggressor without killing him and proportionate force is used). For Suarez, natural law places as much emphasis on the subject's right to act as on the lawful permission to act. But because the right to act is still directed to the end of virtue and qualified by the common good, Suarez's rights are somewhere between Thomas's lawful permissions and Locke's rightful claims to act according to the necessities of preservation without waiting for God's permission. Suarez brings out the natural power to act within the created order sanctioned by God's will and sustained by nature's rational operation.[18]

A further qualification on the natural power to act is the relation of church and state. Suarez defends a limited version of national sovereignty and the pluralism of nations: Christian kings are supreme and independent in the temporal sphere because neither the Holy Roman Emperor nor the pope has direct temporal power; even infidel and unbaptized peoples exercise rightful political authority in their nations. The pope, however, has "indirect" temporal power in all issues relating to the Christian faith (for example, defending missionaries and persecuted Christians) which gives the pope a fair amount of leeway to intervene in nations, including non-Catholic ones. While Suarez expects Christian kings to uphold the true faith in their nations, he explicitly endorses Thomas's teaching on the treatment of unbelievers—that toleration of false beliefs is often a wise policy because it is a "lesser evil" than coercive imposition, as long as the faith of Christians is not endangered.[19] This is prudential toleration, not a right of conscience or religious liberty.

In sum, Suarez develops Thomism by preserving the notion of the universe as an intelligible moral order freely created by God and governed by laws, while diminishing natural hierarchies and emphasizing a political order that originates in the people. One of his boldest innovations is to insist that the divine image in man has democratic implications, thereby turning a spiritual doctrine into the grounds for a political doctrine (though Suarez still respects the Two Cities' distinction between the divinely instituted church and the contractual state). The result is Suarez's eclectic vision in which democratic principles are asserted and then severely qualified by traditional assumptions about the hierarchical church, the primacy of the common good, and the transfer of political power from the people to a strong national king. Such developments move Catholic political thought toward a humanistic Thomism that provides an opening for democracy without making it inevitable or giving it full reign.

THE ENLIGHTENMENT AND LIBERALISM

The fourth major factor in transforming Christianity in a democratic direction is the Enlightenment. Like other factors, this is a complicated subject because the Enlightenment has many, often contradictory, facets. In the political realm, it produced the natural rights and social contract theory of government—otherwise known as liberalism—in the writings of such luminaries as Hobbes, Locke, Rousseau, and Kant. Though attenuated notions of rights and social contract may have existed in earlier movements (such as medieval canon law, the Reformation, and neo-Scholasticism), they never had the revolutionary implications of the Enlightenment theories. Sometimes the Enlightenment theories were defined in opposition to the Christian religion and produced intense hostility, as in Voltaire's cry to "destroy the infamous thing"—meaning Christianity—which culminated in violent attacks on the Catholic Church during the French Revolution. Sometimes the Enlightenment and liberalism sought to accommodate and even to mimic Christianity, either from admiration or from a desire to tame it for worldly purposes. Sorting out the strands of a powerful movement like the Enlightenment requires many subtle judgments, which I will attempt in one small area—the emergence of rational religions and the development of doctrines of God-given natural rights sanctioned by Divine Providence.

To understand these phenomena, it is useful to reconsider the common stereotype of the Enlightenment as the uncompromising enemy of religion—as a movement that sought to abolish religion or to reject religion entirely as nothing more than primitive superstition that could be replaced by modern science. Though this stereotype is not entirely false, it needs to be qualified. Many of the philosophers and scientists of the Enlightenment did not so much call for the abolition of religion as for the transformation of religion into something more reasonable—into a belief in God and universal benevolence that discarded the supernatural and miraculous aspects of Christianity along with the intolerance and persecution associated with irrationalism while preserving a set of core convictions grounded on reason rather than on revelation or Scripture.

Thus, there emerged in the seventeenth and eighteenth centuries the "religions of reason" or rational religions, which took several forms. The most influential, undoubtedly, was Deism—the belief in a rational God who is the Creator and Designer of the rationally ordered universe. Also known as "natural religion," Deism could be interpreted in two different ways. One way was purely scientific and nonprovidential: The belief in God as a "clockmaker" who created the universe and its intricate mathematical laws but who leaves it running on its own like a machine without intervening to direct its course to good or evil ends. A more complex version was providential Deism, sometimes called Theism, which saw God as the Supreme Governor who not only created the universe but also actively and continuously intervenes in it, directing the lives of men and nations, judging their actions, and administering rewards and punishments in this life and the next.

In addition to Deism or Theism, a less naturalistic version of rational religion emerged around the time of the Enlightenment—Latitudinarianism. It was primarily a movement within the Church of England that was influenced by Renaissance humanism and rationalism. Its goal was to broaden the creed of the Christian faith by simplifying its essential beliefs and practices so that all Christian churches could be accepted and tolerated (a forerunner of the ecumenical movement whose aim is to bridge sectarian differences by finding common ground). A third version of rational religion was Unitarianism, originally called Socinianism, which rejected the Christian doctrine of the Trinity (three Persons in one God) as irrational and mystical in favor of the more rational conception of God as one divine person. This belief was often combined with universalism, producing

Unitarian Universalism, which emphasized the salvation of all people rather than the harsh distinction between the saved and the damned. One might also include Arminianism among rational religions (though it is sometimes seen as a liberal version of Calvinism). It emphasized the role of human free will in attaining salvation rather than predestination and irresistible grace. One should also mention Freemasonry when compiling a list of rational religions; it was a highly influential secret society of notable persons dedicated to the cause of Enlightenment and the worldly improvement of humanity.

What all of these movements have in common is the belief that religion can be preserved in the modern age of Enlightenment only by rationalizing and simplifying it to include the belief in one God as the Creator of the universe and the belief in a rational morality of universal benevolence that requires religious toleration, human freedom, and scientific progress. Nearly all other doctrines of traditional Judaism and Christianity—the belief in the Bible as the revealed word of God; in original sin and divine redemption; in chosen peoples and divine election; in the divinity of Christ and His resurrection from the dead; in popes, bishops and priests; in sacraments and sacred rituals; in miracles and supernatural causes; in divine wrath and the torments of hell; in the missionary duty of converting heathens and sinners—were to be discarded as irrational relics of a less enlightened age which modern people, especially educated people, have outgrown.

When described in this fashion, the religions of reason strike many as being superficial or blasphemous, hardly worthy of serious attention. Many Jews and Christians cringe at their brazen rationalism and see them as little more than disguised atheism—"atheism with a blush," as one wit described Unitarianism. Atheists, too, are annoyed by rational religion: Why bother to preserve a fig leaf of religion when the honest and courageous course would be to embrace pure rationalism and secular humanism? Both parties are a bit taken aback, however, when they discover how many great thinkers and leaders of this period adhered to some version of rational religion (although it is always hard to distinguish those who were sincere from those who were merely paying lip service, even to a minimal creed, in order to avoid persecution or the scandal of public atheism).[20] Whatever is the case, I would count among public or private adherents of rational religion some of the most important figures of the late seventeenth and eighteenth centuries: In America, Benjamin Franklin, Ethan Allen, Thomas Jefferson, Thomas Paine, George Washington, John Adams, and James Madison; in England, Lord Herbert of Cherbury, Sir Isaac Newton, John Locke, John Toland, the Earl of Shaftesbury, Anthony Collins, Matthew Tindal, Alexander Pope, and Lord Boling-broke; in Germany, Herman Samuel Reimarus, Gotthold Lessing, Im-manuel Kant, Gottfried Leibniz, Moses Mendelssohn, and possibly Goethe; in France, Voltaire, Diderot, possibly Rousseau, Montesquieu, and Tocqueville. Yet, it is not only the large number of influential fig-ures subscribing to some version of rational religion that forces one to take it seriously. One must also consider the importance of rational re-ligion for modern politics.

Speaking broadly, I would argue that liberal democracy in America and England would not be possible without the religions of reason because they played a decisive role in reconciling Christianity with modern liberal democracy. In America, most of the founding generation embraced Deism or Theism; it enabled the intellectual and political leaders of the day to combine belief in God with a ratio-nal theory of natural rights, producing the American political creed of *God-given natural rights.* Its classic expression is the Declaration of Independence, which I regard as a Deistic natural law document. The Declaration appeals to "the laws of Nature and of Nature's God," which it calls self-evident truths of reason rather than revelations of Scripture. It describes nature's God as the Creator who has endowed all men with unalienable rights to life, liberty, and the pursuit of happiness—rights inherent in the very nature of human beings as creatures of God possessing reason. The Declaration also requires government based on the consent of the people to secure those God-given natural rights and even calls upon the protection of Divine Providence in the struggle for rights, implying that the universe is a rational moral order, designed and governed by a just God who favors the cause of human liberty.

As we have seen, the notion that God created man to enjoy natural rights and to establish government by consent—the founding principles of liberal democracy or republican self-government—is

not in the Bible. Nor is it in the writings of medieval and early Reformation theologians nor in the covenantal theology of the Puritans of
colonial America. Though not wholly incompatible with these traditional views and preserving residual elements of classical and Christian thought, the Declaration of Independence is primarily a product
of the rational religions of the Enlightenment that emphasized God's
support for the freedom of self-governing peoples.[21] This rational-
republican religion supercedes Calvinist-Puritanism in America with
its doctrines of human depravity and original sin, its belief in predestination and the divine election of saints, and its theocratic politics.
Deism replaces such harsh Puritan doctrines with natural freedom,
natural equality, and trust in the people to govern themselves without
the guidance of a spiritual aristocracy. The result is a diluted and
rationalized version of Christianity—a 'kinder and gentler' religion
than Calvinism—that makes possible the God-given natural rights
of the Declaration of Independence and the republican form of
government of the U.S. Constitution.

To understand how America arrived at this republican religion,
one may read with great profit an article by the historian Paul
Johnson titled, "God and the Americans." Johnson's thesis is that
America has always been a religious nation—"a nation with the soul of
a church," in the words of Chesterton. But the American religion is
hard to define because it evolved gradually from the Puritanism of the
colonial era to the Deism of the founding period, producing a republican civil religion that mixed elements of Evangelical Protestantism
and Enlightenment liberalism—a combination of Calvin and Locke,
as it were. It survives today in what is loosely called the Judeo-Christian
tradition which Americans appeal to when they recite the Pledge of
Allegiance to the Flag and pay tribute to the republic as "one nation
under God."

According to Paul Johnson, the common ground of these various
religious currents is the belief that America is a providential nation, a
City upon a Hill, whose original mission was defending religious freedom in order to advance the purest version of the Protestant Reformation (the theme of Cotton Mather's *Magnalia Christi Americana*)
and whose later mission became the spread of democratic human
rights around the world (the message of Woodrow Wilson's "Four-

teen Points"). What makes such a nation possible is the gradual development of a rationalized Christianity that strips away Scholastic theology, miracles, elaborate rituals and dogma, church hierarchies, Calvinist pessimism as well as millenialist utopianism, reducing religion to a simple belief in God and morality: "The form of Christianity which developed in America was a kind of ecumenical and unofficial state religion . . . [that] was itself the civil and moral creed of republicanism." It provided a consensus among Protestants, Catholics, Jews, and even nonbelievers because they could accept "the premise that religion, meaning morality, was essential to democratic institutions."

Only such a creed explains the strong but vague religious beliefs of many American statesmen and citizens—such as John Adams's belief, echoed by George Washington, that our Constitution presupposes "a moral and religious people" without specifying the content of that religion; the appeals of Lincoln to the judgments of Almighty God, even though, as Paul Johnson says, Lincoln was "a man who believed in providence rather than a personal describable God, nominally a Baptist but a member of no regular church"; Ronald Reagan's optimistic faith that God blessed America to be the beacon of freedom and hope to the world; and President Eisenhower's famous statement, "Our government makes no sense unless it is founded on a deeply felt religious faith—and I don't care what it is." In response, Paul Johnson says, of course, Eisenhower did care; but "he could not define it any more than his predecessors Washington and Lincoln had been able to define the heavenly providence which they relied upon to see America right."[22]

If one accepts the Johnson thesis about republican religion in America and looks back at England, one could write a variation on the theme called, "God and the English." For in England, the Anglican Church has been deeply influenced by Latitudinarian Christianity (which in turn was influenced by Renaissance humanism and Deism), and these movements have nurtured the growth of a uniquely English institution: the Church of England, which is an exclusive national church under the Crown and Archbishop that has learned over the past several centuries to accept the *de facto* toleration of other churches and sects while maintaining its nominal preeminence. The Anglican Church has been able to do so mainly because it does not take Christian doctrine too seriously—a latitudinarian approach that is spiritually disheartening but politically beneficial. The result is two nations, America and England, the former with no nationally established church, the latter with its established Anglican Church, that have arrived at similar endpoints. Both are nominally Christian nations whose form of government is republican or parliamentary and whose leadership class has consisted largely of Christian gentlemen. But the content of Christianity has been gradually and almost insensibly transformed from reformed Protestantism to rational religion, making the God-given natural rights of the American republic and the civilized freedom of British parliamentary government under a ceremonial Church of England and a ceremonial monarchy the two great pillars of religiously based freedom in the modern world.

In addition to facilitating the harmony of God and political freedom, rational religion has changed beliefs about Divine Providence and historical progress. Before the Enlightenment and the modern democratic revolutions, Christian thinkers frequently pondered the relation between Divine Providence and the great tides and events of history. Their primary focus was "salvation history": God's plan for the redemption of the world, as seen in the history of Israel, in the birth of Christ, and in the growth and persecution of the Christian Church. The role of the earthly city—of kingdoms, empires, and civilizations from Egypt and Assyria to the Roman empire and early Europe—in salvation history was uncertain. St. Augustine argued that the city of God and the earthly city were intermingled, but their ultimate destinies were different. Other Christian historians saw common destinies, such as Eusebius, whose *Ecclesiastical History* treats the Emperor Constantine as a divine agent for rescuing the church from persecution and establishing its power in the world. In modern times, divine right theorists such as Bishop Bossuet believed that God favored absolute monarchy and even brought royal families to the throne by "particular" providence (meaning the Bourbon monarchy of France was, in a sense, divinely anointed). Following Bossuet's logic more closely than St. Augustine's, modern thinkers who witnessed the great democratic revolutions in America and France began to see the history of the Two Cities pointing toward a common destiny. They began to see the progress of democracy as a sign of God's irresistible providence.

Two important examples of this new thinking were the liberal Catholic, Alexis de Tocqueville, and the heterodox Catholic priest, Félicité Robert de Lamennais. Both were Frenchmen who tried to grasp the religious significance of political events in the 1830s, one generation after the French Revolution. They saw the will of God in history as a providential force turning the world against the "old regime" of monarchy and aristocracy and driving it toward democracy. Their view of Providence marks a change, one might say, *from divine right monarchy to divine right democracy.*

The role of rational religion in bringing about this change in perspective can be seen in Tocqueville's appeal to the will of God in history. As Tocqueville says in the introduction to *Democracy in America,* "God does not Himself need to speak for us to find sure signs of His will; it is enough to observe the customary progress of nature and the continuous tendency of events; I know, without special revelation, that the stars follow orbits in space traced by His finger. If patient observation . . . have led the men of the present day to recognize that both the past and the future of their history consist in the gradual and measured advance of equality, that discovery alone gives this progress the sacred character of the will of the Sovereign Master. In that case, the effort to halt democracy appears as a fight against God Himself."[23] Tocqueville's affinity with rational religion is evident in his claim that it is possible to know God's will "without special revelation" by using an empirical test along the lines of physical science. As the passage indicates, both natural science and historical science are built on the deistic premise of an ordered universe created by God whose will can be known by visible signs. A historian of civilization can infer that a universal, lasting, and irresistible trend in one direction is evidence of the fact that it is providential rather than accidental. Observing such signs, Tocqueville infers that God wills the end of monarchy and of aristocracy and the triumph of democracy.[24]

Among Catholics, this type of providential thinking has led to a reassessment of the French Revolution. For much of the last two centuries, the Catholic Church condemned the French Revolution, including the "rights of man," as anticlerical, anti-Catholic, tyrannical, and atheistic. The French priest and journalist, Félicité Robert de Lamennais, ran headlong into this reactionary sentiment in the 1830s and was crushed by it. A little known figure today, Lamennais stirred a huge controversy in his time. Although he fought against religious indifference and for religious revival in an age of skepticism, he was deeply confused about how to justify the Christian faith and changed his mind about the meaning of Christianity. He began as a conservative or Ultramontane Catholic who favored strict allegiance to the pope and a French monarchy freed from a national church. He evolved in midlife toward liberal Catholicism, defending freedom of religion and speech in a liberal democratic order ("God and Liberty," was the motto of his journal, *L'Avenir*, which flourished in the 1830s). At the end of his life, he switched to socialism and quasi-Christian pantheism, breaking with the Catholic Church and rejecting his priestly vows without being formally excommunicated. What is fascinating about Lamennais is the unifying thought of his several periods: He believed that neither revelation nor individual reason could justify the Christian religion and uphold legitimate authority. Instead, he looked for certainty in the "sens commun" or the common consent of mankind as reflected in the dominant tides of history which he took for evidence of the providential hand of God. At first, he read the tide of common history like the conservatives Burke and de Maistre and affirmed the ancient institution of the papacy. In his middle period, he saw it on the side of liberal democracy; and finally, he saw it favoring the proletariat, the apparent wave of the future that would render the Catholic Church obsolete and transform Christianity into a humanistic religion. By this logic, God turned out to be neither a monarchist nor a liberal democrat but a socialist.

After repudiating his early papal sympathies, Lamennais was put on the defensive by Pope Gregory XVI in his 1832 encyclical, *Mirari Vos*, which attacked liberalism and the French Revolution for leading to relativism and religious indifferentism (the view that all religions were equally true or untrue). Other popes of the nineteenth century made the same point more vehemently, including the famous statement of Pope Pius IX in his 1864 *Syllabus of Errors* which declared that the Church would never accept the prevailing sentiments in favor of "progress, liberalism, and modern civilization." Yet, after a century of conflict and change, the Catholic Church has made its peace with the French Revolution and with Lamennais.

Reflecting this change of heart, the present archbishop of Paris, Jean-Marie Cardinal Lustiger, wrote that the ideals of the French Revolution are now acceptable to Catholics because we can see that they are not simply products of atheistic philosophy: "In the course of two centuries since the Revolution . . . it has been more and more widely recognized that liberty, equality, and fraternity are among the fruits borne by the Biblical and Christian tradition . . . [indeed] the law of God is the only sure guarantee of the rights of man."[25] Cardinal Lustiger's point is that, even though the original proponents of the rights of man may have failed to see the Christian basis of their principles or ignored the necessary moral restraints on human rights provided by Christian ethics, the Church has now discovered the authentic basis of rights in the Christian idea of human dignity. Thus, Tocqueville and Lamennais have been partially vindicated in hindsight and have prepared the way for an extraordinary event: The Catholic archbishop of Paris has just "baptized" the French Revolution! While it would be seriously wrong to infer that the Church has adopted the rational religion of the Enlightenment, it has come to accept some of the political ideas initially proposed by rational religion—such as God-given natural rights and the providential history of democracy. Whether all of these changes have been wisely undertaken is a question we shall examine in later chapters.

STRUGGLES AGAINST OPPRESSION AND THE IDEA OF "SOCIAL JUSTICE"

A fifth factor that has changed Christian attitudes toward democracy are the struggles against oppression—by which I mean Christian responses to the problems of colonialism, slavery, and the exploitation of industrial workers from the sixteenth to the twentieth centuries. From these struggles, the idea of social justice emerged as a dominant theme of Christian politics. By looking back at history, one can see that, even though the precise term "social justice" was not coined until the middle of the nineteenth century (probably by the Italian

Jesuit and natural law scholar Luigi Taparelli), the concerns which gave rise to it began much earlier.[26] The first stirrings can be found in the neo-Scholastics who opposed the Spanish conquest of the Americas, in the Christians who participated in the antislavery movements, and in the Christian trade union and socialist movements that fought against the injustices of modern industrial society. Because these struggles were usually waged in the name of equal rights and an egalitarian social order (with occasional turns toward reactionary corporatism), they gave a powerful impetus to the equation of Christianity with political and social democracy.

The link with democracy must be stressed because protesting the injustices of the powerful on behalf of the powerless is not a new theme in the Christian tradition. St. Ambrose, bishop of Milan at the end of the fourth century, excommunicated the Christian Roman Emperor Theodosius for his mass reprisals against the Greek population at Thessalonica and did not lift the ban until the emperor humbly and publicly repented for his sin against the people. St. John Chrysostom, the bishop of Constantinople in 398, attacked the luxury and moral corruption of the imperial court, built houses and shelters for the poor, and encouraged the manumission of slaves. St. Augustine formulated the theory of "just war" to restrain wars of imperial conquest. The medieval canon law codified by Gratian refined the notion of justice for church officials to use against the misuse of power by emperors and kings. St. Thomas Aquinas said the common good may require rulers to command the rich to share with the poor and permits the poor to take from the rich in extreme necessity. Such protests against injustice drew upon the most powerful moral weapon of the Christian tradition—the concept of "higher law" that is spelled out in the Christian divine law of charity, the Christian natural law of justice, the law of nations (*jus gentium*), and the theory of just war. For most traditional Christians, however, the protest against injustice did not automatically point toward democracy or the social welfare state. Their stance resembled the ancient Hebrew prophets, who denounced oppression and proclaimed the righteousness of caring for the poor, the widows, and orphans while envisioning perfect kingship as the solution. As the prophet Isaiah said after condemning the injustices of his age: "Behold a king shall reign in righteousness, and princes will rule in justice" (Isa. 32:1).

While modern advocates of social justice continue the protests of higher law critics and the Hebrew prophets, they take a new step by linking charity with justice and equating justice with the restructuring of society along democratic lines, including the equal distribution of power and wealth as a matter of human rights. In many cases, the proponents of social justice even demand rethinking the doctrine of the Fall and original sin so that the human condition is not thought of as doomed to injustice, where slavery in some form would always exist and only modest ameliorations of human misery would be possible. The new tendency is to see the human condition as capable of fundamental improvement by state action in ways that may even foreshadow the coming of the kingdom of God on earth. In some of its more audacious forms, social justice is linked to the demand to "democratize the conception of God" so that God does not seem oppressive to human beings.

Obviously, not every modern Christian thinker would favor such radical formulations. In fact, if we go back a few centuries, we can see that the first steps emerged from something fairly traditional—namely, new applications of Thomistic natural law in the sixteenth century by scholars and churchmen who were responding to Spanish colonialism in the New World and to mistreatment of native American Indians. As I mentioned above, Francisco Suarez argued that political authority arose from the consent of the people. Others in the Spanish school of Salamanca deliberately extended the notion of consent to native peoples and to foreigners and developed the humanitarian implications of the Golden Rule. Two central figures were Francisco Vitoria and Bartolomé de Las Casas, members of the Dominican Order of Preachers who were steeped in the works of Thomas Aquinas and canon law. Without ever hearing of Marxism or class struggle or liberation theology, they courageously opposed the most powerful political currents of their time, arguing against the Spanish conquest of America and for the peaceable conversion of the Indians.

Vitoria and Las Casas based their case on two major points. First, they developed Thomas Aquinas's argument about the legitimacy of government and property held by unbelievers, according to which pagan or infidel states already in existence possess a certain lawful "dominion" even over Christian subjects. In their view, God granted dominion over external things to all rational beings; and the human laws of pagan kingdoms have not been negated by the coming of the true divine law, as Christ acknowledged when He paid tribute to Caesar in his sphere even though the emperor was a pagan. Hence, Christians could not lawfully invade and destroy pagan or barbarian nations simply because they, as Christians, possessed the true religion and the pagans were idolaters or practiced immorality. Even the pope does not have temporal jurisdiction over pagan governments and does not acquire spiritual jurisdiction until the pagan nations are converted to Christianity, though he does have a duty to send and to protect missionaries in those lands. Following this logic, Vitoria says in his treatise *On the American Indians*, "before the arrival of the Spaniards these barbarians possessed true dominion, both in public and private affairs."[27] In addition, Vitoria argued that waging a just war requires an injury to be redressed; but the native peoples of America did not perpetrate injuries against the Spanish. By this standard, the American Indians were more justified in waging a just war against the Spanish, who had injured them. Pushing a bit further, Las Casas inferred that the naturalness of "dominion" and the justice of self-defense could be turned into a natural right to consent. He said that, in order for the king of Spain to govern the American Indians, "their consent must be free, made of their own accord, since the decision affects them all and they cannot be deprived of something rightfully theirs by natural law, i.e., liberty."[28] On grounds of natural dominion and the right of consent, the colonial conquest of the Indians was judged to be unjust.

The second major point made by Vitoria and Las Casas was that the American Indians were not Aristotle's natural slaves, as some Spaniards claimed. Las Casas spent much of his life arguing this point, culminating in a public debate with the Spanish Aristotelian Juan Ginés de Sepúlveda, held in 1550 for the benefit of Charles V, emperor and king of Spain, who wanted to know if Spanish colonialism could be justified on the Aristotelian ground of natural superiors ruling natural inferiors. Las Casas argued that the civilization of the Indians, including their government, trade, arts, and religion, showed that they possessed the innate rationality of human beings and did not fit the category of natural slaves. Nor were they barbarians, even though they practiced human sacrifice and cannibalism (which Las Casas, in moments of weakness, tended to excuse as an expression of worship to their gods that was not against natural law).[29] As if to avoid further misunderstandings, Las Casas rejected the Aristotelian claim that any group of human beings fits the category of a natural slave: God's plan of salvation means that everyone must have been created with a "rational nature" that is sufficient to hear and receive the word of God (ibid., II, ch. 2, pp. 35–36). He and other neo-Scholastics further qualified the teachings of the Bible, which said slaves should obey their masters even though slavery is merely a human institution, and the view of Thomas Aquinas, who said slavery was justified by the law of nations (*jus gentium*) as a useful and accepted practice though it was not dictated by natural law (*jus naturale*).[30] The Spanish neo-Scholastics radicalized the Thomistic tradition by pushing it in a democratic direction, appealing to the common humanity of rational beings who could not be subjugated for their own good by those claiming to be wiser (though other forms of hierarchy could still be justified). Las Casas mixed the natural law argument about the rational nature of all human beings with the humanitarian implications of Christian charity, proclaiming that the subjugation of the Indians was wrong because "they are our brothers" made in the image of God and redeemed by Christ's blood.[31]

Did Vitoria and Las Casas develop these arguments into claims of natural or human rights? Not quite. Vitoria made strong statements about lawful dominion by all people; and he included a statement about the lawful permission to own or take property in his commentary on Thomas's *Summa Theologiae*. In the commentary, Vitoria raises the question whether the poor may steal from the rich in cases of extreme necessity, for example, when faced with starvation. Vitoria notes that Thomas justified the actions of the poor in such cases by saying private property reverts to common use for everyone. Vitoria adds that "if therefore all things are common, then I have a right to them" [*Si ergo sunt communia, habeo jus ad illa*].[32] Vitoria has gone beyond Thomas in this formulation and has made property a right; but he still follows the traditional idea that a right is a grant from the common good rather than a claim derived from the primacy of the individual will. Moreover, Vitoria overall is a fairly conservative monarchist who bases the legitimacy of government on an eclectic mix of divine right, natural sociality, consent, and the perfection of rational creatures through virtue.

Las Casas is more radical than Vitoria and with greater plausibility may be seen as a forerunner of modern democracy and even of liberation theology. This is how he is portrayed by the founding father of liberation theology, Gustavo Gutiérrez, in his book, *Las Casas: In Search of the Poor of Jesus Christ.* Gutiérrez argues that Las Casas proclaimed a type of natural law liberty as the justification for democratic consent along with a doctrine of religious freedom that foreshadows the teachings of Vatican II and liberation theology. In support of Gutiérrez's interpretation, one may cite Las Casas's views that religion cannot be coerced and must be based on freely given consent because the model of Jesus Christ in his evangelization was that of gentle persuasion.[33] Yet, Las Casas always insisted on a Spanish presence in the New World in order to convert the Indians, which means he conceived of the primary right as that of hearing the Gospel preached. As Gutiérrez says of Las Casas, he thought that "the proclamation of the Reign of God was the first and last end of what ought to be happening in the Indies."[34] To understand the significance of Las Casas's concept of religious rights, one can imagine how the First Amendment would have to be rewritten to protect the primary right of hearing the Gospel preached and the kingdom of God proclaimed to all. Such a right would include the immunity of conscience from coercion by the state; but it would also include the right to have the culture saturated with religious proselytizing! And it would mean, as Las Casas believed, that once the Indians freely accepted the Christian faith they would come under the spiritual jurisdiction of the Catholic Church and the temporal power of the Spanish king. Thus, the ultimate goal of Las Casas's struggle to free the Indians from Spanish conquest and economic exploitation was the Christianizing of the Americas under proper spiritual and temporal authority. As a Christian Aristotelian, he conceived of freedom as the means for perfecting man's rational nature—"the best and noblest part of the whole universe"—through Christian conversion.[35]

The next phase in the Christian struggles against oppression was aimed at abolishing slavery and the slave trade in America and the British empire. Among Christians, the Quakers and Methodists were early and outspoken abolitionists. As David B. Davis shows in *The Problem of Slavery in Western Culture*, they faced formidable obstacles because many powerful doctrines sanctioned slavery in the Western world—Aristotle's doctrine of natural slavery, the biblical admonitions of Paul and Peter telling slaves to obey their masters and masters to treat their slaves humanely without necessarily emancipating them, and the interpretation of the Fall by conservative theologians who described slavery as a punishment for the disobedience of Adam and Eve and an inevitable consequence of original sin. The Quakers, Davis shows, were vocal and active in their opposition to slavery precisely because they were more willing than other (more conservative) Christians to abandon the doctrine of original sin and the inevitability of slavery in the fallen world. Like the proponents of rational religion who preached natural benevolence, Quakers gained an advantage in the struggle for social justice by their willingness to reject traditional doctrines and to disregard Scripture in favor of guidance from the "inner light."[36]

In surveying such movements, it is sometimes forgotten that there was a middle position between radical pessimism and Quaker optimism, according to which slavery is neither inevitable nor required by natural and divine law. For example, Thomas Aquinas argued that slavery is an issue that falls under the purview of the law of nations (*jus gentium*) rather than natural law; it is a customary practice of nations that usually arises when captives are taken in war and accept servitude in return for having their lives spared. Thus, slavery is mainly a matter of "use" to nations rather than a matter of justice; for "the fact that this particular man should be a slave rather than another man is based not on natural reason but on some resultant utility."[37] A development of this line of thinking could have led to an argument for eliminating slavery without rejecting original sin as the Quakers did or embracing natural benevolence as the rational religions tended to do. The law of nations, after all, is based largely on convention rather than on nature or divine decree; it is therefore open to revision without changing basic theological doctrines. But opposing slavery by revising the law of nations was largely ignored by traditional denominations, which meant Catholics, Lutherans, Anglicans, Presbyterians, and Baptists generally sat on the sidelines of the antislavery movement and watched the Quakers, Methodists, and more radical abolitionists take the lead.

By contrast, the exploitation of industrial workers under modern capitalism posed a challenge that mainstream churches as well as radical Christians took up with energy and originality. In the nineteenth and twentieth centuries, many faced the question: How could Christianity appeal to the working classes and save them from Marxism? The answers ranged from moderate to radical—from the trade unionism of Pope Leo XIII, Cardinal Manning, and Dorothy Day's Catholic Worker movement, to the Chartist movement against laissez-faire capitalism, to the social gospel of Walter Rauschenbusch, to the Christian socialism of Archbishop William Temple and R. H. Tawney, to the liberation theology of Gustavo Gutiérrez and Leonardo Boff, to workers movements allied with civil rights and feminist movements demanding broader social emancipation.[38] From this list of social movements, I shall select two for discussion— Catholic trade unionism and Protestant social gospel theology.

Trade unionism got a great boost from Pope Leo XIII, who changed the course of Catholic social teaching by embracing workers' concerns in his encyclical *Rerum Novarum*, subtitled "On Capital and Labor" (1891). He took a middle ground between unbridled capitalism, which he blamed for the growing disparity between rich and poor, and socialism, which he condemned as a false solution that was worse than the problem. Like the neo-Scholastics before him, Leo XIII was a Thomist who developed the natural law tradition. For the first time, he incorporated into Catholic social teaching the doctrine of natural rights—specifically, the natural right to property which he called "sacred and inviolable." While Leo used the Lockean theory that labor gives a title to property, he also sought to detach private ownership from possessive individualism. His main justifications for property rights were in fact not Lockean but Aristotelian and Thomistic: God's grant of dominion over external things to all rational beings; the priority of the family to the state and the necessity of fathers to support their families by working and owning property; the need for personal wealth to exercise the virtues of generosity and charity; and the natural inequality of talents. While using these arguments to justify the natural right to property, Leo qualified private ownership with the traditional Catholic insistence on the primacy of the common good, including limited state intervention for the sake of establishing a just wage for working families and decent working conditions. But, above all, Leo endorsed trade unions, especially church-sponsored unions, as the best means for protecting the working classes—making him the "workers' pope" and positioning the Catholic Church between unregulated capitalism and state socialism.[39]

The centrist approach of Catholic trade unionism seems tepid compared to the Protestant "social gospel" of Walter Rauschenbusch (1861–1918) and the "liberation theology" of Latin American Catholics. What is radical about them is not simply their support for a left-wing brand of politics—socialism or social democracy—and the inevitable centralization of state power that accompanies nationalizing industry, redistributing wealth, extensive social welfare guarantees, and, in some cases, class struggle and violent revolution. What is radical is the demand for a democratic revolution in theology to justify the revolution in politics. On this point, I find Walter Rauschenbusch's treatise, *A Theology for the Social Gospel* (1917), to be one of the most revealing documents because it states with perfect candor the premises of progressive Christianity for the next century. Its central thesis is that Christianity is a social construction that must be changed in accordance with the times: "The social gospel . . . is the religious reaction to the historic advent of democracy"; "the worst thing that could happen to God would be to remain an autocrat while the world is moving to democracy. . . . God must join the social movement."[40]

What is astonishing about this demand is the ease with which Rauschenbusch accepts the historicist assumption that religion is merely a product of its times, that "the conception of God . . . is a social product" (ibid., 167). Almost no attempt is made to sort out the unchangeable core of Christianity from the changeable elements—to distinguish what is permanent and necessary from that which is subject to the circumstances of time and place because it is left open by divine law and a legitimate matter of prudence. Instead, the goal is to reconstruct the whole of Christianity in accordance with social democracy. Above all, Rauschenbusch says, "we must democratize the conception of God" (ibid., 48). Earlier conceptions of God reflected the imperial Roman social world and the feudal social order; now God must reflect democratic sentiments: "The old conception that God dwells on high and is distinct from our human life was the natural basis for autocratic and arbitrary ideas about him. On the other hand, the religious belief that he is immanent in humanity is the natural basis for democratic ideas about him" (ibid., 179). In addition, Christ's sacrifice on the cross should no longer be thought of as atonement for sins against the Father. Atonement is outdated; "our dominant ideas are personality and social solidarity . . . the problems which burden us are the social problem[s]," namely, oppression and exploitation. Hence, Jesus died to "achieve his own personality" and to overcome the evil and injustice of "social sins" (ibid., 244, 260–61). In democratizing and socializing God, Rauschenbusch's social gospel prepares the way for future liberating theologies that will seek to dethrone the patriarchal Father and to portray Christ as the Emancipator as well as the Savior.

In addition to democratizing God, Rauschenbusch calls for redefining the kingdom of God, the central concept of the social gospel. Admittedly, the kingdom of God has always been an elusive teaching of Jesus in the Gospels, referring to a condition of perfect faith, love, and justice that is present both here and now and more fully in the world-to-come. But Rauschenbusch emphasizes "social salvation" in this world instead of the invisible communion of saints or personal salvation in the world-to-come (ibid., 7). His definition of the kingdom of God reminds one of Kant's description of the "kingdom of ends" which Rauschenbusch acknowledges by observing that "Kant first recognized the importance of the kingdom of God for ethics" (ibid., 139, note 1). At the core of the social gospel's conception of the kingdom is "democracy and social justice"—a social order in which equality reigns and human personality flourishes (ibid., 136). As Rauschenbusch says: "The kingdom of God . . . tends to a social order which will best guarantee to all personalities their freest and highest development. This involves the redemption of social life from the cramping influence of religious bigotry, from repression . . . in the relation of upper and lower classes, and from all forms of slavery in which human beings are treated as mere means to serve the ends of others. . . . [It also involves] the redemption of society from political autocracies and economic oligarchies; the substitution of redemptive for vindictive penology; the abolition of constraint through hunger as part of the industrial system; and the abolition of war as the supreme expression of hate . . . the redemption of society from private property in the natural resources of the earth and from any condition in industry which makes monopoly profits possible. The reign of love tends toward the progressive unity of mankind, but with the maintenance of individual liberty and the opportunity of nations to work out their own national ideals. . . . It is the supreme end of God [and] the purpose for which the Church exists" (ibid., 142–43).

The appeal of Rauschenbusch's social gospel is the idealism of transforming the world in accordance with social justice, understood as equality, freedom, and the end of exploitation and war. Deeply influenced by Kantian idealism and utopian socialism, it presents a modern Christian version of the kingdom of God. Its radical premise is a notion of historical relativism that makes God a creation of man rather than man a creation of God and that allows politics to drive theology rather than requiring theology to set the terms for politics. Of course, not every Christian version of social justice goes to such an extreme; but it remains a perpetual temptation in the modern movement to democratize Christianity.

THE TOTALITARIAN EXPERIENCE

A sixth factor in changing Christian attitudes toward democracy was the experience of totalitarianism in the twentieth century. With the rise of communism and fascism, the modern world faced a new situation in which the centralized power of state was expanded to every area of life. The totalitarian state sought to draw all associations, including the churches, into its orbit and to transform human nature according to a revolutionary ideology that would bring about the universal classless society of Marx or the domination of the world by the master races. The challenge of totalitarianism confounded Christian churches and individuals. Some bravely resisted and became martyrs, and some collaborated. Many were confused by ideologies that sounded idealistic in theory but were horrible in practice; and the churches often acted out of a narrow instinct to protect themselves as institutions by making agreements with the new totalitarian powers. One long-term consequence, however, was a reaction to the totalitarian experience that led to a much deeper alliance between Christianity and democracy—to the demand that Christians shed forever their nostalgia for the hierarchical and authoritarian political regimes of the past (whether it be for emperors and kings or medieval corporatism) and take a clear stand on the only two regimes that appeared viable in the modern world, totalitarianism or democracy. From these sentiments, the theory of "Christian democracy" was developed by philosophers such as Jacques Maritain and Reinhold Niebuhr; and Christian democratic political parties were formed in Europe and Latin America.

The most successful party was the Christian Democratic Union led by Konrad Adenauer. It governed West Germany for a generation after World War II and brought Germany into the family of democratic nations by turning it away from the Nazi past while firmly resisting the communist threat from the East. The key to Adenauer's conception of Christian democracy was the belief that democracy must be based on a "*weltanschauung*"—a worldview—that provides a complete account of the universe, man, and politics. Adenauer realized that part of the appeal of totalitarianism was the promise of a complete worldview, in contrast to democracy which was seen as a formal procedure that was neutral about outcomes or that simply managed the clash of competing interests. While communism and fascism offered complete worldviews, they were based on "atheistic materialism" which Adenauer steadfastly opposed for reducing the individual to a mere automaton of the state. As he saw it, politics was the struggle between competing *weltanschauungen;* and democracy could be firmly established in Germany only by possessing a worldview that could compete successfully with Marxism and Nazism.[41] What it needed was a spiritual worldview to replace atheistic materialism and to prevent its own degeneration into egoistic materialism.

Fortunately, Adenauer argued, Western democracy had such a worldview in Christianity. As he said in 1945, "Christianity denies the dominance of the state and insists on the dignity and liberty of the individual. . . . This conviction would give our party the strength to raise Germany from the depths. Hence, the new party had to be a Christian party, and one that embraced all denominations. Protestant and Catholic Germans, indeed all who knew and valued the importance of Christianity in Europe should be able to join—and it goes without saying that this also applied to our Jewish fellow-citizens."[42]

What is striking about Adenauer's position is that he viewed the formation of the Christian Democratic Union in 1945 as a nondenominational party open to all people, while insisting on a platform that stated: "The Christian foundation of the Democratic Union is the absolutely necessary and decisive factor. We want to replace the materialistic ideology of National Socialism with a Christian view of the world. . . . Only Christian precepts guarantee justice, order, moderation, the dignity and liberty of the individual and thus true and genuine democracy. . . . We regard the lofty view that Christianity takes of human dignity, of the value of each single man, as the foundation and directive of our work in the political, economic, and cultural life of our people" (ibid., 49–50). The puzzling feature of this statement is its mixture of nondenominationalism and explicit Christian foundations. The puzzle is deepened when we learn that Adenauer himself was a devout Catholic and former member of the Catholic Center Party—the party that was created in the 1870s during Bismarck's *kulturkampf* (culture war) against Catholicism and that continued through the Weimar Republic which the Center Party strongly supported (nine chancellors from 1923–33 were from the Catholic Center Party). Moreover, Adenauer was deeply influenced by the social teachings of the Catholic Church expressed in papal encyclicals, especially Leo XIII's *Rerum Novarum* and Pius XI's *Quadragesimo Anno*, which he read and studied while under Nazi house arrest in 1933. Adenauer discovered in them a "comprehensive and coherent program inspired by belief in an order willed by God which was perfectly practical in terms of modern society."[43]

To resolve the puzzle in Adenauer's position, one must see that his affirmation of a Christian Democratic Union that was nondenominational—open to Catholics, Protestants, Jews, and secular people alike—was possible because it offered a moral vision to all people: the belief in the innate dignity of every human being as the basis of democratic equality and freedom, and the grounding of this principle on faith in God and the Western heritage of Christianity. Adenauer believed that all people could rally around this conception of human dignity and could accept its democratic implications as a common basis for sacred and secular outlooks. Nor was this hope confined to Adenauer. It became the crucial article of faith in modern Christianity, a faith that was more and more explicitly articulated by political leaders, churches, and theologians in the course of the twentieth century. The crucial insight is that Christianity and liberal democracy are two sides of the same coin—the sacred and secular sides of a common conception of human dignity that is in principle accessible to believers as well as nonbelievers, even if the ultimate source and foundation is Christian.

While Adenauer applied this vision in practice, others worked out the theory. One of the most influential theoreticians was Jacques Maritain, the French Catholic philosopher of the previous generation (1882–1973), who wrote many books defending Christian democracy. Interestingly, Maritain did not come to the theory of Christian democracy all at once. His earliest political thinking took place in the shadow of nineteenth-century Catholic teaching that still favored Christian monarchy and was just beginning to change when Pope Leo XIII grudgingly admitted in 1885 that "no one of the several forms of government is in itself condemned . . . neither is it blameworthy . . . for the people to have a greater or lesser share in the government."44 In this atmosphere, Maritain flirted with monarchism and the right-wing politics of *Action Française* until the organization was condemned by Pope Pius XI. Starting around the 1930s, Maritain confronted the totalitarian threat directly and sided clearly and irrevocably with democracy.

In his wartime works, *The Rights of Man and Natural Law* (1943) and *Christianity and Democracy* (1944), and in his postwar book, *Man and the State* (1951), Maritain presented an argument for Christian democracy and human rights based on the innate dignity of the "human person" as a rational and spiritual being. In Maritain's eyes, a democracy of the person—or "personalist" democracy—was superior to bourgeois democracy based on materialistic individualism and to the totalitarian regimes of communism and fascism which crushed human dignity. Maritain also forged links with non-Christian democrats, most notably by helping to draft the United Nations "Universal Declaration of Human Rights" in 1948, which echoes Maritain in declaring its "faith in fundamental human rights, in the dignity and worth of the human person."[45]

Maritain's arguments and the experience of totalitarianism had a significant impact in moving official Catholic teaching to embrace liberal democracy. Pope Pius XII delivered a wartime Christmas address in 1942 on "The Internal Order of States and People" and another in 1944 on "True and False Democracy" that supported democracy based on the dignity and rights of human persons; he contrasted this true version of democracy with false democracy based on the "shapeless mass of individuals" who were simply the passive pawns of despotic rulers or public opinion. The changing attitudes to democracy were eventually embraced as a matter of principle by Pope John XXIII and ratified in the documents of the Second Vatican Council in the early 1960s. The Council endorsed religious liberty and constitutional democracy as principles for the first time in the history of the church, grounding them in the inherent dignity of the human person as a rational and spiritual being. Reflecting on these developments, it is evident that the battles against totalitarianism in World War II and the Cold War played a decisive role in cementing the alliance between Christianity and modern liberal democracy.

As one looks back on the evolution of Christian politics over the past three or four hundred years, one is struck by the gradual but relentless impact of the six major movements that I have described. While the various Christian denominations moved at different paces in accepting democracy and human rights, all eventually arrived at the same destination. The first steps were taken by the radical Protestant reformers—the 'left-wing' Puritans and free-church Anabaptists—with Lutherans, Presbyterians, and Anglicans going much slower. Catholics were also slow to change, except where they were persecuted minorities (as in America and Germany); and they did not really settle the issue until the latter part of the twentieth century. Eastern Orthodoxy has been the last to change, in some cases waiting until the fall of communism to accept democratic constitutions (with some hedging in Russia, where a privileged position for the Russian

Orthodox Church has been preserved). Nevertheless, it is safe to say that at the beginning of the third millennium nearly all Christians believe that the form of government most compatible with their ethical and spiritual teachings is liberal democracy.

THE IMPACT OF KANT AND THE NEW *IMAGO DEI*

While I have argued that many forces chipped away at the traditional hierarchical patterns of authority and opened Christianity to democratic vistas, I think that it is possible to isolate one as having a greater and more lasting impact than the others. In my judgment, a particular strand of Enlightenment liberalism, namely, Immanuel Kant's philosophy of freedom, has been the decisive factor. How could the philosophy of one eighteenth-century German thinker be so important for changing Christianity?

The answer, I believe, is that Kant offered the most explicit formulation of the ethical principles of human dignity that now shape Christian politics—namely, the infinite and absolute worth of every human being, the unconditional duty to treat everyone as an end not merely as a means (in Kant's language as a "person" rather than as a "thing"), and the moral imperative to respect the rights of persons in a liberal democratic political order. On a superficial level, one can see the impact of these Kantian ideas on the ethical discourse of modern Christians who now speak as much or more about "persons," "dignity," "rights," and "respect" than about sin, redemption, compassion, Heaven, and hell. One can also see the impact of Kant on the way modern Christians think about politics.

When making political judgments, modern Christians proceed in a way that is qualitatively different from traditional Christians. As I demonstrated in chapter two, the traditional approach was guided by the doctrine of the Two Cities and by prudential politics. In this approach, the spiritual realm is guided by divine law, which Jesus summed up in the two great commands of love or charity; but the commands of divine law were not understood as mandates for a specific civil or legal code, in contrast to the divine law in Judaism and Islam; nor did they require a specific political regime. For most traditional theologians, the main choices of the temporal realm—about the best form of government, the best economic system, the arrangement of social classes, and the rules of warfare—were largely matters of *prudence* in which human law was formed by applying natural law to concrete situations. Thus, the command to love one's neighbor, especially the poorest among us, required acts of charity; but it did not necessarily contain an imperative to set up a democracy in which the poor ruled or to establish a social welfare state; nor did it mean that one automatically had to abolish all class distinctions or social inequalities. In this view, God's revealed law did not require specific political and social structures, though God did sanction the political authority in general. The choice of political and social structures were practical decisions about the best means to the ends of the temporal common good which included civil peace, moral virtue, and some kind of civic piety or Christian orthodoxy. Because the choice was prudential, no single regime was absolutely required in all circumstances. A variety of regimes could be legitimate, depending on how well they served the temporal common good in the given situation, though most traditional Christians thought that mixed regimes—mixed monarchy or aristocracy mixed with democratic elements—were best in most cases.

By contrast, modern Christians do not view the choice of the political regime as a prudential choice of the temporal realm. They see it as a 'categorical imperative' of Christian ethics that requires one and only one legitimate political regime in all circumstances, namely, a democratic form of government based on human rights. This conception of politics is no longer prudential because it diminishes the independence and flexibility of the temporal realm and makes political choices a direct deduction from first principles of the spiritual realm. Politics becomes an unconditional duty flowing from the Christian notion of human dignity—a direct deduction from the claim that all are made in the image of God or that all are children of God. I infer, therefore, that a change in the interpretation of the *Imago Dei* is the decisive factor underlying the dramatic change in Christian politics, resulting in a new spiritual and ethical imperative for democracy. No longer is democracy one among several legitimate regimes—not to mention a second or third choice compared to other, more hierarchical regimes. Instead, democracy is a Christian moral duty, almost a religion—*the sole regime consistent with the dignity of man in his full moral maturity.* As Jacques Maritain said, democracy is evangelical or Gospel inspired; it is the profane name of the Christian ideal. This exalted view of democracy could not have occurred without a change in the understanding of human dignity from its original spiritual and intellectual conception to a political conception. The change can be seen in the three distinct views of the *Imago Dei* that have evolved gradually over the course of the Christian tradition.

The first is derived from the Bible, which (I argued in chapter two) equates the divine image in man with the original immortality of Adam and Eve before the Fall and with the capacity for holiness that enables the faithful to recover their original perfection by becoming holy like the Holy One of Israel or like the Savior who is God incarnate. This view of human dignity is essentially spiritual, focusing on man's capacity to relate to God by obeying or disobeying His commands. It is not inherently democratic in a political sense, since it underlies God's command to Moses to establish a theocracy and to Samuel to establish a kingship by anointing Saul and David as well as the commands of the New Testament to obey Caesar in the temporal realm. For Christians, it means that everyone has infinite worth as a creature of God with an immortal soul and an eternal destiny. And it means that human beings must be loved in relation to that eternal destiny, not simply as rational beings who are ends-in-themselves or bearers of rights. Since the biblical *Imago Dei* refers to something supernatural or mystical about every human being and is compatible with 'divine election' as well as with spiritual and political hierarchies, it does not necessarily entail democracy and human rights.

The second interpretation of the *Imago Dei* is that of the early church fathers and the medieval theologians, who used Greek philosophy to define the divine image as the possession of a rational soul that is ordained to return to God as the source of its being. This view is essentially spiritual as well, although it adds an intellectual dimension because human dignity is equated with the possession of a rational soul that has a supernatural destiny: Everyone has a soul with intellect and free will that can gain or lose eternal life by knowing and loving God properly and that may be elevated by contemplating the rational order of God's created universe. This conception of dignity points to a hierarchy of perfection in the spiritual realm and permits kingship and undemocratic regimes as prudential choices in the temporal realm because they are the best means for perfecting man's sinful but rational nature.

The third interpretation of the *Imago Dei* has been added by modern theologians. It equates the divine image in man with being a "human person"—a creature possessing reason and free will who is created not only to recover lost immortality (as in the Bible) and to return to God as the source of its being (as in Scholastic theology) but also to claim inalienable human rights and to assert those rights on behalf of others. This modern view of the divine image establishes a connection in principle between Christian ethics and a specific political order. It claims that human beings are creatures made in the image of God whose innate dignity must be respected by the state and fellow citizens, which means setting up a democratic political system that protects human rights. By this logic, a spiritual, intellectual, and ethical conception of human dignity takes on the added dimension of an unconditional political imperative that demands universal implementation.

To illustrate the new political conception of human dignity, I would like to quote from two powerful statements, one by Archbishop Desmond Tutu of South Africa and another by Pope John XXIII. In an article titled "Religious Human Rights and the Bible" (1994), Bishop Tutu says: "The basis of the egalitarianism of the Bible . . . is that all are of equal worth in God's sight. . . . That is what fired our own struggle against apartheid—the incredible sense of the infinite worth of each person created in the image of God . . . inviolate, possessing a dignity that is intrinsic, with autonomy and freedom to choose, that are constitutive of human personality . . . that is what invests them with their preciousness and from this stems all kinds of rights."[46]

Similarly, Pope John XXIII in his influential encyclical, *Pacem in Terris* (1963) declared: "Every human being is a person: His nature is endowed with intelligence and free will. By virtue of this he has rights and duties of his own, flowing directly from his very nature, which are therefore universal, inviolable, and inalienable . . . [including] the right to respect for his person. . . . From the dignity of the human person there also arises the right to carry on economic activities" and other rights, including religious freedom and democratic participation.[47]

By listening carefully to these statements, one can detect the influence of Kantian ethics on Christian theology. For it was Kant who stated most clearly in his second formulation of the categorical imperative that human beings are "persons," rather than "things," and that persons must be treated as ends-in-themselves rather than as mere means to another's pleasure or profit.[48] And it was Kant who said that human persons possess infinite dignity or absolute worth, not because they possess immortal souls, but because they can transcend the determinism of Nature and enter an intangible realm of Freedom through the exercise of their rational wills. And it was Kant who said that such persons possess inalienable human rights that must be recognized in a legal and political order, from which he drew the momentous conclusion that "*the one and only legitimate constitution is a pure republic*"—meaning a representative democracy that protects human rights in the name of the people.[49]

This conception of the human person has given birth to the most influential philosophies of freedom in the modern world—to Kantian liberalism, Hegelianism, phenomenology, existentialism, and the various neo-Kantian theories of justice that dominate liberalism today. Despite their differences, all accept the Kantian distinction between Nature and Freedom and locate the dignity of the person in the ability to create a human world outside of biological and physical nature through assertions of the will; and nearly all draw the political inference that the dignity of the human personality justifies inviolable human rights. In one form or another, this conception has been incorporated into Christian theology and transformed it dramatically. Sometimes the influence of Kant is openly acknowledged; and at other times it is not acknowledged because Kant carries the taint of the Enlightenment which in some religious circles is embarrassing and because Kant's conception of the person as an autonomous self poses difficulties for many religious believers. Nevertheless, the ethical idealism of Kant is widely accepted and, in my view, has been the most important factor in changing Christianity because the other potentially liberal or democratic tendencies within Christianity—in medieval canon law, radical Protestantism, or neo-Thomism—would not have led to a conception of democratic human rights on their own. Why not?

The answer, I believe, is that Christianity strongly affirms the dignity of every human being as a creature made in the image of God and recognizes the limited nature of the state compared to the spiritual realm. But Christianity actually has a deep resistance to the concept of human rights. As shocking as it may sound today, there are numerous and profound reasons why this is so. In the first place, Christianity places duties to God and duties to one's neighbor before individual rights and cannot easily accept the proposition that people have the right to pursue happiness as they see fit, especially if that right leads to societies that are indifferent to God. Second, Christianity's foundation on divine revelation implies a duty to accept transcendent truth as well as authoritative pronouncements about truth by a hierarchical church rather than to accept the dictates of individual conscience wherever they might lead. Third, the Christian notion of original sin implies distrust of weak and fallible human beings to use rights properly; it instills a keen sense of how freedom can go awry and ultimately must view political freedom as a conditional rather than an absolute good. Fourth, Christianity puts the common good above the rights of individuals, and its emphasis on the family and man's social nature conflicts with the individualism and privacy of rights. Fifth, the Christian teaching about charity—whose essence is sacrificial love—makes the whole notion of rights seem selfish, as if the world owes something to me when I declare, "I have my rights!" Ultimately, of course, Christians cannot accept the premise of human autonomy or the natural freedom of the autonomous self that underlies most doctrines of rights.

Despite all of these reservations and difficulties, Kant has made the idea of human rights respectable to modern Christians. For Kant separated rights from utilitarian calculations of self-interest and defended them in immaterial terms, appealing to an intangible realm of freedom that transcends psychological egoism and that sounds spiritual. He made it a duty to respect other persons and their rights because persons are ends-in-themselves, rather than respecting them out of enlightened self-interest. Kant even called the human personality "holy" and respect for the moral law holiness, linking them with an idea of historical progress toward perpetual peace and justice under international law that sounds like building the kingdom of God on earth. For these reasons, Kant's ethical idealism is highly attractive to modern Christians.

It is precisely the incorporation of such idealism into Christian theology that lies behind the two most significant developments in modern Christianity that I have just described—the end of the prudential approach to politics and the new emphasis on the human person as a bearer of inherent rights. The first development points to Kant as the source because the turn from a "politics of prudence" (to borrow from Russell Kirk), which permits a variety of legitimate regimes, to a "politics of moral imperatives" (to borrow from Kant himself), which demands liberal democracy as the sole legitimate regime, is now viewed by modern Christians as a deduction from human dignity. The second development also points to Kant because it depends on changes in the understanding of "person" or "personality"—a shift from the metaphysical view of the person found in medieval Scholasticism to the moral and political emphasis of modern Kantian culture.

Today, the term "person" refers to a human being with a duty to forge his or her own identity or moral personality by an assertion of the will. In the earlier discourse of Scholastic theology, the term "person" was used primarily in a metaphysical sense: it meant a substance capable of separate existence. Hence, the famous Scholastic definition of Boethius: A person is "an individual substance of a rational nature." Though a general metaphysical term for separate existence, person was applied almost exclusively to God in the doctrine of the Trinity, where God is three *persons* in one Being (the Father, Son, and Holy Spirit) separated by different relations or origins but not by essential differences. In recent years, however, "person" has become a moral term applied to human beings, meaning a rational and free agent who possesses inherent dignity and rights.

"Personality" in this new sense means moral agency through the will—the creation of a moral identity by rising above biological and physical processes through conscious willing. In reference to the self, personality is the self-determination that gives unity to the whole moral agent—either through the rational will, as Kant himself argued, or through the irrational will, as various neo-Kantian and existentialist philosophers have argued. In relation to others, personality is the unified self that is capable of finding fulfillment in social activity, especially in freely giving one's self to others. While some theologians (especially Catholic neo-Thomists) see a fairly smooth transition from the metaphysical person to the moral personality—arguing that "person" has always referred not only to a type of "substance" but also to a type of "relation" between beings—I think that the equation of moral relations with asserting one's rights and respecting the rights of others is a new dimension. By making separate existence something that is willed and claimed as a right that must be recognized by others, personhood moves outside the sphere of Thomism and even of Christian charity into the realm of Kantian liberalism.[50] Indeed, the emphasis on the rights and dignity of the person in the Kantian sense has become so important that much of modern theology has turned its focus away from metaphysics (how things exist) toward morality and politics (social ethics and social justice).

Taken as a whole, the Kantian influence on modern Christianity is so deep and pervasive that I believe it makes sense to speak of three great periods of Christian theology, each associated with a dominant philosopher. (1) The first period is the Platonic or Neoplatonic Christianity of the early church fathers; (2) The second is the Aristotelian Christianity of medieval or Scholastic theology; (3) and the third is the Kantian Christianity of the modern age. (A similar division could also be found in Judaism, whose earlier theologians were Neoplatonic and Aristotelian but whose greatest modern spokesmen—Moses Mendelssohn, Hermann Cohen, and Martin Buber—have sought to combine belief in the Jewish God with the freedom and universality of Kantian ethics.)

If this generalization is correct, then the key to modern theology is to see its various developments as synthetic efforts—as new combinations of metaphysical realism grounded in the traditional theologies of St. Augustine or St. Thomas and ethical idealism derived from Kant's theory of moral personality and philosophy of freedom. Such theological syntheses can be observed in many examples of modern Catholic, Protestant, and Eastern Orthodox, as well as modern Jewish, theology.

Among Catholics, it is found in "personalism"—the dominant school of Catholic theology in the twentieth century, developed above all by Jacques Maritain but also in different fashions by Emmanuel Mounier, Gabriel Marcel, Heinrich Rommen, John Courtney Murray, Michael Novak, and John Finnis; it can also be found in the documents of Vatican II and the encyclicals of Popes John XXIII, Paul VI, and John Paul II. Catholic personalism is a complex idea, but at its core one can find a synthesis of Thomas and Kant—the natural law teaching of traditional Thomism, featuring man as a rational and social animal with transcendent longings for God, combined with the Kantian theory of moral personality, featuring man as an acting and willing agent claiming a host of social, economic, and political rights. Catholic social teaching has thus retained natural law but redefined its content. Instead of emphasizing virtue and constitutional monarchy, as traditional Thomism did, it now teaches "the rights and dignity of the human person" in a liberal or constitutional democracy.

This dramatic change was ratified in the Second Vatican Council and can be found in its key documents. As noted above, "The Declaration on Religious Freedom" (*Dignitatis Humanae*) states that the Church is now embracing the principles of religious liberty and constitutional democracy in accordance with the growing "sense of the dignity of the human person [that] has been impressing itself . . . on the consciousness of contemporary man" (par. 1). The declaration says that "the right to religious freedom has its foundation in the very dignity of the human person" (par. 2) and "the protection and promotion of the inviolable rights of man ranks among the essential duties of governments" (par. 6, 13). In another important document, "The Constitution of the Church in the Modern World" (*Gaudium et Spes*), the Council also speaks of the "growing awareness of the exalted dignity proper to the human person, since he stands above all things, and his rights and duties are universal and inviolable" (par. 26). At the same time that it affirms the Kantian-like rights of persons in a constitutional democracy, the document makes it clear that the human person is a creature made in the image of God whose "innermost nature is a social being" and whose destiny as a spiritual being finds its true fulfillment in Christ (par. 12, 22–23, 41, 75).[51] In similar language, the new *Catechism of the Catholic Church* says that "the human person . . . is and ought to be the principle, the subject, and the end of all social institutions" (par. 1881) and "respect for the human person entails respect for the rights that flow from his dignity as a creature" (par. 1930). Even Christian charity is redefined in terms of human rights: "Charity is the greatest social commandment. It respects others and their rights. It requires the practice of justice . . . [and] inspires a life of self-giving" (par. 1889).[52] In these statements, one can see the pervasive influence of Catholic personalism and its new combination of Thomistic metaphysics and Kantian rights.

Among Protestant theologians, the lines of modern development are less clear than in Catholicism due to sectarian divergences. Moreover, the preferred doctor of theology among Protestants is St. Augustine rather than Thomas Aquinas, which means theological innovations tend to grow out of the Augustinian doctrines of sin and grace rather than out of Thomistic natural law, producing more amorphous notions of "personhood" than Catholic personalism. Nevertheless, many Protestant theologians follow similar patterns, forging new links between Augustine and Kant that support democratic human rights. I already mentioned the social gospel of Walter Rauschenbusch, whose kingdom of God is patterned after Kant's kingdom of ends, and Archbishop Desmond Tutu, whose statement about the struggle against apartheid refers to the rights and dignity of the person which he finds in the Bible but are more accurately located in Kantian liberalism. I would also cite Martin Luther King, Jr.'s famous "Letter from Birmingham Jail" (1963) to illustrate the new developments in Christian theology.

King's letter includes an appeal to the traditional doctrine of higher law found in Augustine and Thomas Aquinas while adding a Kantian and an existential conception of human dignity. In defending civil disobedience to unjust laws, Doctor King says, "I would agree with St. Augustine that 'an unjust law is no law at all.' [But] what is the difference between the two? . . . A just law is a man-made code that squares with the moral law or the law of God. An unjust law is a code that is out of harmony with the moral law. To put it in the terms of

St. Thomas Aquinas: An unjust law is a human law that is not rooted in eternal law and natural law. Any law that *uplifts human personality is just.* Any law that *degrades human personality is unjust.* All segregation statutes are unjust because segregation distorts the soul and *damages the personality.* It gives the segregator a false sense of superiority and the segregated a false sense of inferiority. Segregation, to use the terminology of the Jewish philosopher Martin Buber, substitutes an 'I-it' relationship for an 'I-thou' relationship and ends up relegating *persons to the status of things.*"[53]

In reading Martin Luther King's description of higher moral law, one can see another version of Christian personalism. It combines the Augustinian and Thomistic concept of eternal law with Kant's ethical imperative to treat human beings as "persons" rather than as "things." Interestingly, King formulates the ethical imperative in terms of Martin Buber's Jewish existential personalism, which distinguishes an "I-thou" relationship from "I-it" in exactly the same way that Kant distinguishes the treatment of "persons" from the treatment of "things." However the new moral law is formulated, it commands respect for the human personality as an end-in-itself possessing human and civil rights.

In another variation of modern Protestantism, Glenn Tinder develops a Lutheran strand of Augustinianism by combining it with elements of Kantian and existential freedom. Tinder has written an influential book, *The Political Meaning of Christianity*, in which he argues that the central message of Christianity is respect for the "exalted individual"—respect for the infinite worth and dignity of all human beings because of their unique and irreplaceable identities. Everyone is exalted, Tinder says, because God commands "you to do what your authentic being or destiny requires. God commands you to be truly yourself." The concept of the exalted individual is the "spiritual center of Western politics," according to Tinder. He also feels that it is the only sound basis of liberal democracy because it contains the moral imperative that "governments should be considerate, egalitarian, and universalist." In other words, the love and respect for the authentic personality that God calls each one of us to be leads to the political conclusion that "Christianity implies democracy"; it is the only legitimate form of government because it alone recognizes and respects the exalted dignity of the individual.[54]

What is fascinating about these trends in Christian theology is the high degree of common ground that Protestants and Catholics have found in certain features of Kantian liberalism.[55] It is also interesting to note the convergence of modern Christian teachings with recent tendencies in secular liberal philosophy which are powerfully influenced by Kantian and neo-Kantian ideas of "equal concern and respect" for every human being. The crucial difference, of course, is that most secular philosophers deny that there is any ultimate foundation for human dignity and embrace the radical autonomy of the unencumbered self, while Christians always bring human dignity back to a foundation in the *Imago Dei*. But the *Imago Dei* has now been given a Kantian twist: It includes the ethical imperative to affirm the rights and dignity of the self-defining person.

EVALUATING KANTIAN CHRISTIANITY

Having sketched the development of Christianity in the modern period, I would like to conclude this chapter by attempting to evaluate the theological revolution that has occurred. What should one think of the opening of Christianity to democracy and human rights now that one can see its culmination in a new theological paradigm— a paradigm that combines Kantian liberalism with the doctrines of St. Thomas Aquinas and St. Augustine? Is it a valid synthesis of old and new ideas and a wise move? Or, is it a liberal 'sell-out,' a surrender of Christian faith to modern liberalism? Much is at stake in these questions, and answering them involves careful and difficult judgments.

As I see it, the validity of the new synthesis depends entirely on one issue: the ability to control Kant, to keep 'Kant-in-a-box,' as it were. For pure Kantianism is incompatible with Christianity: The Kantian person, taken by itself, is an autonomous being who lives solely by self-imposed laws, which means it denies the real existence of divine law or of natural law sanctioned by God, and it denies man's supernatural destiny. The implication is that only a qualified acceptance of Kant could be legitimate for Christians; and the conditions of acceptance must be clearly spelled out. If a given Christian theologian is careful to keep Kant subordinated to Augustine and Thomas—that is, if the theologian understands the freedom of the person to serve higher ends than autonomous reason and does not treat the human personality as an end-in-itself—then the theologian has created a valid synthesis in which God's law remains superior to human personality. But if a Kantian conception of autonomy prevails, then God has become the servant of modern humanism and the synthesis is invalid. To clarify this crucial point, I will conclude with two cases from modern Christian theology. The first case is Pope John Paul II, who creates a valid synthesis by keeping Kant subordinated to Thomas Aquinas. The second is Reinhold Niebuhr, who attempts to synthesize Augustine and modern freedom but allows the Kantian element to predominate, creating an invalid synthesis.

Turning first to the pope, we encounter a wise and holy man who may well be named 'John Paul the Great' by the Catholic Church when his pontificate is over. Yet, many Catholic intellectuals in America and Europe regard him as a cranky old conservative, as a Polish authoritarian who is stuck in an old-world mind-set that fails to appreciate modern liberal societies. In reality, however, the pope is a sophisticated scholar who develops Catholic personalism in a way that judiciously blends traditional and modern ideas and preserves the true hierarchy of ends.

On the one side of the pope's theology is traditional Thomism, as reflected in his natural law teachings on moral virtue and sexual ethics which have consistently opposed abortion, contraception, and homosexuality. The pope also views the Church in traditional terms, as the divinely ordained hierarchical magisterium with full teaching authority over the faithful and with a priesthood guided by the continuous deposit of faith that cannot be changed simply to conform to modern opinions. On the other side, the pope has incorporated into Catholic theology important aspects of the modern philosophy of freedom—particularly, the phenomenology of Max Scheler and elements of Kantian ethics. From these traditional and modern schools of thought, the pope has formulated the "dignity of the human person" as the leading principle of the Church's social teaching. For Pope John Paul II, the dignity of the person is first and foremost a spiritual view of man, a being made in the image of God with an eternal destiny and a capacity for self-giving love, as well as a rational and social being. But the "personalistic principle" of the pope also includes the conception of man as an active agent who possesses inalienable rights, such as freedom of conscience and other political and economic rights.[56]

The pope's synthesis of Thomas Aquinas with Max Scheler and Immanuel Kant is clearly documented in *The Acting Person,* a philosophical work written in the 1970s by Cardinal Karol Wojtyla before he became Pope John Paul II. In the Preface, he says: "The present study owes everything to the systems of metaphysics, of anthropology, and of Aristotelian-Thomistic ethics on the one hand, and to phenomenology, above all in Scheler's interpretation, and through Scheler's critique, to Kant, on the other hand."[57] Given the synthetic nature of the pope's thought, the critical question is which element of the synthesis predominates.

The clearest answer was given later by the pope in his encyclical, *The Splendor of Truth* (1993). The purpose of this work is to define the true meaning of freedom, which the pope emphatically describes as a conditional good: Freedom is not an end-in-itself but must serve the truth about God and the truth about the dignity of man. If freedom does not serve the truth about God and man, then it is relativistic and amoral or immoral. From this position, we may infer that the pope has a qualified view of freedom: Freedom has an end beyond itself prescribed by divine law and natural law, which means it cannot be used for actions that the pope calls "intrinsically evil"—actions which are wrong regardless of circumstances and intentions because they go against the objective moral order decreed by God and prescribed by eternal and natural law.[58]

This view of freedom does not mean the pope is against liberal democracy based on human rights, including rights of conscience and property. As the whole world knows, the pope is a champion of human rights against tyranny and a defender of democracy, including democratic capitalism over socialism and totalitarian communism. But his arguments in favor of freedom and democracy are always qualified: Freedom must lead to a "culture of life" rather than to a "culture of death"; freedom is designed to enable people to fulfill "their duties and responsibilities towards the family and the common good . . . and cannot be given without responsibility and accountability . . . it must seek the higher purposes of life in concert with others . . . and afford protection to the most vulnerable . . . [to] the unborn, the sick, and the old."[59] Indeed, the pope does not hesitate to say that "democracy . . . is a means and not an end; its 'moral' value is not automatic, but depends on conformity to the moral law . . . [and] on the morality of the ends which it pursues."[60] From these statements, one can see that the pope's brand of Catholic "personalism" is a combination of Thomas and Kant, with the Thomistic elements predominating.

The second case I would like to use for the purpose of evaluation is Reinhold Niebuhr—the influential Protestant theologian of the previous generation. Niebuhr's great achievement was in developing the doctrine of "Christian realism" that provided a hard-headed rationale for American Protestants to support liberal democracy against fascism and communism during World War II and the Cold War. The basis of Niebuhr's Christian realism is a synthesis of Augustinian politics and the Kantian idea of the free personality, which looks unobjectionable and even inspiring at first glance. But when carefully scrutinized, one can see that it falls into the error of making the freedom of the human person an end-in-itself.

In a famous essay entitled, "Augustine's Political Realism," Niebuhr takes his characteristic stance against soft-headed liberal Protestants who equate Christianity with sentimental humanitarianism, forgetting the evil and sinful nature of man. Niebuhr endorses the teaching of St. Augustine on this point, calling him "a more reliable guide than any known thinker." Augustine's superiority lies in his distinction of the Two Cities, with its contrast between the perfection of the heavenly city and the radical imperfection of all politics in the earthly city. Niebuhr praises Augustine for seeing that evil lies in the rebellious human will (in self-love) rather than in the body as Plato taught or in oppressive social institutions as Rousseau taught. But Niebuhr is also critical of Augustine. He says Augustine's "realism was indeed excessive," meaning Augustine was too cynical about politics and not fearful enough of tyranny. This criticism is the entry point for Niebuhr's modern conceptions of personality, freedom, and democracy.

Niebuhr likes to see Augustine pointing the way himself by putting Christian love over the rigid precepts of law and by sensing the radical freedom of man from nature. But he says Augustine was misled by Neoplatonic otherworldliness, which directs all love to God and denigrates love of human personality for its own sake: "Augustine makes the mistake of never being concerned whether . . . we rise to the point of loving the other person for his own sake . . . [or] for God's sake . . . [Augustine] compounds this error by insisting that the love of neighbor must express itself not so much in meeting his needs, as in leading him to God." In other words, Niebuhr thinks Augustine did not appreciate persons for their own sake (as ends-in-themselves) but as creatures to be led to God for their own salvation and for our salvation.[61]

This Kantian twist, loving persons for their own sake, is given a theoretical basis in *The Nature and Destiny of Man* where Niebuhr takes up Christian anthropology—the enduring dispute about the meaning of *Imago Dei*. What, he asks, does it mean to be made in the image and likeness of God? After rejecting the Thomistic view of the divine image as the possession of a rational soul, Niebuhr offers his own formulation: The divine image is man's "indeterminate self-transcendence." Now, this is obviously a difficult term to understand. Niebuhr tries to clarify the meaning of indeterminate self-transcendence by calling it a type of freedom over nature that is undefined about its end. He says that "man is self-determining . . . he transcends natural processes . . . and must choose his total end" and that "[the] human capacity for self-transcendence is the basis of human freedom and the uniqueness of the individual." Interestingly, Niebuhr cites the influence of Max Scheler, Søren Kierkegaard, and Martin Heidegger on his view of man's divinely endowed freedom.[62] But, if I were to characterize his view more precisely, I would say that he has arrived at a type of Kantian freedom mixed with existentialism, for he describes a self-defining human personality that is able to transcend the biological and material processes of nature and to find dignity in determining its own end. This means that Niebuhr combines Augustinian realism with a modern conception of freedom. But, unlike the pope, Niebuhr has tipped the scales in favor of human autonomy that overstates man's independence from God and detaches the free personality from an objective hierarchy of ends.

My conclusion, therefore, is that the modern synthesis of Christianity and Kant's philosophy of freedom is not inherently wrong. Like all syntheses, its validity depends on the precise formula for putting the different elements together. But one must be very careful how it is done. It can be justified if Kantian freedom is carefully quali-fied and controlled—if the rights of the human person are clearly di-rected to higher ends, such as virtue, the common good, the duty to protect the weak and the innocent, and the supernatural destiny of man. If rights are not controlled and directed upward to the higher ends of virtue and charity, then they become ends-in-themselves and subordinate Christian faith to human personality. They can then be used to subvert legitimate authority as well as to oppose tyranny, dis-guising themselves as neutral freedom of choice about the good life while actually imposing a specific way of life slanted toward secular-ism or one-dimensional materialism or moral depravity.

Though some versions of the modern synthesis are justified, one may well ask if the whole strategy of incorporating the Kantian theory of rights and dignity into Christian theology is a wise or necessary move. Even when it is carefully qualified by responsible theologians or by the magisterium of the Catholic Church, it has a tendency to get out of control—to be misunderstood by people who are constantly bombarded by 'secular liberalism' as opposed to 'Christian liberal-ism' and who easily forget that human dignity does not lie in au-tonomy or personal identity but in the possession of an immortal soul with an eternal destiny that permits only conditional notions of free-dom and rights. For political freedom to be true and authentically Christian, it must be controlled freedom—freedom that is guided and restrained by a host of institutions so that the characters of free persons are properly formed to choose wisely and well.

Awareness of this problem explains why premodern Christian theologians could speak boldly about spiritual freedom and freedom of the will but generally oppose political and personal freedom, except as an element of a corporate hierarchy that constrained the will and directed it upward to authorities higher than the popular will and to goods higher than personal satisfaction. Such prudential wisdom should not be forgotten. If we look back to the premodern tradition, above all to St. Augustine's Two Cities, we can find there a justification for limits on the power of the state that are based not on individual rights but on recognition of the supremacy of the spiritual realm over the entire temporal realm. It is this idea that I shall now try to develop as an alternative to modern Kantian Christianity.

CHAPTER FOUR

RETHINKING CHRISTIAN POLITICS: THE TWO CITIES IN THE MODERN AGE

In the preceding chapters, I presented an overview of the Christian tradition that showed its evolution from the illiberal and undemocratic views of the past to a positive acceptance of democracy and human rights in the modern age. I argued that many factors contributed to the change: the unified sovereignty of the divine right of kings, the democratic spin-offs of the Protestant Reformation, the theory of popular sovereignty developed by neo-Scholastics, the rational religions of the Enlightenment, the struggles against oppression, and the totalitarian experience of the twentieth century. I also claimed that the primary influence was a specific strand of Enlightenment liberalism, namely, Kant's philosophy of freedom, which brought the rights and dignity of the person into Christian theology and made liberal democracy an unconditional duty of Christian ethics—the only form of government worthy of man as a creature made in the image of God. I ventured the generalization that the Kantian influence on modern religion is so pervasive and profound that one may speak of three great periods of Christian theology: the Platonic Christianity of the early church fathers, the Aristotelian Christianity of the Middle Ages, and the Kantian Christianity of the modern age. I concluded by asking if it is wise to incorporate so much of Kant's philosophy of freedom into Christianity, and I answered that it depends on the precise formulation. Those that carefully control Kant are defensible, but those that let Kant out-of-his-box, as it were, elevate human autonomy and personal identity above the law of God and the common good.

As a preliminary judgment, the distinction between proper and improper uses of Kant is extremely important. But I think we need to go much further and ask if the whole way that modern Christians approach politics—as a Kantian-like moral imperative of human dignity that extends spiritual precepts into the political realm without relying on prudence—is really the best way to make political decisions. We also need to ask if the characteristic way of life promoted by liberal democracy and human rights (along with associated structures such as capitalism and industrial society) are compatible with the Christian faith. Though these issues seem to be settled by a new consensus, they were once fiercely contested; and I propose reopening the debate in order to see if the perspective of older theologians can be applied today and provide an alternative approach. What I would like to propose, in short, is a comparison of Augustinian Christianity with Kantian Christianity on the great issues of politics. My goal is to recover the original meaning of the Two Cities in order to see how democracy looks when it is treated, not as a moral imperative of human dignity or as a secular reflection of a sacred ideal, but as a prudential choice of the temporal realm—as a regime that may be a reasonable option in the present age but that is not the best regime simply or even the one most compatible with Christian faith. We need to consider the possibility that modern democracy may be nothing more than a transient phase in the rise and fall of the earthly city rather than the high point of moral progress or a step toward building the kingdom of God on earth.

Assessing Christian Democracy

To arrive at a fair assessment of the present age, we should begin on a positive note and consider the benefits of believing that Christianity contains an ethical imperative for democracy and human rights. The main advantages, in my judgment, are political rather than religious. As many important figures have attested, the belief that Christianity requires democracy strengthens and ennobles liberal democracy.

When human rights are held as God-given rights—as endowments of the Creator—they take on a sacred quality that imbues freedom with a sense of moral responsibility; individuals and nations feel that they are accountable to the Supreme Governor of the universe who will judge them for their righteousness. This makes citizens and leaders conscientious in the performance of their duties. In addition, believing in the Christian origins of democracy, as Tocqueville observed 160 years ago and as Konrad Adenauer argued in the twentieth century, serves as a powerful check on atheistic materialism and on the corrosive selfishness that is inherent in the democratic ethos of individual rights. More generally, the belief in Christian democracy puts restraints on permissive freedom, limiting the idea that anything goes as long as it does not violate the letter of the law or that law itself should continuously push back the boundaries of decency to allow for greater self-expression. The Christian notion of man's dual nature—his dignity and his depravity—instills in democracies a healthy sense of human fallibility and an awareness of the many ways that freedom can go awry.

As for the political effects on the churches, the belief in a close connection between Christianity and modern democracy has the benefit of placing the churches squarely against totalitarianism and dictatorship, ending the confusion and waffling that was seen in the twentieth century when fascism and communism posed genuine threats to the world. The new consensus checks the unrealistic hopes of some conservative Catholics, Anglicans, and Eastern Orthodox believers for a restoration of the "ancien régime" of Throne and Altar in the present age (which even Jacques Maritain entertained at the beginning of his career, before he went on to become a champion of Christian democracy). In addition, the recent conversion of Christian churches to the cause of human rights benefits Christianity by helping to restrain its historic zeal for persecuting heretics and waging religious sectarian warfare. In the spirit of civil religion which makes the moral education of citizens and statesmen the highest priority, it seems wise and beneficial to say that Christianity teaches democratic human rights as a secular reflection of a sacred ideal because it strengthens the democratic state and humanizes the churches.[1]

The crucial question, however, is whether in the long run it is wise for Christianity to be identified closely with any political regime, especially with liberal democracy. I believe that it is not wise to establish such intimate connections. The primary reason is that the Christian faith is weakened from within by embracing democratic human rights as an inference from the dignity of the person or from a new interpretation of the *Imago Dei*. When Christianity associates its spiritual and ethical teachings so closely with democratic politics, the Christian faith eventually turns into a mirror image of modern political ideologies, such as liberalism or socialism, that sap its spiritual energy and eventually undercut even the political utility of religion. Why does this happen?

There are many ways to explain the phenomenon. One explanation is the 'secularization' of religion—the gradual abandonment of Christian 'otherworldliness' under the influence of modern ideas and the growing belief that improving life in this world is more important than the salvation of souls in the world-to-come. While secularization is a useful thesis to explain broad patterns of change, it is too general because it does not pay sufficient attention to the political dynamics of the change. Most modern Christians do not believe they have compromised the supernatural destiny of man or the belief in eternal salvation by embracing modern democracy; they sincerely believe that they are developing Christian teaching in accordance with the times and are enlightening their faith as well as ennobling liberal democracy. Their mistake lies in drastically misjudging the negative side effects of this move—in underestimating the corrosive effects of a culture of rights and the leveling effects of mass democracy on the human soul and on the institutions that are necessary to sustain a sense of the sacred. Instead of being alarmed by a convergence of the Two Cities, they seem pleased that the city of God and the earthly city are now operating on the same democratic wavelength, as if the original democracy of the Gospels was finally being realized after centuries of misguided authoritarianism. In the process, however, modern Christians are diminishing the supernatural destiny of man, not by repudiating the higher spiritual realms, but by channeling religious obligation toward the progress of democracy in the church as well as in the state and by treating political restructuring as the new path to salvation. The result is a declining interest in the otherworldly and mystical aspects of religion combined with a restless urge to democratize everything—from the clergy to the forms and style of worship to the translations of Scripture. The first and greatest commandment—to love God with all one's heart, mind, and soul—is gradually superceded by the second great commandment—to love one's neighbor as one's self—now understood as respecting the rights of persons in an enlightened and democratic setting.

To see how this happens, let us reflect candidly on the negative side effects of advocating democratic human rights. Such reflections are difficult and unpopular because the negative side effects are inseparable from the inspiring beauty of human rights as weapons against oppression. The central problem is that human rights are not only powerful weapons against tyranny; they also carry skeptical and subversive assumptions that undermine all authority. Rights challenge and subvert authority because they carry premises of natural freedom and natural equality which imply, as Rousseau said, that "Man is born free, but everywhere he is in chains," or, as the Sons of Liberty cried during the American Revolution, "Don't Tread on Me!" How is it possible to prevent these claims from undermining legitimate authority as well as tyranny? The very same rights which help to protect people from tyrants—from the Hitlers and Stalins of the world—can also be used, and indeed have been used, to subvert good and just authority—such as the authority of parents, teachers, political rulers, canonical writings, and the church itself. The skeptical baggage of rights is so intimately tied to conceptions of autonomous freedom that it is nearly impossible to stop human rights from subverting all authority and social cohesion. They even cast doubt on the very idea of an objective Good, undermining belief not only in God, virtue, and the common good but also in the doctrine of rights themselves. Nor is it individual rights alone that work against authority; even group rights (under the present banner of multiculturalism or identity politics) tend to subvert all authority, whether that authority is arbitrary and tyrannical or necessary and just.

Of course, the most thoughtful Christians in the contemporary world are painfully aware of the problem and seek to overcome it by making crucial distinctions—between "true" rights and "false" rights or between noble and degraded democracy. True rights, they say, are not merely negative assertions against authority; they free people to pursue higher ends and to serve objective goods. True rights are "perfectionist" or "teleological" because they direct citizens to the ends that make freedom worthwhile, namely, virtue and salvation. And true democracy rejects the notion that the will of the people is absolutely sovereign or that majority rule is always right; democracy is justified only when it is held accountable to higher moral law and remains open to the spiritual and transcendent destiny of man.

Yet, these distinctions are almost impossible to sustain while remaining within the horizon of democracy and rights. If democracy and rights are not ends-in-themselves but are justified only as means toward realizing an objective hierarchy of ends, then they are not 'rights' properly speaking. They are conditional goods subservient to higher goods; and there would be no justification for claiming that individuals have a natural right to pursue happiness as they see fit. Many great theologians seem genuinely stumped by this problem and inevitably wind up compromising their position by arguing that freedom takes precedence over higher goods.

For example, in his popular work, *The Children of Light and the Children of Darkness,* Reinhold Niebuhr distinguishes Christian democracy from bourgeois democracy. The former is good because it preserves a sense of man's sinful nature and need for spiritual authority, while the latter is bad because it is based on materialism, individualism, and naive assumptions about the natural goodness of man. Yet, in the effort to make Christianity more hospitable to democracy, Niebuhr defines freedom as "indeterminate self-transcendence," meaning the ability to rise above physical and biological processes and determine our own ends and direction. This definition leaves freedom unprotected from misuse by the evil tendencies of sinful human nature that Niebuhr so forcefully describes.[2] It means that Niebuhr's effort to distinguish true democracy founded on Christian principles from false democracy founded on materialism and individualism is negated by the need to keep freedom open-ended.

A better strategy for defending modern democracy and freedom is to link them directly to the higher ends that they must serve in order to be legitimate. In a recent book, *Making Men Moral,* Robert George calls this approach "perfectionist liberalism" because it directs freedom to moral perfection. In his view, perfectionist liberalism permits democratic freedom; but it also justifies some laws that curtail civil liberties in order to promote public morality and social responsibility. In order to reassure his readers that he is committed to genuine pluralism rather than moral authoritarianism, George calls his own theory of liberal democracy "pluralist perfectionism."[3] The same idea was developed earlier by Jacques Maritain, who argued that Christian democracy is "personalist" (based on the dignity of the person as a rational and spiritual being who seeks higher purposes) while "bourgeois" democracy is individualistic, materialistic, and spiritually indifferent. The implication in both cases is that "true" democracy and rights are not directed against the family, the church, traditional educational institutions, the state, or the military chain of command. True democracy does not include rights to abortion, free sex, homosexual marriage, disloyalty, pornography, or excessive capitalism. Distinctions such as these are supposed to keep liberal democracy from degenerating into immorality or vulgar self-expression or a consumer-worker society of soulless materialism. Yet, one must ask: Is it possible to avoid the moral confusion and still remain within the horizon of democratic human rights?

I do not think so. Even when rights are accompanied by clear directions to higher ends and the human "person" is distinguished from the selfish individual, the doctrine of rights will not lead to the intended results. The rights to personal satisfaction and to personal identity—driven by the self-love that is part of our fallen nature—take over. Rights eventually swallow up higher ends and subvert all higher authorities, including the churches and theologians who defend them while trying to avoid their negative side effects. Speaking humorously, I would compare the Christian proponents of human rights to the lady described in a popular limerick who thought she was safe while riding a tiger. In the words of the limerick: "There once was a Lady from Riga / Who smiled as she rode on a tiger. / They came back from the ride / With the lady inside / And a smile on the face of the tiger." Modern Christians are like the Lady from Riga because they, too, are riding a tiger—the movement for democratic human rights. Now they are smiling, confident that they are in control and pleased to be in tune with modern culture; but it is only a matter of time before they will be swallowed up by the culture of rights!

The mistake lies in vastly underestimating the *subversive power* of rights. Modern Christian theologians naively believe that rights can be detached from their subversive premises and regrounded on the Christian idea of human dignity—on the idea that man is a creature made in the image and likeness of God—in order to avoid the misuses of freedom and lead people to a sense of gratitude and duty to God. But rights do not work that way. Once they are claimed, their subversive premises take over. That is because rights are essentially ungrateful claims against authority, either for protections and immunities against the interference of authority or for entitlements from authority. The deep premise of rights is the natural freedom and natural equality of the autonomous self—the belief that man is born free and can determine his own destiny without being dependent upon others or beholden to higher powers. As I argued in chapter one, the implicit assumption of such natural freedom is distrust of Divine Providence—the belief that God is stingy, that God does not provide sufficiently for man by giving clear signs about who should rule or by providing sufficient abundance in nature for human survival and well-being. The stinginess of Providence requires man to provide for himself—to act on his own without waiting for God's permission, justifying the natural right to self-preservation and other freedoms. Following this logic, man cannot rely on higher powers but must construct the state by an artificial social contract; and instead of feeling gratitude toward nature, man provides for his survival by conquering and transforming nature through human labor and technology. As Locke said, we cannot afford to wait for God's permission to act; the necessities of our condition give us the right to act on our own.[4] And as Kant argued with chilling logic, the autonomous person should avoid gratitude at all costs because gratitude implies indebtedness to others and dependence on powers outside ourselves.

Rights, therefore, are great weapons in the struggle against tyranny and other forms of exploitation because rights encourage positive action rather than passive suffering. They help to move Providence along, as it were, under the assumption that 'God helps those who help themselves.' Modern Christians and other religious believers are attracted to this idea because it helps in the defense of powerless people and even encourages the powerless to defend themselves. For example, by speaking of "the right to life," Christians are aided in their duty to protect unborn children against abortion. And by speaking of the rights of conscience, all religious believers are helped in defending themselves against the totalitarian state. And the right to property encourages the poor to improve their lot or to demand a fair distribution of wealth. And, persecuted people, such as the Jews, gain strength by appealing to the right of self-determination; it has enabled modern Zionists to claim that building the nation of Israel by human agency hastens the promised messianic redemption (in contrast to traditional Jews who believe in patiently waiting for the Messiah to do it miraculously). Rights have this power and attraction because they encourage human agency to help along Divine Providence. Their premise, therefore, is not atheism *per se* but impatience with God's providence. Modern religious believers adopt human rights because they have learned from bitter historical experience that it is too dangerous to wait for God to intervene and to protect people from their murderous enemies. How could this attitude be wrong? Does God object to a little help from His friends?

The problem is not with human agency as such but with human agency as a "right": It makes people feel that God and the world owe them something, and it easily turns into a belief in human self-sufficiency. Thus, proclaiming a right to life easily turns into the claim that biological existence is sacred or that mere life has absolute value, regardless of whether it is the life of an innocent unborn child or the life of a heinous criminal. And the claim that life is a "right" diminishes the claim that life is "gift" from God: How can a gift be a right? Proclaiming a right to life eventually leads to the mistaken idea of a "seamless garment of life" that is indistinguishable from complete pacifism or a total ban on taking life, including animal life, even for just and necessary causes. It also makes one forget that the good life, not to mention the afterlife, is a greater good than merely being alive in the present world—an unintended but significant depreciation of Christian otherworldliness.

In order to defend the unborn, the infirm, and the weak, Christians would be wise to avoid the language and logic of rights. Instead, they should appeal to the hierarchy of being and to the duty of Christian charity which teach that the innocent are "better"—that is, closer to God—than the guilty. Hence, the innocent are to be loved and protected more fully than the guilty. The implication is that one should oppose the taking of innocent human life, as in abortion or euthanasia, while recognizing that it is sometimes necessary to take the lives of unjust aggressors and murderers. Thus, it is perfectly logical for Christians to oppose abortion, on the one hand, and to support the theory of just war and the logical extension of just war, capital punishment, on the other hand. The former protects the innocent while the latter punishes the guilty. But the right to life as a blanket proposition tends to obscure the crucial moral difference between the innocent and the guilty, suggesting a false moral equivalence between protecting a child and protecting a murderer. Yet, how can a sincere Christian think that an unborn child and a hideous criminal like Charles Manson both have an equal right to live? Let us not forget that Jesus Christ sharply distinguished the treatment of innocent children and guilty human beings when He said, "whoever causes one of these little ones who believe in me to sin, it would be better for him to have a great millstone fastened round his neck and to be drowned in the depth of the sea" (Matt. 18:6). And Jesus also said that Judas His betrayer "would have been better . . . if he had not been born" (Matt. 26:24). If rights were the ultimate horizon, then Jesus could not have uttered these words; for His words clearly distinguish between innocent people, whose lives demand protection, and guilty people, whose crimes can be grave enough to justify forfeiting their right to life. Jesus' very words require us to distinguish between higher and lower human beings and imply that fundamental human rights can be negated in order to satisfy the demands of divine justice.

When Christians embrace Kantian-like human rights, they also become confused about the nature of Christian charity. In the contemporary world, Christian charity—the command to love one's neighbor—is now equated with respecting the rights of others and affirming their personal identities. The older understanding of Christian charity emphasized compassion for man as a fallen being who stands in need of divine redemption and human help; but this idea has faded into the background because it seems too condescending in a culture based on the rights and dignity of the individual. Yet, if we consider classic lessons of the Bible about charity, such as the story of the Good Samaritan, then the older concept of compassion seems closer to the mark. For the Bible says that the Samaritan saw an unfortunate man who was robbed and beaten and left to die by the side of the road; and the Samaritan "took pity" on him and showed "mercy" toward him (Luke 10:33–37). This is not the same as respecting his rights and dignity as a person; the unfortunate man did not claim medical attention as a right and his posture was that of someone in need rather than someone asserting his dignity as an autonomous agent. The Good Samaritan was motivated by compassion rather than by justice understood as defending human rights.

In an interesting book called *The Idea of Christian Charity,* Gordon Graham reflects on this distinction. He is critical of contemporary efforts by Christians to equate charity with social justice and human rights: "Christian moralists increasingly prefer talk of justice and rights to talk of misfortune and charity." Rights are preferred because they fit the autonomy of adults, while charity seems to imply dependence, "an affront to human dignity." He argues for the need to rediscover charity as a divine command—"an active concern to help others . . . [based on] the gracious acknowledgment of our dependence."[5] I take this to mean that Christian charity is not simply giving to others what they claim to be owed as a matter of rights. Charity is compassion for man as a fallen being who stands in need of divine redemption and sometimes also in need of spiritual and bodily help from fellow human beings. But this does not automatically mean respecting people's rights, although it is not necessarily inconsistent with certain kinds of freedom. The incompatibilities arise when rights become ungrateful demands. They also arise when charity itself requires 'tough love' for weak and sinful beings—which often implies the moral duty of imposing on others to improve and to correct their behavior, to teach them virtue and save their souls, rather than simply affirming who they are as a person.

Instead of truly helping people, the affirmation of a person's rights encourages him to believe that the world owes him something, that he has entitlements from society and even from God. This feeling often makes modern people believe that everyone has a right to be happy, even to be eternally happy in the world-to-come—a notion that is, in principle, infinitely selfish. As Alexander Solzhenitsyn has pointed out, the Western concept of human rights lacks an inherent principle of self-denial or self-limitation; it tends to multiply claims indefinitely, often at the expense of others. It is not an accident that the history of rights is a record of indefinite expansion, from the rights of man to women's rights to workers' rights to children's rights to animal rights. And, within rights themselves, they begin as legal protections from arbitrary power and expand into entitlements from government, including rights to virtually every worldly good (including jobs, housing, education, medical benefits, leisure time) in order to ensure that all needs and desires (from the cradle to the grave) are guaranteed satisfaction.[6] Thus, human rights are not so noble or just or harmless as they first appear, even when they are invoked to oppose tyranny and to help Divine Providence along in protecting the powerless. Rights cannot be stopped from endorsing the infinity of desire and the pride in human autonomy which leads modern people to deny their dependence on God's providence and God's grace as well as to deny their duties to neighbors and society. In this way, rights themselves become tyrannical.

When human rights are joined with democracy, creating the regime of liberal democracy, many of these problems are compounded. Democracy tends toward 'leveling'—toward reducing all hierarchies and inequalities to the same level of equality and uniformity, usually to the lowest common denominator of mass taste and popular culture. Together, the subversive thrust of rights and the leveling effects of democracy undermine the hierarchical doctrine of the Two Cities, undermining the primary claim of the city of God over the earthly city and bringing the spiritual and temporal orders close together. Obviously, this would not be bad if it meant that the temporal realm were being elevated to a higher spiritual plane and everyone became more holy and godly. But the trend is in the opposite direction. The city of God is becoming less transcendent and more political under the assumption that the political order—in this case, democracy—has spiritual significance. This diminishes the importance of holiness, understood as the vertical relation with God, attained through such activities as contemplative prayer, the celebration of sacred mysteries, ascetic practices, and gratuitous charity for the needy. When holiness recedes, political and social change moves to the center stage of Christian faith and spiritual life is diminished.

Of course, balancing the spiritual and political realms is always difficult; but the transcendent order loses power in the modern democratic age precisely because it is associated with democracy. For example, a change in the definition of the Catholic Church that downplays the traditional view of the Church as "the mystical body of Christ" and emphasizes instead the modern view of the Church as "the People of God" suggests a more political and indeed a more democratic view of the Church. The new definition diminishes the mystical or divine foundations of the Church and elevates (or creates the public perception of elevating) popular will and public opinion. It encourages a change of tone in worship from the celebration of sacred mysteries to a community gathering—from a solemn worship instilling sacred awe to a civic assembly or communal meal of the people of God. Instead of offering an alternative to the prevailing secular culture by inspiring reverence and an otherworldly vision of celestial beauties, the Church becomes a mirror image of modern society and weakens its ability to stand as a counterculture to the world.[7]

The culture of rights and democratic leveling also turn against the hierarchical authority of the church. The Protestant churches have been wrestling with this problem since the beginning of the Reformation when they rejected the sacramental priesthood in favor of the priesthood of all believers: Is worship merely a social gathering in which the faithful hear the Word read and preached, or is God actually present in some form? Now the Catholic Church faces the same problem (and the Eastern Orthodox will soon follow suit if, after its liberation from communism, it embraces democracy with the same spiritual fervor with which it once embraced emperors and tsars). In the case of the Catholic Church, it seems inconsistent to defend democratic rights in the political realm as a moral imperative of human dignity and then argue that such rights do not apply with the same force to the Church and the spiritual realm.

Yet, the endorsement of democracy and human rights as a moral imperative of human dignity is undoubtedly the major cause of confusion today about the authority of the Church and the Catholic priesthood in particular. In modern countries like America and the Western European democracies, the Catholic Church and priesthood are no longer seen as divine authorities, instituted by Christ and the Apostolic Succession and affirmed by the continuous deposit of faith. Like other forms of authority in the democratic age, the priesthood is seen as a political issue about individual rights or a technical issue about individual competence. The relentless pressure for women's ordination in the Catholic Church is a consequence of thinking that the Church is a mere protector of the rights of the people of God rather than the mystical body of Christ which cannot be measured by political standards because it is divinely ordained by Scripture and tradition. According to divine authority, there is no right to be a priest; it is a type of divine election beginning with the Apostles and continuing with their successors. But democratic cultures find this thought inconceivable and view the priesthood as a profession like all others, which anyone should be allowed to choose if he or she wants to, subject only to the limitations of talent and motivation. How could a just and loving God be exclusive rather than inclusive in establishing the structures of the Church?

The traditional Christian answer, of course, is that no one has a right to be a priest or a holy person because no one *deserves* anything from God, although we may deserve some things from our fellow men as a matter of justice. In the true perspective, God is everything and man is nothing, which means we are not entitled to anything, not even to complain about suffering. As Leszek Kolakowski says in his new work on Pascal and Augustine: *God Owes Us Nothing.*[8] This awesome thought negates all rights as a matter of spiritual and moral principle. Reflecting on the implications, I wonder if there is a modern Christian or Jew who could write a book about suffering like the Book of Job, in which a righteous man loses everything for no apparent reason except God's desire to test his faith and about which Job is told he has no right to complain. Can modern Christians understand the Book of Job as anything other than an existential statement of meaningless suffering or a bewildering account of a victim of a tyrannical God? In the political world, could modern Christians understand the statement of Martin Luther when he said that Christians should not go to court to sue on their own behalf—that lawsuits are immoral and un-Christian except to protect others but not to redress one's own grievances?[9] How strange these sentiments sound in a culture of rights, where one feels that God and the world owe us something like a right to happiness and that God cannot exclude someone who wants inclusion. But God's exclusions are part of the concept of 'divine election,' which runs throughout the Bible as well as the Jewish and Christian traditions. It is justified in the Bible by the idea that God is an omnipotent Creator with a mysterious will who will be merciful to whom He will be merciful, however incomprehensible it is to us. If an institution is based on divine election—whether it be the election of Israel to be the chosen people or the election of the Apostles to succeed Christ or the election of men to the Church's priesthood—then one must acknowledge that certain kinds of exclusion and inclusion are compatible with divine justice while universal claims of rights are not.

A similar confusion surrounds the right to religious freedom. Most modern churches have accepted religious freedom as a human right in order to protect religious believers from the coercion of hostile states or from the persecution of religious zealots, grounding the right of conscience in the dignity of the person as a free agent. Yet, they have not answered satisfactorily the major objection against it: How can the right of all religions to equal liberty be accepted without diminishing the superior claims of the One True Religion? How can people accept the pluralism of religions as a right without demoting Christianity to mere "denominational" status or relegating it to a private association?[10] Does error really have the same rights as the ultimate, cosmic truth? From the perspective of ultimate truth, pluralism is a sign of imperfection that should be overcome rather than frozen in place as a right to diversity. Of course, one can always 'tolerate' error as a matter of prudence, based on the recognition that error and sin are intractable problems of the fallen world. But from the perspective of ultimate truth, diversity is not a right; it is a sign of imperfection, a condition which one may patiently combat with reason and moral example rather than with coercion, while recognizing that Christianity is the fullness of truth. The loss of this grand and exhilarating perspective is another casualty of modern Christianity and its principled embrace of human rights.

For all these reasons, it seems unwise for modern Christians to adopt a Kantian imperative for liberal democracy and to close the gap between the Two Cities, allowing the transcendent and otherworldly demands of the faith to be absorbed and marginalized by the earthly city. It seems like a repeat of earlier mistakes when Christians forged close links between the churches and a specific political regime—for example, (1) when Eastern Orthodox churches embraced emperors and tsars as divinely sanctioned heads of the church, and the Russians saw their nation as the "third Rome" with a messianic mission, which led to the servility of the Orthodox Church to the modern tsars; or (2) when Anglicans and Gallicans adopted the divine right of kings, making kings the vicars of God on earth in place of bishops or popes and elevating the nation-state over the universal church; or (3) when American Puritans adopted a version of Calvinist theocracy which equated church membership with citizenship and even deified America as a New Jerusalem. Such views gave the state or the nation a spiritual significance that it does not deserve in the proper hierarchy of being; such views not only tend to deify nationalism, they inevitably bring the church under the thumb of the state.

In the modern democratic age, the political dominance of religion is more subtle. The church is given freedom of worship but comes under the thumb of the 'culture of rights' and the cult of democracy, creating an obsessive fascination with dismantling spiritual hierarchies (as if promoting democracy were a form of 'atonement' for the authoritarianism of the past) and subjecting ultimate, cosmic truths to majority rule. Christianity then becomes indistinguishable from the modern world and allows itself to be swallowed up by democracy without a struggle. In the last analysis, this may cause the demise of liberal democracy itself, since the reliance on God to legitimize its authoritative institutions seems less and less necessary to democratic nations and legitimacy comes to rest solely on the ability to deliver material prosperity and technological mastery. Since fulfilling these promises is inevitably subject to market fluctuations and technical failures, one must conclude that treating religion as a personal or private right puts modern democratic civilization on the most fragile foundation it could possibly devise.

RECOVERING THE TWO CITIES

If this diagnosis is correct, then the highest priority of religious believers (indeed, of all concerned citizens) in the present age should be to restore the proper balance between the spiritual and political orders and to reestablish proper hierarchies in each order. I can think of no better way of restoring the proper order of things than by recovering St. Augustine's doctrine of the Two Cities—the distinction between the city of God and the earthly city—and applying it to the modern age. This is actually a fairly radical proposal, the equivalent of replacing the Kantian Christianity which predominates today with Augustinian Christianity in one form or another.

At first glance, it may be difficult to understand what such a proposal would mean because everyone pays lip service to the doctrine of the Two Cities. Every writer on Christian politics acknowledges that Christ distinguished the duties to God from the duties to Caesar and asserted the primacy of the spiritual over the political realm when He said that His kingdom is not of this world. Hence, all agree that the Christian message cannot be reduced to a political ideology or a social theory, whether it favors monarchy or democracy, capitalism or socialism. While denying any simplistic equation of spiritual and political ideals, however, many modern Christians develop arguments that give spiritual significance to democracy and wind up insisting, as Kant and other modern thinkers have done, that the consent of the people and human rights are the sole legitimizing principles of political authority.

For example, as I noted above in several places, Jacques Maritain argues for the distinction of two orders and the primacy of the spiritual over the temporal realm. But Maritain also says that democracy is spiritual in the sense of being "evangelical" or inspired by the Gospel—a translation of the Christian idea of the equal dignity of all human beings before God into a profane political order.[11] A similar, though more circumspect example, is John Courtney Murray, who distinguishes the spiritual and the temporal realms but then gives a privileged status to democracy in Christian natural law thinking. Murray looks back to the distinction between the two powers made by Pope Gelasius in the fifth century and by John of Paris in the fourteenth century as evidence for the fact that medieval Catholicism acknowledged a certain separation of the state from religion, even though the idea remained undeveloped in the Middle Ages. Murray also says that modern constitutional principles, like the First Amendment rights of the U.S. Constitution, are merely legal "articles of peace" to keep the several churches from harming each other rather than "articles of faith." Yet, Murray ultimately thinks that Anglo-American liberal democracy is the only political order consistent with Catholic teaching about the dignity of the human person, which makes "popular sharing in the formation of the collective will . . . a natural-law principle."[12] Another example is Stanley Hauerwas. He rejects the equation of Protestant Christianity with liberalism or Americanism; but he also says the "church is the polis," by which he means a democratic religious community whose need for a "narrative" story is the ultimate validation of Scripture.[13] Likewise, Glenn Tinder argues that the political meaning of Christianity is not a specific political ideology but a "prophetic stance" that treats everyone as an "exalted individual"; yet, he says explicitly that "Christianity implies democracy."[14] And in a more subtle version of the same idea, the new *Catechism of the Catholic Church* says: "The diversity of political regimes is morally acceptable provided they serve the legitimate good of the community." It then goes on to define the legitimate good of the community (or common good) as the "inalienable rights of the human person" and "the sum total of social conditions which allow people, either as groups or individuals, to reach their fulfillment" (par. 1901–1912). When these qualifications are added up, the initial reference to the diversity of political regimes is negated by the strong suggestion that liberal democracy is the only legitimate political choice.

What I infer from these examples is that contemporary Christians are trying to have it both ways. In deference to the traditional doctrine of the Two Cities, they maintain that the Christian message cannot be reduced to a particular political order or ideology and is compatible with a variety of legitimate regimes. But they also insist on an intimate connection, even a moral equivalence, between Christianity and liberal democracy based on inalienable human rights.

To recover the true meaning of the Two Cities—and therewith the proper foundation of Christian politics—one must be brave enough to sever the Christian-democratic connection and start all over again. One must begin by acknowledging that Christianity is an otherworldly religion whose primary mission is saving souls in the world-to-come rather than constructing political regimes and whose distinction between the spiritual and temporal realms means that no specific form of government or social order is required by divine law. In this regard, Christianity is less inherently political than Judaism and Islam, whose spiritual teachings and divine law are closely tied to politics and lend themselves readily to the theocratic unification of religion and the state. In Judaism and Islam, the divine law itself contains a political teaching; and the chief prophets, Moses and Mohammed, were not only spiritual leaders but also political rulers, lawgivers, and warriors. As monotheistic religions, of course, Judaism and Islam acknowledge the absolute Lordship of God over the created universe, which implies a distinction between the absoluteness of God's rule and the conditionality of all human rule. But the content of divine revelation in Judaism and Islam is essentially political, including a legal code that organizes religious, political, social, and family life into an integrated whole. Moreover, Judaism is defined by God's covenant with Israel that identifies a specific people and territory as holy or set apart; and its divine law or *halakah*, includes a civil code (although the end of the Davidic kingship and the rise of rabbinic Judaism in exile have permitted greater political flexibility than in earlier days, and the modern Jewish state of Israel has a secular as well as a religious justification). Similarly, Islam's divine law or *sharia* includes a comprehensive civil code for an Islamic state, with some distinction between clergymen who are legal scholars (*ulama*) and political rulers who traditionally have been kings but could also be elected representatives. Despite these complexities, the comparison with Judaism and Islam shows that Christianity is essentially transpolitical, not only because Christ distinguished God's realm from Caesar's realm and said His kingdom is not of this world (thereby rejecting the Davidic model of a warrior-king) but also because the divine law in Christianity is reduced to two great commands of love—loving God and one's neighbor—which put charity above justice and eliminate the many civil and ceremonial statutes of the old Mosaic law. Thus, the concept of a Christian state is less clear or necessary than a Jewish state or an Islamic state (and all monotheistic religions are less tied to the state and sacred rulers than pagan or polytheistic religions).[15]

Yet, the transpolitical character of Christian spirituality does not mean that the state is entirely secular. A more accurate statement of the Christian position is that its doctrine of the Two Cities implies *a distinction but not a separation* of the spiritual and temporal realms. In other words, God does not require a specific form of government or spell out a precise legal code or anoint specific political rulers; but government in general is instituted by God. As Paul said in his classic statement in Romans 13, "There is no power but from God and all power is instituted by God" and political rulers are "God's ministers." This means government is God-given, not merely a human social contract or a product of natural inclinations; and the obligation to obey political rulers is a religious duty. Yet, the state itself does not have a religious function and is not a sacred order. Nor is Caesar a god or a sacred king or even a priest-king. A subtle paradox is at work in Christianity: God ordains the state, but God ordains the state for nonreligious ends, namely, the limited purposes of the temporal realm.

Thus, for Christians, the state is inherently limited because God has given the state as a remedy for the Fall—for the negative purpose of restraining man's sinful nature and, more positively, to direct man's sinful nature upward toward virtue and piety while recognizing that ultimate redemption is spiritual rather than political. Hence, the state is not directly involved in the salvation of souls or in the messianic redemption of the world. Nor is there a principle of divine law—such as, the duty of charity, the kingdom of God, the new covenant, the *Imago Dei,* or even universal brotherhood—that translates into a specific political order (though some of these ideas may have indirect political consequences).

In more precise terms, the distinction of the Two Cities means that the spiritual and the political realms are instituted by God and accountable to God; but they are guided by different kinds of law and serve different ends. The spiritual realm, or city of God, is guided by divine law and an order of charity, holiness, and grace that serves the highest end, eternal salvation. The temporal realm or earthly city is guided by natural law which prudence formulates into human or civil law for the secondary ends of the temporal realm. The significance of this distinction, I believe, is that the institutions and activities that are prescribed by God for the spiritual realm—such as the church, the family, and works of charity—are governed by divine law, with little flexibility for prudence to adapt them to time and place. But the temporal realm is of a different character. There, God has not clearly revealed a principle of divine law to determine the major choices; God thus leaves a huge opening for prudence to operate in politics, economics, social relations, and military matters. God has not clearly indicated which form of government is best (monarchy, aristocracy, or democracy); which economic system is best (feudalism, capitalism, or socialism); which arrangement of social classes and distribution of wealth is best (pure equality or various degrees of inequality); and which organization of the military and which rules of diplomacy and warfare are best. Since God's will is not clearly specified by divine revelation in these areas, prudence must decide what is best on natural or human grounds, taking into account the fallen but rational nature of man and serving the secondary and limited goals of earthly happiness.

If this analysis of the Two Cities is correct, then we may infer that the minimum requirements of Christianity for legitimate political authority are twofold: the recognition of God's sanction for government and the limited nature of government, which may be put together in a single formulation, *limited government under God.* As I see it, the principle of limited government under God should be regarded as the general rule that guides Christian politics rather than the demand for a specific form of government or a specific theory of social justice or a doctrine of human rights. But what precisely is meant by limited government under God?

One interpretation can be found in St. Augustine's *City of God,* which shows that God ordained the state as a remedy for the Fall but confined it to the modest goal of "tranquillity of order." Augustine also argued that obedience to established political authorities is a conscientious duty, with the qualification that the state cannot require immorality or impiety and "provided no hindrance is presented to the religion which teaches that the one supreme and true God is to be worshiped."[16] Augustine's formulation for the proper sphere of

God-given political authority sets minimal guidelines for a variety of legitimate political regimes and a variety of legitimate arrangements between church and state. Over the centuries, the great Christian theologians who followed Augustine's Two Cities approach—including Aquinas, Luther, Calvin, and Hooker—applied those guidelines in different ways; but all had a sense of what Gerhart Niemeyer meant when he said that "Augustine is the intellectual father of the concept of limited government."[17] It is this sense that needs to be recovered and applied to the modern age.

What it means, in the first instance, is that the political realm is part of the hierarchy of being established by God's created order and man's fallen condition; and this hierarchy sets up a distinction between the city of God and the earthly city as well as the primacy of the former over the latter. A state is therefore legitimate to the extent that it respects the distinction and gives God and Caesar their proper due. If we try to spell out the implications for legitimate authority more precisely, the most obvious point is the rejection of any political regime that attempts to unify sovereignty under one head, thereby denying the proper distinction between the Two Cities and the proper balance of the spiritual and temporal orders. Thus, the Two Cities doctrine may not require a particular form of government by divine law; but it acts negatively to prohibit certain forms—namely, those which seek to abolish the distinction of the two realms by unifying power under one head. This rules out totalitarian regimes, in which the all-powerful state tries to absorb the church, and theocratic regimes, in which the all-powerful church tries to absorb the state. A proper understanding of the Two Cities makes the unified sovereignty of both totalitarianism and theocracy illegitimate. Let me elaborate this crucial point.

The totalitarian states of the twentieth century would be illegitimate because they attempt to usurp God's power with the overwhelming power of the secular state, leading to state-imposed atheism and the promotion of neopagan ideologies that deify the nation and the political ruler. Under totalitarianism, the state attempts to destroy the independence of the church and the rest of civil society by bringing them into its orbit and to transform human nature in accordance with utopian political ideologies, whether it is the universal classless society of communism or the dominance of the master race under fascism and Nazism. This type of evil cannot be adequately understood or explained by modern liberals, who conceive of evil mainly as the absorption of a private sphere of rights into the public realm or the subordination of the individual to a larger collective whole. But the subordination of individuals can be justified in some instances, for example in military organizations and religious societies dedicated to higher goods. What liberals miss is that the real evil of totalitarianism is its impiety—the worship of the state as an idol and the aspiration of rulers to play God, which intoxicates them with power and leads them to believe they have a license to commit mass murder. Sometimes, of course, even secular liberals speak of the lust for power as the aspiration 'to play God,' which means they are implicitly endorsing the teaching of the Two Cities and its condemnation of impious regimes.

The Two Cities also excludes lesser forms of state idolatry than totalitarianism, such as the Roman Empire's elevation of the emperor to the status of a god (as distinguished from the Roman imperial system itself, which may be a legitimate type of moderate authoritarianism when detached from emperor worship, as the early Christians correctly grasped in their intuitive application of the Two Cities). And it excludes secular theories of unified sovereignty, such as those developed by Hobbes and Rousseau, whose primary ambition was to obliterate the distinction of the spiritual and temporal realms and to subordinate the church to the political sovereign or to the general will of the nation for purely earthly ends.

On the other side of the coin, the Two Cities excludes theocracy in the sense of regimes directly ruled by clergymen, priests, bishops, or popes. Clerical or theocratic rule is illegitimate because it tries to unite the two realms under the church, thereby absorbing the state into the spiritual order and denying the legitimate but circumscribed independence that God gives to Caesar in the temporal order. The violation of the Two Cities in the name of theocracy has been a powerful temptation of Christian churches and clergymen over the centuries. In the High Middle Ages, it appeared in the extreme advocates of papal power, from Pope Gregory VII to Pope Boniface VIII, who claimed that the pope's "plenitude of power" is the sole source not only of spiritual authority but also of the state's temporal authority, making the state a mere appendage of the church and denying its God-given sphere of competence. The violation of the Two Cities has been part of the Caesaro-Papist tradition of Eastern Orthodoxy as well. It has promoted theocratic unification of state and church, sometimes by reducing the state to a tool of the church, but more often by conceding primacy (somewhat paradoxically) to the state on the grounds that emperors have religious or mystical authority. Theocratic unification has also been attempted by radical Calvinists who believed that the visible saints should rule the church and the commonwealth directly, placing the two realms under a single spiritual aristocracy. While theocracy is a lesser evil than totalitarianism because theocracy reflects the true hierarchy of being—the primacy of the duties to God over the duties to Caesar, whereas totalitarianism elevates Caesar over God—both are forms of sinful pride. Theocracy is illegitimate spiritual pride and totalitarianism is illegitimate political pride, both of which violate the Two Cities by unifying sovereignty under one head and denying the God-given function of each realm.

Following the guideline of respecting the proper spheres of the Two Cities, one may infer that several forms of government may be legitimate—including monarchies, mixed regimes, tempered democracies or republics, and even moderately authoritarian regimes. What makes them legitimate is their acceptance of the inherently limited nature of the state out of respect for the sovereignty of God and for the imperfections of fallen human nature. Of course, not all regimes that accept this crucial point are equally good; and a ranking may be established by prudence, indicating minimally acceptable regimes and optimal regimes depending on how well they serve the God-given ends of the temporal realm in the particular circumstances of time and place. To make those prudential judgments, one needs a clear conception of those ends.

Many battles have been fought about the proper ends of the state and the exact boundaries of the spiritual and temporal realms. In general terms, one can say that God has ordained the spiritual realm to serve the highest ends, eternal salvation and messianic redemption, while the temporal realm, including the state, has been ordained by God to serve the lesser ends of temporal or earthly happiness. If we search the New Testament and the writings of the premodern Christian theologians to identify those temporal ends (as we did in chapter two), then we can enumerate at least three: (1) civil peace, sometimes called the "tranquillity of order" or "unity in peace"; (2) a modicum of moral virtue that shapes the characters and souls of citizens so they may exercise responsible freedom and justice; and (3) certain religious duties that include civic piety and some concern with Christian orthodoxy (this point is the most difficult one to resolve). These three ends constitute a hierarchy of goods that must be balanced and weighed together to form the temporal common good.

One of the simplest statements of those ends can be found in the influential passage of the New Testament, 1 Pet. 2:13–17: "Be subject for the Lord's sake to every human institution . . . to the emperor as supreme or to governors as sent by him to punish wrong doers and to praise those who do right. . . . Live as freemen, yet without using your freedom as a pretext for evil; but live as servants of God. . . . Honor all men. . . . Fear God. Honor the emperor." This passage on the Christian view of the state indicates that God sanctions political authority as a human institution without specifying the precise form or organization that it should take. Peter's task is not to specify the form (although the Roman emperor and Roman citizenship are taken for granted) but to clarify the ends of the state and the type of obedience it requires. Like the enumeration above, this passage identifies three basic ends: (1) maintaining order by punishing the wicked and rewarding the good; (2) promoting moral virtue so that citizens may "live as freemen . . . without using . . . freedom as a pretext for evil," meaning the inculcation of moderation, courage, and a sense of justice to exercise responsible freedom; and (3) commanding certain religious duties, which in this case should be called "civic piety" because it includes the cultivation of reverence and awe for public officials as ministers of God, along with a salutary fear of God as the source of all authority, while stopping short of calling for the establishment of Christianity as the state religion. One might say that the passage outlines a Christian theory of the state without requiring a Christian state.

The implication is that the state should cultivate fear of God and God's ministers, the rulers and governors of the state, even though the state is not theocratic. It does not have to establish the Christian religion and to enforce Christian orthodoxy; but the state needs proof, so to speak, of its sanction by higher authority. In the Middle Ages, this was interpreted to mean that spiritual authorities, popes or bishops, actually crowned kings and emperors—officially signifying that political authority flowed from God to the church to the king.[18] But the actual passages in Peter (and Paul) might be interpreted more accurately to mean that the state needs the sanction of a "civil religion"—a sanction that most states have publicly recognized, usually by establishing a sectarian or confessional religion. The descriptions in 1 Pet. 2:13 and Paul's Romans 13 are less sectarian and less denominational than the historical examples; the apostles seek to inculcate a general fear and awe of God as the providential governor of the world—the source of all political authority and the sanction for good and evil conduct.

As I noted in chapter three, Americans are familiar with this kind of civil religion as the nondenominational 'theism' or 'deism' that pervades American public life; the English have also cultivated a slightly different version in the latitudinarian establishment of the Church of England. Another example can be found in the preamble of The Canadian Constitution Act (of 1982) which begins: "Whereas Canada is founded upon principles that recognize the supremacy of God and the rule of law . . ." The aim of such appeals to God in public life is to promote nondenominational piety and reverence for public authorities as reflections of higher authority rather than a confessional state; their purpose is not to lead people to salvation (that is the job of the church) but to remind citizens that the state is divinely sanctioned and that citizens have a religious duty to obey political rulers rather than a mere contractual obligation. As I also noted in chapter three, Americans have fashioned their republican civil religion out of a diluted version of Christianity and rational religion—emphasizing belief in God and basic morality without denominational creeds or elaborate rituals. The only rituals are the Pledge of Allegiance to the Flag that affirms one nation under God, nondenominational prayer at public ceremonies and (formerly) in public schools, swearing on the Bible in the courtroom, and national holidays such as Thanksgiving that instill the virtues of gratitude and piety by asking citizens to thank God for the blessings of American abundance and to share those blessings with others. This constitutes a civil religion that Protestants, Catholics, Jews, and even rationalists can publicly affirm in order to remind everyone that government is given by God for the proper ends of the temporal realm. While true Christian believers must never forget that this is merely Caesar's civil religion, not real Christianity, it is compatible with Christian faith as long as it is properly viewed as a partial truth or as an incomplete version of monotheism. Thus, it would be permissible, even a civic duty, for Christians to pray in public ceremonies in the nondenominational words of public chaplains: "O Supreme Governor of the Universe, give our political rulers the wisdom to rule justly and compassionately," while praying in their churches and families in the specifically Christian words: "Our Father who art in Heaven" and "Glory be to the Father, and to the Son, and to the Holy Spirit."

These guidelines indicate that a recovery of the Two Cities doctrine is possible in the modern world. Its contemporary application implies opposition to totalitarian and theocratic states and gives sanctions to all constitutionally limited governments under God, even those that are not based on human rights or social contract theory. The recovery and application of the Two Cities thus has the advantage of supporting constitutional government without carrying the subversive baggage of rights or encouraging the leveling effects of mass democracy.

SOLZHENITSYN AS A GUIDE TO THE TWO CITIES

To gain greater clarity about the application of Augustinian political principles in the modern world, I would like to discuss Alexander Solzhenitsyn, the former Soviet dissident and now-returned Russian exile. He is the primary inspiration for the view I am developing and may be the greatest Augustinian political thinker of the modern age, although he is not usually understood in such terms. Nevertheless, I think that the label "political Augustinian" fits Solzhenitsyn very well because the basic intellectual framework of his political thinking is the doctrine of the Two Cities, which he evidently took from the Gospels and from the residual Augustinian heritage in the Russian

Orthodox tradition. He uses this framework to understand the evils of communism as well as the moral decay of the West, fashioning a distinctive set of political views that opposes all forms of unified power— both totalitarian and theocratic—while also rejecting the modern Western theory of human rights (to the surprise and consternation of many Westerners). Solzhenitsyn's alternative to Soviet totalitarianism and Western liberalism has been worked out in several books over his career and provides a powerful illustration of the Augustinian principle of limited government under God and the prudential approach to politics that flows from it.

In an early work, *From Under the Rubble* (1974), Solzhenitsyn praises "the Blessed Augustine" for saying that a state without justice is no better than a band of robbers. He also develops Augustine's view that most states never achieve justice but still must be obeyed, although there is a point beyond which injustice becomes unbearable. To determine that precise point, Solzhenitsyn appeals to the doctrine of the Two Cities. He says: "In relation to the true ends of human beings here on earth . . . the state structure is of secondary significance. That this is so, Christ himself teaches us. 'Render to Caesar what is Caesar's'—not because every Caesar deserves it, but because Caesar's concern is not with the most important thing in our lives. . . . The state system which exists in our country is terrible not because it is undemocratic, authoritarian, based on physical constraint—a man can live in such conditions without harm to his spiritual essence. Our present system is unique because over and above its physical and economic constraints, it demands total surrender of our souls . . . [to] the conscious *lie*. To this putrefaction of the soul, this spiritual enslavement, human beings who wish to be human cannot consent. When Caesar, having exacted what is Caesar's, demands still more insistently that we render unto him what is God's—that is a sacrifice that we dare not make! The most important part of our freedom, inner freedom, is always subject to our will. If we surrender it to corruption, we do not deserve to be called human."[19]

At first glance, this appeal to God over Caesar seems to imply indifference to political freedom and political regimes, an error commonly attributed to St. Augustine himself. But Solzhenitsyn is not indifferent to politics (and neither was St. Augustine). What they believe, in precise terms, is that the "state structure is of secondary significance" compared to the spiritual realm. This is not indifference. It means the state has a definite but limited purpose which it may not legitimately exceed and which justifies resistance if it is exceeded. Yet, the standard of legitimacy is confusing to modern Western intellectuals because it is not set by an inviolable sphere of private rights in which one is free to do as one pleases. Rather, it is set by a permanent hierarchy of ends ordained by God, which makes the spiritual things of the soul and its "inner freedom" primary and relegates the material things of earthly happiness to secondary status, including the "external freedom" controlled by the state. Herein lies a criterion for distinguishing legitimate and illegitimate regimes that is derived from the Christian doctrine of the Two Cities rather than the Enlightenment doctrine of natural or human rights.

According to the Christian doctrine, a regime is legitimate if it respects the distinction between the Two Cities and confines the state to the limited ends of the temporal realm, even while recognizing that political leaders and nations are accountable to God for their actions. In contrast, a regime is illegitimate if it violates the distinction between the two realms by unifying sovereignty under one head—either in totalitarian fashion (where the secular state tries to absorb the church and the rest of social life); or in theocratic fashion (where the church tries to absorb the state by clerical rule or by making the tsar the head of the church). This is the most important practical application of the Two Cities: It does not require a specific form of government, but it does exclude those forms that destroy the distinctive roles and proper hierarchy of the Two Cities.

Accordingly, Solzhenitsyn is most vehemently opposed to totalitarian communism, because it raises the state to primary significance and attempts to crush the church and spiritual life with state-imposed atheism. He views totalitarianism as radically evil because it makes an idol of the secular state, allowing Caesar to usurp God's realm and corrupting the soul by destroying its inner freedom. Such tyranny is evil not only, or even primarily, because it suppresses external freedom and kills the body; it is evil because it causes spiritual enslavement to materialistic ideologies and kills the soul. Hence, it must be resisted or overthrown.

While highly critical of totalitarianism, Solzhenitsyn is also strongly opposed to theocracy, especially the Caesaro-Papism of the Orthodox tradition, because it, too, violates the distinction of the Two Cities. He says in *The Mortal Danger* (1980), "I have been repeatedly charged with being an advocate of a theocratic state, a system in which the government would be under the direct control of religious leaders. This is a flagrant misrepresentation. . . . The day-to-day activity of governing in no sense belongs to the sphere of religion. What I do believe is that the state should not persecute religion and that religion should make an appropriate contribution to the spiritual life of the nation. Such a situation obtains in Poland and Israel and no one condemns it; I cannot understand why the same thing should be forbidden in Russia."[20] Though this position may sound 'theocratic' to Western liberals who favor a completely secular society, it is actually a consistent application of the Two Cities doctrine, which requires distinct spheres and distinct personnel (civil vs. religious leaders) but not the elimination of religion from national life.

In Solzhenitsyn's view, the failure to maintain a proper distinction is precisely what has misled the Russian Orthodox Church over the years. In his *Lenten Letter to Patriarch Pimen* (1973), he rebukes Church leaders for surrendering the independence of the Church to the tsars over the past centuries and suggests that this attitude prepared the leaders of the Orthodox Church for collaboration with the communist authorities.[21] Solzhenitsyn's critique of the church's servility towards tsars and commissars sometimes looks backwards to the premodern age when religious purists, like the Old Believers, resisted the alliance of church and state. Yet, it is consistent with views expressed in *Rebuilding Russia* (1991) that look forward to the postcommunist age: "The Church will be helpful to our social recovery only when it . . . frees itself completely from the yoke of the state and restores a living bond with the people."[22] The implication is that the premodern relation of church and state is a model for the postmodern relation in recognizing a proper balance of the Two Cities—opposing state absolutism and secular totalitarianism as well as rejecting theocracy and messianic pretensions of the state, while preserving a vital role for spirituality in Russian national life.

From this perspective on church and state, Solzhenitsyn is prepared to be flexible about forms of government. As long as the state is limited, in the general sense of avoiding the unified sovereignty of totalitarianism or theocracy, and confines itself to the modest ends of the temporal realm while permitting the spiritual realm to flourish, it has a basic legitimacy. Under this generic notion of limited government, however, Solzhenitsyn recognizes a crucial difference between regimes that are restrained solely by the limited ideological ends they pursue and 'constitutional' regimes that deliberately limit power by law, institutions, and moral self-restraint. This leads him to a prudential ranking of three legitimate regimes that may be chosen as circumstances permit: (1) the least desirable choice (though still a "liveable or bearable" regime) is the moderate authoritarianism of traditional tsarism; (2) the most desirable choice is the constitutional monarchy of the early twentieth century under Tsar Nicholas II and Prime Minister Stolypin; and (3) a reasonable second choice is the constitutional democracy proposed in *Rebuilding Russia.* Let me comment briefly on each of these regimes in Solzhenitsyn's writings and explain his political judgments.

In the early works, *Letter to the Soviet Leaders* (1973), *From Under the Rubble* (1974) and *Mortal Danger* (1980), Solzhenitsyn advocates moderate authoritarianism as a transitional regime for Russia from communist totalitarianism to a new society. This is prudential in the sense of being tactically wise or expedient: It is a way of getting the existing authorities to renounce communism without having to give up their power. It also reflects a rather favorable view of traditional authoritarianism as well as a distrust of modern democracy, indicating an Augustinian pessimism about politics that few Western liberals would dare to think, let alone express. The only comparable view is Jeane Kirkpatrick's distinction between "authoritarian" and "totalitarian" regimes. She argues that moderately authoritarian regimes are legitimate because they are limited in scope, confining themselves to national security and civil order (even if they sometimes use repressive measures) while leaving alone the religion, customs, property relations, family structures, and cultural life of the nation; examples of this type of regime were the Iranian monarchy under the Shah, the

Somoza regime in Nicaragua, the Marcos regime in the Philippines, and Pinochet's Chile. In contrast to authoritarianism is totalitarianism. The latter is illegitimate, according to Kirkpatrick, because it is unlimited in scope. It uses the centralized power of the state to wipe out all secondary institutions and attempts systematically to transform human nature according to an ideological blueprint that inevitably leads to mass murder and concentration camps.[23] Like Kirkpatrick, Solzhenitsyn views traditional Russian tsarism as liveable or bearable because even its worst rulers had limits imposed by religion, rival elites, and local councils: "If such systems have functioned for centuries on end in many states, we are entitled to believe that, *provided certain limits are not exceeded*, they, too, can offer people a tolerable life, as much as any democratic republic can"; and "the majority of governments in human history have been authoritarian, but they have yet to give birth to a totalitarian regime" as did the weak democracies of Russia, Italy, Germany, and China.[24] Simply put, centuries of tsarism did not destroy whole classes of the Russian people, while seventy years of totalitarian communism nearly succeeded in doing so.

Yet, in subsequent writings, Solzhenitsyn indicates that traditional authoritarianism is a minimal standard and that constitutionally limited governments are preferable, as long as the true meaning of freedom is clearly understood. This point is often missed because Solzhenitsyn is so critical of Western societies for establishing legal structures of human rights without preserving a religious basis for. moral self-restraint. Indeed, Solzhenitsyn rejects the modern theory of rights as the basis of constitutional government because it has no inherent principle of self-limitation or self-sacrifice: "'Human rights' are a fine thing, but how can we be sure that our rights do not expand at the expense of the rights of others? . . . Most people in a position to enhance their rights and seize more will do precisely that. . . . Human freedom, in contrast, includes voluntary self-limitation for the sake of others." And, as Solzhenitsyn emphasizes, this is precisely "the true Christian definition of freedom."[25] The dilemma for Solzhenitsyn is that constitutional government requires legal limits to protect freedom, but such government is endangered by legalistic rights and requires a Christian basis that restricts the scope of freedom.

The reason for the dilemma is that political freedom is not an absolute good or an end-in-itself but a conditional good whose value is determined by the ends it serves. If freedom merely serves material well-being, it loses its value and becomes illegitimate. If it serves higher spiritual goods (the goods of the soul), its value and legitimacy are enhanced. But the goods of the soul that freedom is supposed to serve are often nurtured by severe forms of unfreedom—including imprisonment, war, suffering, and spiritual discipline that cultivate inner strength by suppressing external freedom or that develop the soul by repressing the body ("Bless you, prison, for nourishing my soul," Solzhenitsyn says at the end of *Gulag II*). The same paradox is expressed in another powerful statement by Solzhenitsyn: "Freedom of action and prosperity are necessary if man is to stand up to his full height on this earth; but spiritual greatness dwells in eternal subordination, in awareness of oneself as an insignificant particle."[26] Political freedom, then, is a first step toward higher ends because it gives man the pride and dignity to stand on his own and to be responsible for himself. But attaining the highest spiritual ends demands unfreedom in the sense of subordinating the self to a permanent hierarchy of being in which one is merely an insignificant particle.

Obviously, there is no perfect political solution to the paradoxical demands of freedom and higher obligation. They are as different as pride and humility. They can be perfectly reconciled only in a world where freedom is used for self-limitation in service to the highest good—a condition that would require a new historical stage, one that would replace the modern world as it has existed since the Renaissance in the West and inaugurate a Christian revival based on voluntary religious obligation.[27] Meanwhile, in the imperfect world of late modernity where the West is spiritually exhausted and Russia is in ruins, political freedom must be granted. But it must be accompanied with strict conditions, giving people political responsibility while surrounding them with political controls and cultural norms that encourage moral and spiritual development rather than materialism and laxity. Solzhenitsyn describes two constitutional regimes that establish the proper institutions and cultural atmosphere for controlled political freedom.

The best possible regime is the constitutional monarchy that existed in Russia during the Duma period of reform in the first decade of the twentieth century, nominally under Tsar Nicholas II but actually governed (from 1906 to 1911) by an extraordinary prime minister named Peter Stolypin. Solzhenitsyn analyzes this regime in a long chapter of *August 1914: The Red Wheel* devoted to Stolypin, who is clearly Solzhenitsyn's heroic ideal of a great statesman. The greatness of Prime Minister Stolypin was his courageous effort to "persuade Russia that the epoch of constitutional government was here to stay," even while resorting to extralegal action on occasion to achieve this goal. His program was a balancing act that sought to preserve the traditional basis of Russian authority in tsarism and Orthodox Christianity while implementing modern reforms—above all, land reform that would create a new peasant class of bourgeois citizens who would own and cultivate their own land and participate in local councils. This difficult combination of old and new—of tsarism and Jeffersonian democracy, as it were—required a fearless crackdown on revolutionary terrorists that put Stolypin and his family at great risk (eventually costing him his life) as well as astute political maneuvering to persuade the emperor of his plans and have them approved by the Duma. Solzhenitsyn's account of Stolypin describes the heroic statesman in the grandest terms: "His qualities were, in truth, kingly; a second Peter ruled Russia—as energetic as the first . . . as radical a reformer but with an idea that distinguished him from Peter the Great: 'To reform our way of life without damage to the vital foundations of our state and the soul of the people'." His assassination by terrorists, Solzhenitsyn concludes, was a tragedy for the whole twentieth century because only Stolypin could have saved Russia and the world from communist revolution.[28]

The Stolypin regime obviously depended on chance—on the survival of a single great man as well as the peculiar circumstances of a liberalizing autocracy—and could not serve as a durable model for Russia. Thus, when Solzhenitsyn finally published his concrete proposals for the postcommunist age in *Rebuilding Russia* (1991), he recommended neither tsarist authoritarianism nor constitutional monarchy but constitutional democracy. His frank admission that "the future Russian Union . . . will need democracy very much" indicates a change in practical judgment but not a break with his fundamental principles.[29] For he justifies democracy on prudential grounds, as a realistic approximation of Stolypin's vision in new and different circumstances.

Solzhenitsyn's prudential approach is evident in the denial that democracy or any regime is the ultimate form of government. Why, then, choose democracy? In the first place, he says, "we cannot be said to have much of a choice: The whole flow of modern history will unquestionably predispose us to choose democracy"—meaning it is an inevitable fact of the modern age; there is no going back to monarchy at the present time. But he warns against glorifying democracy, as some do by elevating it from a "particular state structure into a sort of universal principle of human existence, almost a cult." To make himself absolutely clear, Solzhenitsyn says we must choose democracy "as a means, not as an end in itself . . . not because it abounds in virtues, but only in order to avoid tyranny."[30] Its purpose, in the first place, is to establish stable order by protecting the people against tyrannical government and then to direct democratic freedom to moral and spiritual development as much as possible within the earthly city.

To achieve this balance, he says (in an echo of the Two Cities) that the Orthodox Church should be independent of the state so the church does not glorify the state or permit politics and nationalism to become primary. For "the more energetic the political activity in a country, the greater the loss to spiritual life. Politics must not swallow up all of a people's spiritual and creative energies." The same goes for economics: "Neither a market economy nor general abundance constitutes the crowning achievement of human life."[31] These arguments are the most sober endorsement of democracy that I have ever read. They do not appeal to the collective wisdom of the people or to the sovereignty of the people or to the rights of man; rather, they suggest that a constitutional democracy in which religion is disestablished while politics and economics remain secondary to spiritual activity— to Christian faith, family, and artistic life—can provide a tolerable or decent temporal order. To enhance that possibility, Solzhenitsyn sketches three crucial features of a future Russian democracy.

The first two features are derived from Stolypin's reforms adapted to the democratic age: "Stolypin believed that it is impossible to create a state governed by laws without first having independent citizens," meaning landowners who were also self-governing citizens. Thus, in postcommunist Russia, the first task is to restore private ownership of land and houses. Solzhenitsyn defends private property and free enterprise in "modest amounts . . . which [do] not oppress others" because they are "an integral component of personality." Private property and limited capitalism are necessary because they nurture mystic ties to the Russian land and strengthen the family, especially when men make an adequate salary so "women have the opportunity to return to their families to take care of the children." Private property and free enterprise also contribute to stability and a sense of fairness among people.[32] The second element of the Stolypin plan, which Solzhenitsyn advocates for the new democratic order, is local government, beginning with the long task of recreating the Russian village through local councils and face-to-face moral leadership. His models are the conservative cantons of Switzerland and the *zemstvoi* of nineteenth-century Russia applied to the village level. The whole scheme depends on these two elements—land ownership and village councils—because democracy must be built from the bottom up.

The third element is the national government, which should resemble a mixed regime rather than a purely democratic structure. The national legislative body should be a people's assembly chosen indirectly by the tiers of the *zemstvoi* system, each of which chooses the next higher level. The popular assembly will be balanced by an upper chamber consisting of "highly respected individuals of lofty moral character, wisdom, and rich experience" whose mission is to provide moral wisdom about legislation and to represent the different "estates" of society—a quasi-aristocratic advisory body that sounds like ancient Sparta's *gerousia* of venerable elders. Their purpose is to raise the tone of society above the popular tastes of mass democracy. A strong presidency will also be needed to assure national cohesion. The best guarantee for a unifying figure is a selection process that begins with nominations of candidates from the national assembly and offers the people a limited but genuine choice while avoiding divisive party campaigns.[33] The general vision is that of a Russian nation organized as a corporate hierarchy from the bottom up with participatory bodies at all levels for people of different kinds to make a contribution. Unlike most Western models, this is constitutional democracy with a corporatist character that seeks to establish a moral order among the people.

In making these proposals for the future of Russia, Solzhenitsyn provides a practical application of the Augustinian doctrine of the Two Cities. He shows how a Christian thinker can reject totalitarianism without embracing the Western theory of human rights and still advocate constitutionally limited government under God. Though he thinks that constitutional monarchy is the best regime, he recognizes its dependence on the special historical circumstances of the early twentieth century which no longer prevail. Therefore, Solzhenitsyn adapts his model to the present age and endorses a tempered and corporatist version of constitutional democracy as the best option for postcommunist Russia. It offers the best hope for protecting people from tyranny while directing democratic freedom to moral and spiritual development.

The Two Cities in the Modern Age

While many modern people might have misgivings about rethinking Christian politics and proposing an Augustinian alternative to Kantian human rights, I believe that the Two Cities doctrine and the hierarchy of being are not more dangerous foundations for political order than contemporary liberalism. Though liberalism may seem less frightening because it expresses skepticism or modesty about knowing ultimate ends, those expressions are actually a form of false modesty that disguise a rigid and stultifying dogmatism. The professed neutrality of the liberal state about the Good Life is merely a pretext for imposing an exclusive view of the Good Life. Though claiming to take no stand on the ultimate purpose of life, modern liberal democracy in fact promotes a life dedicated to middle-class materialism, popular entertainment, and secular humanism which it imposes through the aggressive marketing of modern culture in public education, the universities, the courts, mass media, and other instruments of opinion formation that many critics of mass society have aptly described as social tyranny. Even when liberal democracy is supported by Christian churches and theologians as an ethical imperative of human dignity rather than as materialism and secular humanism, it tends to produce the same results and even subverts the Christian faith by sapping its vital spiritual energies. Only by restoring belief in the true hierarchy of ends and treating modern liberal democracy as a prudent choice of the temporal realm, rather than an end-in-itself, can democracy be properly defended against its totalitarian enemies and its own tendencies toward degraded conformity. This is the important lesson that I have learned from the greatest Augustinian-Christian of our times, Alexander Solzhenitsyn.

My conclusion, therefore, is that there should be no reason to fear a revival of the doctrine of the Two Cities, the hierarchy of being, and prudential politics as an alternative to the belief in human rights and social contract that currently underlie liberal democracy. Not only is there no danger of tyranny in replacing Kantian Christianity with Augustinian Christianity, there is also hope for deliverance from democratic despotism. For the doctrine of the Two Cities opposes unified sovereignty and concentrated power in all its forms (whether totalitarian, theocratic, or democratic); and it promotes limited government under God, offering all the benefits of constitutionalism without the subversive baggage of liberalism. To complete this argument, I will attempt in the last chapter to develop a more detailed theory of Christian constitutionalism and to explain its superiority to contemporary alternatives.

CHAPTER FIVE

THE EARTHLY CITY: CONSTITUTIONAL GOVERNMENT UNDER GOD

E very historical age has convictions that are so deeply held that they seem beyond question or reproach. At the beginning of the twenty-first century, liberal democracy and its associated structures (such as market economies) are so widely accepted that questioning their justice and benevolence seems foolish or disloyal. Even the Christian churches and theologians who once fiercely opposed them now embrace them and have allowed spiritual and ethical teachings to be reshaped by them. I have called this development Kantian Christianity because it has brought the rights and dignity of the person into Christian theology, reshaping views of church and state as well as the practice of Christian charity. I also pointed out the problems with Kantian Christianity, especially its tendency to promote individual rights at the expense of spiritual hierarchies and to diminish the mission of otherworldly salvation in favor of social and political change. In order to restore the proper balance of the spiritual and political orders, I proposed recovering Augustine's doctrine of the Two Cities and offered a contemporary reformulation which I illustrated with the political teachings of Alexander Solzhenitsyn. In this chapter, I would like to refine the Augustinian alternative by developing it into a Christian theory of constitutional government and showing its advantages over other theories.

My principal claim is that Christianity does not require a specific form of government (such as democracy) nor a specific theory of social justice (such as human rights); but it does have a distinctive view of politics that can be summarized in the phrase "limited government under God" and that we can recognize today as a type of "constitutionalism." I am supported in this interpretation by several modern scholars who have found in Augustinian Christianity a theory of constitutional government.[1] One of the most impressive accounts is by H. Richard Niebuhr (the brother of the famous Reinhold) who wrote an essay titled "The Relation of Christianity and Democracy," in which he argues (much like I have been arguing in this book) that Christianity has no specific teaching about forms of government and that Christ "did not require a new government in place of the Roman monarchy." But, according to Niebuhr, this apparent indifference to forms of government does not imply the rejection of political responsibility. It means that Christianity elevates the spiritual above the political and opposes all attempts to absolutize or divinize political power, thereby fostering a "constitutionalist frame of mind." In Niebuhr's view, "the effect of prophetic faith has always been the limitation of government. . . . Early Christian martyrs who refused to worship Caesar, the monks who maintained their independence by abandoning all things over which despotism could exercise power, the Roman church with its self-sufficiency and its principle of natural law, Protestantism with its loyalty to the Scriptures, the sectarians with their resolute obedience to conscience—all these have barred the path to absolutism. The existence in human societies of a community which maintains . . . a loyalty beyond political loyalty always prescribes a limit to state power. . . . Thus, constitutionalism, the limitation of political power by written law considered as prior to the power, has been reinforced by a faith which seeks to obey a God whose will is known by revelation and reason."[2] The only point that needs to be added to Niebuhr's fine statement is that, even though God forbids man to absolutize political power, God also recognizes the necessity of political authority for maintaining civil peace and moral order and strengthens the state by making political obedience a religious duty. Thus, a Christian theory of constitutionalism upholds the state as God-given while limiting and tempering its powers.

From this formulation, one can see the points of similarity and difference between Christian constitutionalism and the dominant

conception today, namely, liberal constitutionalism. Both agree on
the need for limited government and for protections against the
tyrannical temptations of rulers and peoples. Hence, both agree on
the need for some kind of safeguards against abuses of power and for
removing certain spheres of life from the competence of the state.
While sharing common ground, however, the two conceptions differ
dramatically on the reasons for upholding and limiting the state and
on drawing the boundary lines for political power.

Christian constitutionalism is rooted in piety—in respect for the
absolute Lordship of God and the inherently limited ends of the temporal realm compared to the spiritual realm as well as the inherently
imperfect or corruptible nature of politics in the fallen world. The
underlying assumption is that God has established an order of being
made up of two different realms or "cities," with activities in the spiritual realm that are independent of and higher than the state and
those in the temporal or earthly realm that are a necessary and
natural part of the political order. The liberal conception of constitutionalism does not recognize this hierarchy of being. It is based on the
theory of natural rights or human rights which exist prior to the state
and must be protected by an artificial social contract that separates a
private sphere of civil society from the public sphere of the state. The
underlying assumption of liberalism is not a God-given hierarchy of
being but natural freedom and equality that make freedom an end-
in-itself or a means for enjoying the safety and security that accom-
pany protections from state power. Even when liberalism conceives of
natural rights as endowments of the Creator, the state recognizes an
inviolable private sphere in which one is free to pursue happiness as
one sees fit as long as one does not violate the law or take away the
rights of others.

Thus, the Christian theory of constitutionalism cannot be reduced
to the liberal distinction between a public sphere of legitimate state
authority and a private sphere of rights. The Christian distinction
between the spiritual and temporal realms means that the state is a
necessary, and even a noble, institution, requiring the support and
participation of citizens, soldiers, and statesmen; but the state is nevertheless of secondary importance compared to the spiritual realm.
The many facets of spiritual life that are not subject to the state are

off-limits because they transcend politics and are required by divine law, not because they are part of an inviolable private sphere of rights that inhere naturally in people. Although the liberal distinction between 'the public and the private' (or between 'state and society') may look like the Christian distinction between the 'temporal and spiritual,' the two theories are based on different conceptions of reality. The Christian conception is based on a hierarchy of being that is distorted when it is absorbed by, or adapted to, liberalism because liberalism treats what is higher and nobler as something that is merely 'private' or 'personal' and, therefore, in a sense lower than the state. The contrast is further evident in the fact that Christian constitutionalism subdivides the spiritual and temporal realms into multiple spheres of authority that resemble corporate bodies with hierarchical ruling elements, instead of free associations of individuals organized along democratic lines. At the root of these different constitutional theories are different conceptions of the order of being, the Christian one ascending from earthly to heavenly things and the liberal one confined to one-dimensional worldliness.

To illustrate more clearly the Christian conception of constitutionalism, I will show that it consists of two great realms, the spiritual and the temporal—the former guided by divine law and the latter by natural and human law—with subdivisions in each realm made up of diverse corporate bodies. On the one side, the spiritual realm consists of the church, the family, and the organizations and activities of Christian charity that are not merely private-voluntary associations (as liberalism would have us believe) nor 'mediating structures' (as neo-conservatives prefer to call them) but corporate spheres of spiritual authority derived from divine law. They are part of God's created order, existing prior to, and independently of, the state and often outranking the state in moral worth even though they may be subject to the jurisdiction of the state in certain external respects. Moreover, the spheres of spiritual authority are not inherently governed by principles of democratic consent or majority rule but have their own internal ordering principles from God's law that give them supernatural authority and mystical beauty. In addition to upholding spheres of spiritual authority, Christian constitutionalism upholds spheres of temporal authority, which exist as a consequence of the Fall and of man's social and rational nature. The latter make up the political regime in the broad sense, including the state, the economy, social classes, and the military. These institutions are not specifically determined by divine law and are allowed greater latitude than spiritual matters; they are left to prudence or practical applications of natural law which seek to establish the best possible means to temporal happiness in accordance with the fallen but rational nature of man.

The picture I shall draw of these diverse corporate bodies resembles in certain respects the "spheres of justice" approach of the secular thinker Michael Walzer. However, my deepest inspiration is the notion of "sphere sovereignty" developed by the Dutch Calvinist Abraham Kuyper and the Catholic doctrine of "subsidiarity," both of which try to articulate the appropriate associations for each level of political authority.[3] When brought together into a coherent theory of two realms, the diverse spheres make up a hierarchy of being that is the metaphysical basis of Christian constitutionalism.

CHURCH, FAMILY, AND CHARITY: THE SPHERES OF SPIRITUAL AUTHORITY

The distinction between spiritual and temporal realms is often easier to state in theory than to determine in practice. How do we know which institutions belong to which realm or where the lines should be drawn? A shorthand answer equates the distinction between spiritual and temporal realms—between the things of God and the things of Caesar—with the distinction between church and state. This is not sufficient, however, because the things of God are not confined to the institutional church. A more complete account would include everything that is spelled out in the New Testament as specifically instituted by God for the spiritual welfare and salvation of mankind and commanded by divine or revealed law (as distinguished from the natural law known by human reason). Using these criteria, I would argue that the spiritual realm is made up of the Christian church, the Christian family, and the activities of Christian charity. These institutions and activities are different from those of the temporal order because they are not merely 'from God' in a general providential sense nor are they simply products of human nature. They are spelled out with a higher degree of specificity in the New Testament than the state or the economy and embody an order of holiness and grace that other institutions cannot attain and are not designed to attain. The spheres of spiritual authority usually have a higher moral status than the temporal powers and must be respected and protected by them, not as elements of an inviolable private sphere, but as institutions of divine law that limit the state by their supernatural authority.

As institutions of divine law, the church and the family require conformity to a divine order of being that is above the human will. Thus, when we learn from the Bible and the Christian theological tradition that these institutions are not essentially democratic nor based on human rights but are corporate hierarchies based on reciprocal obligations (with only secondary elements of consent), we cannot simply dismiss the teachings of divine law as undemocratic and refashion them according to our own tastes. This point is not easy to admit today when all institutions are assumed to be social constructs whose legitimacy stems from majority rule or from the equal rights of all members. But the Gospels, Epistles, and the Christian theological tradition indicate that the Christian church and the Christian family are intended to be hierarchical, even patriarchal, in character; and this is not something we can ignore or rewrite because it offends modern democratic sensibilities.

Consider the Christian church. While its proper organization and structure have been disputed since its beginnings, all Christians hold that the foundation of the church is divine, supernatural, or mystical. Though human elements may have been added to it through custom, tradition, and conscious choice, the church is based on divine authority and exists for the sake of spiritual ends which it reveres as sacred mysteries. The disputes about its organization have produced many denominational claims; but, ultimately, they boil down to two models—the apostolic and the congregational models. The apostolic model holds that Christ personally established the institutional church through the Apostolic Succession (giving the Apostles sacramental powers and institutional authority which they then passed on to bishops and priests as their successors). The congregational model holds that the Holy Spirit instituted the church through the congregation which, on its own or in coordination with other congregations, chooses its ministers (who are primarily preachers of the Word and secondarily ministers of the sacraments). The apostolic model of authority is accepted by Roman Catholic, Eastern Orthodox, Anglican, and many Lutheran churches, while the congregational model is accepted by the reformed Protestant churches in a wide variety of forms (Calvinist or Presbyterian, Congregationalist, free-church Baptist and Anabaptist, Quaker meetings, and so forth).

It is not possible or necessary to examine here the many facets of this momentous debate about church organization in order to explain the principles of Christian constitutionalism. The main point is to acknowledge the existence of a sphere of divine origin, standing prior to and independent of the state, which is not merely a private-voluntary association but a mystical body—the "body of Christ," in Paul's words—possessing supernatural authority. Though this is the crucial point for constitutionalism, it may be useful to indicate why Catholics such as myself find the apostolic model of church authority more persuasive than the congregational model, making the church an essentially hierarchical structure that provides an important counterweight to the democratic cultures and totalitarian states of our times.

At the risk of reigniting some of the sectarian fires of the Reformation, I would argue that a preponderance of scriptural and historical evidence supports the view that Christ Himself founded the institutional church by choosing the Apostles and giving them spiritual authority and sacramental powers which they then passed on to their successors, the bishops of the church. Some of the influential passages of Scripture supporting the Apostolic Succession are the following: Christ's statement that Peter is the rock on which the institutional church will be built and His grant to Peter of spiritual authority over the church as represented by the keys to the kingdom of Heaven (Matt. 16:18–19); Christ's grant of authority to all the Apostles to settle disputes in the church in the Father's name (Matt. 18:17–18); Christ's grant of sacramental powers to all the Apostles, specifically the powers to forgive or to retain sins (John 20:22–23), to institute the Eucharist understood as His own body and blood (Luke 22:19–20;

John 6:48–58), and to baptize disciples in all nations (Matt. 28:19). Building on Christ's grant of spiritual authority and sacramental powers, the Apostles, especially Peter and Paul, then passed on His authority by the laying on of hands or other outward signs to special persons, as in the apostolic designation of Stephen by laying on of hands (Acts 6:5–6), Peter's laying of hands on certain Samaritans (Acts 8:14–18), Paul appointing elders in every church in Antioch (Acts 14: 23), and Paul designating Titus to appoint bishops and presbyters in every town of Crete (Titus 1:5–7). In this way, the Apostles designated as their successors those who became bishops (*episkopoi*, a title that originally meant overseers or stewards and was not always clearly distinguished from *presbyteroi* or elders in the Book of Acts), giving them spiritual authority by divine institution.

While the historical record beyond the New Testament is sketchy, it indicates that the Apostolic Succession was developed into the formal office of bishop or episcopal authority by the end of the first century or the beginning of the second century after Christ. According to the Eastern Orthodox tradition, the bishops were direct successors to the Apostles who first established the Christian church in five great cities (Rome, Constantinople, Alexandria, Antioch, and Jerusalem); those bishops eventually received the title Patriarch in recognition of their authority over a major ecclesiastical realm. Among the church fathers of the first and second century, the office of bishop was described and defended by important figures such as Clement of Rome (*Letter to the Corinthians*, sect. 42, 44), Irenaeus (*Against the Heresies*, III, ch. 3.1–3.4; IV, ch. 26.2), and Tertullian (*Rulings on Heresies*, sect. 20, 21, 32); and in the third and fourth centuries, by Cyprian (*On the Unity of the Catholic Church*, sect. 4–6; and *Letter* 33.1) and Eusebius (*Ecclesiastical History*, Bk. IV, chs. 19–27). Of these early authors, Irenaeus summarizes the succession most succinctly: "We can enumerate those who were appointed bishops in the churches by the Apostles, and their successors, down to our own day"; he then proceeds to name the succession in Rome established by Peter and Paul through twelve bishops and claims that the same may be done for the church in Asia minor (III, 3.1–3.4).[4] As both defenders and critics have shown, the doctrine and practice of episcopal authority led to a hierarchical church governed by bishops with recognition of the primacy of Peter, the bishop of Rome, and his successors, the popes—a church structure frequently described as the 'monarchical episcopate.'

While the claims of episcopal and papal hierarchy predominated, they were always contested in some fashion by models of church authority that were more congregational or consensual. For the Book of Acts shows not only the model of Apostolic Succession, but also the council of Jerusalem presided over by Peter and the Apostles that included the whole congregation in some decisions and other Christian communities outside of Jerusalem converted by Paul that made consensual decisions as congregations (Acts 1:23–26; 15:6–23). In addition, all Christians were charged with the apostolic mission of spreading the faith and were included in Paul's description of the church as the "body of Christ," whose various parts are motivated by the same Holy Spirit to work together like the organic parts of the body. One might also note the historical fact that appointing bishops in the early church occurred not only by the designation of the Apostles and fellow bishops but sometimes included the input of emperors, priests, and local people. Yet, at best, this shows that the early church in some instances acted as a mixed form of government—a combination of hierarchical elements from above and popular elements from below (as in the description in Acts 15:22, "it seemed good to the apostles and the elders, with the whole church, to choose men . . . and send them to Antioch"). To sustain the congregational model, one must take a part of the story and turn it into the whole story, exaggerating the influence of the democratic elements and denying entirely the apostolic hierarchies and sacramental priesthood instituted by Christ Himself.

Thus, the hierarchical church, called by Paul the "body of Christ," has the preponderance of scriptural and historical evidence on its side. Of the several apostolic churches—the Anglican Church, headed by the archbishop and king or queen of England; the Eastern Orthodox Church, headed by the patriarch of Constantinople and the various national patriarchs; and the Roman Catholic Church, headed by the pope in communion with the bishops—the Roman Catholic is the most centralized and hierarchical. But even the

Catholic Church resembles a constitutional monarchy rather than an absolute monarchy because it possesses elements of consent and has limitations set by canon law and tradition. The elements of consent, worked out through tradition and theology, include the use of General Councils to define doctrine and the election of the pope by the College of Cardinals representing the whole Church. The Church is thus a corporate hierarchy that includes the entire community of the faithful and that is limited by divine law, canon law, and tradition (understood as the continuously evolving deposit of faith). This organization means that the pope is not an absolute monarch who can decree whatever he wants (even the pope and the councils together could not change the doctrine of the Trinity to become four persons in one God or change the number of sacraments from seven to ten). Instead, the Catholic Church is a spiritual power organized as an elective constitutional monarchy and bound by the ancient and continuous deposit of faith.

As the most important corporate body of the spiritual realm, the institutional church, in all of its forms and varieties, plays a crucial role in Christian constitutionalism by acting as a counterweight to the democratic cultures and totalitarian states of modern times. We are most familiar with the churches as counterweights to dictatorial regimes—for example, the decisive role of the Catholic Church in opposing communism in Poland and central Europe, in opposing the Marcos regime in the Philippines, and, more generally, in promoting what Samuel Huntington calls the "third wave" of democratization among the nations of the Third World.[5] We are also familiar with the role of the Anglican and Evangelical churches in opposing apartheid in South Africa and of the black Baptist churches in coalition with other churches leading the civil rights movement in America. We are less familiar with the idea that, in the age of mass democracy, the church as a hierarchical institution with a nonsecular foundation stands as a bulwark against the leveling tendencies of democracy. It performs this role by repeatedly insisting that the church's positions on doctrines and morals are not subject to majority rule and that its selection of ministers, priests, and bishops should not be subject to secular notions of professional calling or individual rights. This antidemocratic stance of the church is an important facet of constitutionalism that goes beyond the ordinary checks and balances of a legal order and opposes the social tyranny of public opinion with the higher claims of divine authority. Nothing is more important for limiting political power and social tyranny in the democratic age than to remind the people continuously that their will is not entirely sovereign—that there exists a higher spiritual world, governed by divine law and church authority, that is beyond their jurisdiction to determine.

The second major institution of Christian constitutionalism that lies in the spiritual realm is the family. It may sound strange to refer to the family as a sphere of spiritual authority when it has natural roots in biology, psychology, and economics: The family is a naturally occurring union of male and female that exists for the purposes of procreation and child rearing, for the psychological well-being provided by shared love and a sense of belonging, and for other natural needs such as economic production and consumption. While the natural basis of the family is undeniable and natural law governs it in certain respects, nature does not reveal the whole truth about the family.

For the sexuality that lies at the heart of the family—namely, male-female sexual differentiation—cannot be understood by natural causes alone. It is a divine mystery. Male and female are not merely natural categories because nature does not absolutely require two sexes in order to provide for the continuation of the human species (nature could have devised other modes, such as asexual reproduction or multisexual reproduction). The Bible points to the divine mystery of sexuality in Genesis by teaching that the creation of male and female and their union for procreation are part of God's created order. In fact, the Bible teaches that the two sexes are part of the "image of God" intended for reproduction and dominion over the earth: "So God created man in His own image . . . male and female he created them . . . and said to them, 'Be fruitful and multiply, and fill the earth and subdue it.'" The implication is that the human power to procreate is an image of the divine power to create. It foreshadows the biblical teaching that childbirth is a miracle and gift of God rather than a purely natural process (as every infertile couple, from the time of Abram and Sarai to the modern world, are painfully forced to recognize when they discover that childbirth is beyond natural and even technological powers to control). The Bible also teaches that human procreation is different from animal reproduction because humans seek not merely to continue the species but to acquire personal immortality through their children which, after the Fall, becomes a way of recovering some of the lost immortality of the first parents. Thus, the second reference to the image of God in Genesis (5:1–3) says: "When God created man, He made him in the likeness of God. Male and female He created them . . . and named them Man [adam]. . . . When Adam had lived a hundred and thirty years, he became the father of a son in his own likeness, after his image, and named him Seth." In this passage, the spiritual basis of the family emerges from its biological covering: Just as God makes male and female in His image, so, with God's blessing, they make children in their personal image which continues beyond their death. Human beings may therefore resemble the apes in certain outward aspects of reproduction, but a higher dimension of reality is operating in human procreation. Human sexuality is a divine creation and mystery that points not only to the miracle of childbirth but also to the desire for personal immortality and therewith to conscious awareness of the supernatural destiny of man.

For these reasons, the institution of marriage is divinely commanded and highly exalted in Judaism and Christianity. Marriage begins monogamously with Adam and Eve but is temporarily distorted by polygamy in the Old Testament. The probable reason that God allows polygamy among the Israelites, while intending monogamy as the ideal, is to increase their numbers in accordance with His promise to Abraham to make his descendants as numerous as the stars. The emphasis on immortality through the extended family and tribe is a physical or carnal image of God's eternity in the people Israel which will be superceded, but not abolished, by the spiritual immortality promised by Christ. In accordance with the new promise, the original monogamy of Adam and Eve is restored; and marriage is elevated by Christ to the dignity of a sacrament: a sacred union made by God intended to last forever. As the Gospel states, "What God has joined together, let no man put asunder" (Matt. 19:6)—a clear indication that monogamous marriage is not a social contract nor merely a natural association but a divinely ordained indissoluble union. From these biblical injunctions, we may infer that the Christian family is a heterosexual and monogamous union commanded by divine law for the sake of procreation and love, an image of God in human beings in their longing for immortality and self-giving love.

These features alone make the Christian family controversial in modern democratic society where gay rights, abortion rights, and feminism challenge the natural and divine foundation of the family. But these are not the only challenges it faces. The Christian family is also controversial because it is undemocratic in its structure of authority, that is to say, it is patriarchal in some sense of the word. I remind people of this inconvenient fact because one cannot deny that a fair reading of the Bible and the Christian theological tradition indicates that God has appointed the father to be the head of the household. How many times does it say in the New Testament that wives should obey their husbands as a duty to the Lord?[6] Having reminded people of the admonition, I must add that it is important to be clear about what it means. The scriptural passages do not say that the father is appointed head of the household as a natural superior in practical intelligence, as the Greek philosopher Aristotle argued. Nor does Scripture simply say that the father is head of the household in order to perform service-leadership, as the Christian men's movement, the "Promise Keepers" have emphasized.[7] Rather, the father is divinely appointed to be an 'authority figure' for the family. Thus, it is said that wives are obligated to obey husbands not as natural superiors but as "a duty to the Lord," meaning God has created a certain hierarchical order of things which fathers, mothers, and children are supposed to respect because it is God's will and command. It is an impersonal duty to the Lord rather than a personal submission to a man. Accordingly, Paul adds the strong language of divinely ordained hierarchy to describe the family: As God is the head of Christ, and Christ is the head of man, so man is the head of woman (1 Cor. 11:3–9). To this statement of hierarchy, Paul immediately adds the notion of mutual dependence, "Nevertheless, woman is not independent of man nor man of woman, in the plan of the Lord" (ibid., 11:11). Though it offends modern democratic sensibilities to hear these statements, they indicate that the family is designed to follow a corporate order of divine creation based on reciprocal obligations.

It should also be noted that the hierarchical ordering of the family has been accepted by nearly all cultures of the world for most of recorded history, including America as recently as one generation ago. This practice reflects a widespread consensus that is often overlooked by the 'multiculturalists' who advocate greater appreciation of non-Western cultures, which should give them a greater appreciation for Asian, African, and Middle Eastern cultures which follow patriarchal patterns of authority in the family. Yet, the logic behind this near-universal pattern, to reiterate my point, is not purely natural, although sex roles in traditional societies fit the natural patterns of masculinity and femininity far better than the modern claim that men and women are interchangeable. It is undeniable, for example, that fathers play a decisive role as natural 'authority figures' in most well-ordered families. One only has to read about the proneness of fatherless young men to crime, gangs, and other social pathologies to acknowledge the point that a masculine father figure provides a type of authority that mothers or female teachers cannot provide.[8] But the harmony between God's order and the order of the cultural and natural worlds is not the only point to consider. The crucial point behind the biblical view of the family is that obedience to a divinely ordained pattern makes the submission dignified rather than servile: It is a duty "to the Lord" not to a particular human being, and all parties are bound by higher obligation. In following an impersonal order of creation, the heart is freed from the arrogance of rule or the resentment of obedience and becomes more capable of sustaining a loving partnership in mutual dependence than it is under the contested claims of rights where everyone seeks to be free of dependence and obligations.

While the Christian view of family authority requires impersonal obedience to the Lord's plan rather than to individual desire, the actual choice of marriage partners is personal; and this selection requires the consent of husband and wife. Christian marriage is therefore partly impersonal or handed down from above, and partly personal or freely chosen. In recognition of the Christian ideal of marriage as the voluntary consent to wed another for the sake of a

higher good, most Christian churches have held that marriage is
not legitimate unless the partners freely consent to the union. Even
the Scholastic theologian Thomas Aquinas argues that marriages
arranged by parents or by masters of servants may be rejected by children or servants if they choose a celibate life instead of marriage or
oppose the arrangement. Thomas's teaching is that no one may be
married against his or her will (*S. Th.*, II-II, 104.5).

In sum, the Christian family is a partnership in love, voluntarily
entered into in accordance with divine law, which recognizes the
father as the head of the household and requires husband and wife to
cooperate in the procreation and raising of children. It has a divine
status because it is formed from a man and a woman who are made in
the image of God and whose union provides a partial means of recovering the lost immortality of humanity in this life, while pointing to
our supernatural destiny and spiritual immortality in the world to
come. The divine status of the family is so deeply embedded in Christian theology that the Savior Himself is part of a Holy Family, and the
language of the Holy Trinity, used to describe God's inner relations,
includes the language of Father and Son. Thus, it may be said that
both the Christian family and the Christian church have origins in the
mystery of divine love, permitting an order of charity in the church
and in the family to a greater degree than in other institutions
(though, of course, there are many rotten families and many rotten
churches that are far from the image of God). Nevertheless, it cannot
be said of most other institutions that they are the image of God or the
body of Christ. The state, the economy, social classes, and the military,
as we shall see, are natural or conventional institutions established
for temporal welfare rather than authorities ordained by divine law
for spiritual ends.

A third type of institution that qualifies as a sphere of spiritual
authority is formed for the purpose of promoting Christian charity.
Like the church and the family, the works of charity are directly commanded in the New Testament as part of divine law. Just as Christ
declared Peter to be the rock on which the institutional church should
be built, and just as Christ proclaimed marriage to be an institution
that "God has joined together . . . [which] no man can put asunder," so
Christ says that, in order to attain eternal life, one must feed the

hungry, give drink to the thirsty, clothe the naked, welcome the stranger, comfort the sick, and visit the imprisoned (Matt. 25:34–46). These actions, traditionally referred to as 'corporal works of mercy,' can be done individually, of course, and do not necessarily require charitable organizations or spiritual societies; but they frequently take institutional forms. Some of the most familiar ones that have been established by Christian societies over the centuries are: hospitals, foster homes, orphanages, relief agencies for victims of natural disaster and human abuse, homeless shelters, soup kitchens, societies for the redemption of slaves, prison chaplaincies, and missions for reforming souls and spreading the Gospel. We still recognize these today as nonprofit or charitable organizations. Many are run by lay people, but many take the form of religious orders devoted to charity—the Franciscan orders, practicing evangelical poverty and dedicated to the relief of the poor, or the Sisters of Charity, founded by Mother Theresa for the purpose of caring for the destitute.

To gain some idea of the scope of these charitable organizations and religious orders in Christian civilization, one may turn to an impressive work called *The Genius of Christianity*, written by a Frenchman named Chateaubriand in 1802 for the purpose of defending the Christian religion against modern skepticism by describing its benefits to civilization—its contributions to morality, politics, philosophy, art, science, and benevolence or humanity. One chapter is devoted to showing how Christian civilization has incorporated charitable organizations into the fabric of society as a direct consequence of Christian divine law, challenging the ancient pagan practices of treating unwanted people by inflicting infanticide, slavery, or prostitution on them and replacing the cruel pagan practices with institutions of charity. Among the most moving accounts of charitable organizations that Chateaubriand describes are: the Hospitals dedicated to St. Lazarus, attended by monks of the order of St. Basil, who "received such leprous persons as, renounced by their relatives, were languishing in the streets of the cities, to the horror of the passers-by"; the Order of Religious Penitents in Germany and France which "rescued from vice unfortunate females who were in danger of perishing from want" after leading lives of prostitution; the Hospital of the Holy Ghost in Rome where "it is forbidden to follow such persons as come to deposit orphans at the door"; the orders of St. Vincent de Paul, "founder of the Foundling Hospital, the hospital for the aged poor, the hospital for the galley-slaves at Marseilles . . . and the fraternities of Charity . . . [who with] Mademoiselle Legras, instituted [in 1633] the Daughters of Charity." Also described by Chateaubriand are the unknown sisters of the Hotel Dieu who cared for the sick with such devotion that they "habitually live with a slow fever which consumes them . . . from the vitiated atmosphere they breathe" and the monks who lived "in the mines of the New World, at the bottom of which, amid eternal night, they have founded hospitals for the unfortunate Indians" forced to work there.[9] These heroic acts of charity by religious orders constitute spheres of spiritual authority and provide models for ordinary acts of charity by individuals and organizations.

Unlike the church and the family, the institutions of Christian charity have no fixed rule of organization laid down by divine law. While they are inherently communal or fraternal in their cooperative endeavors, they are not intrinsically hierarchical or democratic in structure, though many are founded and organized by single individuals of saintly character who often possess extraordinary energy, charisma, and towering moral authority. Whatever their internal structures, charitable organizations, like the church and the family, are commanded by divine law and are prior to and independent of the state. The state, therefore, has an obligation to protect the Christian church, the Christian family, and the practices of Christian charity, although there is no fixed or precise rule for how this should be done. Greater or lesser degrees of support may be required depending on the circumstances.

Minimally, protecting the spheres of spiritual authority would mean 'Doing No Harm'—permitting freedom of exercise without persecuting or suppressing them. In the case of the church, this is a crucial point because it would mean that divine law does not absolutely require the special privilege of religious establishment; but divine law does require some freedom to operate, a policy that St. Augustine formulated in *The City of God* (19.17) as a minimal policy of "no hindrance" to the true religion of the heavenly city as it dwells like a pilgrim in the earthly city. Maximally, some have argued that the divine law mandating spheres of spiritual authority means creating a confessional state or theocracy—establishing the Catholic, Calvinist, or Orthodox religion by law. But, as I argued in chapter four, though these views have been prominent at different periods of history (in the Catholic Middle Ages, in Calvinist Geneva, in Puritan America, in Orthodox Russia, and so on), they are not absolutely required by the Gospels, Epistles, or the doctrine of the Two Cities which create a distinction, though not a separation, of the spiritual and political realms and view the state as a divinely ordained institution for the limited ends of the temporal realm. From these observations, I infer that the maximal position the state might adopt in accordance with the Two Cities and its corollary, constitutional government under God, could include but does not require the religious establishment of a specific confession or church. Indeed, as a general rule, religious establishment is not a wise idea; the Christian state operates well in most circumstances when it promotes, not confessional orthodoxy, but a nondenominational brand of civic piety—publicly acknowledging the existence of God as the divine source of created order and the foundation of all human authority without requiring state officials or laws to confess denominational creeds. The most one should legitimately demand of the temporal realm (especially in the present historical circumstances) is the expression of nondenominational piety by state officials and state policies which promote the unhindered flourishing of the Christian church, the Christian family, and Christian charity. This posture would create a positive climate of opinion among the citizen body that is open to the transcendent demands of spiritual life—a climate beyond a materialistic culture, in which the Creator of the universe is recognized as the foundation of the state and in which religious beliefs and holy days permeate the culture without making the state responsible for the salvation of souls (which is the job of the church rather than the state).

In this day and age of democratic equality and aggressive secular culture, even the minimal position of 'no hindrance' or 'doing no harm' to the spheres of spiritual authority may entail some firm, countercultural measures. The legislative and judicial bodies of the modern democratic state need to lower the wall separating church and state in order to permit the traditional practices of nondenominational prayer in public schools, graduation ceremonies, official state events, courtrooms, military parades and funerals, as well as permitting faith-based prison chaplaincies and welfare programs. The state also needs to protect the Christian family by promoting profamily legislation—such as the Defense of Marriage Act passed by the U.S. Congress in 1996, defending monogamous heterosexual marriage as the norm for official state purposes. It should promote prolife legislation in order to protect the sanctity of innocent human life; and it should make divorce extremely difficult or nearly impossible in order to protect the union of male and female and to encourage the procreation and proper rearing of children. Protecting the family would also mean some curbs on contemporary feminism to ensure that the divinely ordained and natural distinctions between men and women are not lost in today's unisex society. This would mean, for example, opposing the military experiment of gender-integrated training and permitting women in combat. And it would entail reeducating modern citizens to reject the unnatural and unspiritual idea that men and women are simply interchangeable and that motherhood and homemaking are unworthy tasks of modern educated women. The confusion of sexual roles that disrupts modern societies is a direct result of the one-dimensional materialism and hyperdemocracy of modern life that has virtually shut down the spiritual spheres of authority and equated personal worth with nothing higher than a marketable technical skill.

In addition to defending the church and the family, the state must protect the institutions and activities of Christian charity from the intrusions of state power that might subvert them for secular ends. For example, a socialist or communist government that shuts down religious charities and attempts to replace them (however inadequately) with state agencies must be opposed. A culture of capitalism that emphasizes work-for-profit as the only honorable activity and makes voluntary Christian charity seem foolish or unproductive must also be resisted. Even though private wealth is a precondition for the exercise of charity, one must be critical of arguments developed by neoconservatives such as Michael Novak which treat free-market economics as an inherently spiritual activity. As we shall see, the economy is largely a prudential choice, a matter of finding the best means to manage temporal goods rather than a way of promoting spiritual goods.

In recognition of the spiritual bodies that properly limit the centralized state and restrain the marketplace, Catholic social teaching in the twentieth century developed the doctrine of subsidiarity. Literally, "subsidiarity" means sitting back in reserve in order to help if needed. Politically, it means that the centralized state should be held in reserve and should not take over functions which lower levels of government and nongovernmental associations can properly perform. As the *Catechism of the Catholic Church* (par. 1885) says: "The principle of subsidiarity is opposed to all forms of collectivism; it sets limits for state intervention"; it also curbs individualism by recognizing that people need associations to rise above their isolated selves. In accordance with the modern turn in Christian theology, the Church now justifies the doctrine of subsidiarity in terms of the "rights and dignity of the human person" and shies away from traditional arguments for limiting the powers of government derived from the Two Cities and the hierarchy of being. The Church has chosen to speak in the language of Kantian Christianity about the human person rather than in the language of Augustinian or Thomistic Christianity about the inherently limited ends of the temporal realm. Thus, Catholic social teaching justifies subsidiarity by saying, "the human person is . . . the principle, the subject, and the end of all social institutions."[10] This strategy has a certain rhetorical advantage in a world that knows and respects only modern categories of thought; it encourages the decentralization of power out of respect for the rights and responsibilities of the human person.

Though attractive in many ways, the strategy of justifying social doctrine by appealing to the "human person" rather than to the "Two Cities" may be a short-term advantage. For the Church must remind people repeatedly that the human person is not simply a material individual focused on personal fulfillment but a spiritual and social being directed to supernatural ends and the common good. This means, of course, that the human person cannot be adequately understood without reference to the true hierarchy of being and the priority of the spiritual over the temporal realms. And, in fact, the discussion of subsidiarity in the *Catechism* is immediately followed by a reminder that, in organizing society, "respect must be accorded to the just hierarchy of values, which 'subordinate physical and instinctual dimensions to interior and spiritual ones.'"[11] Would it not be wiser to face this issue at the beginning of the discussion of subsidiarity rather than at the end? Would it not be better to say that the Two Cities defines the principle and ends of social institutions and that the human person is derived from it?

Unless the rights of persons are clearly specified from the outset as serving the true hierarchy of ends, those rights will be seen in contemporary secular terms and will weaken subsidiarity by increasing demands to expand the centralized bureaucratic state. It would be wiser to say that rights are not so much attributes of the human person as they are duties or obligations which divine law makes on the state to limit its power—commands to the state to respect the corporate bodies of spiritual life rather than to protect a blanket right for persons to pursue happiness as they see fit. If this is not understood by modern citizens, the rights of the human person will relentlessly subvert the spiritual authorities—the church's divine foundation, the family's divine and natural structure, the charitable spirit of self-giving love—that subsidiarity is meant to protect. In short, it is the corporate spheres of spiritual authority that are the real justification for subsidiarity—for limiting government and decentralizing power. Such spheres appeal to higher goods rather than to private rights and arise from the supernatural and mystical basis of society that cannot be absorbed by the state.[12]

This Christian conception of constitutionalism may sound like theocracy to secular liberals rather than a version of limited government. It may even frighten them insofar as it is makes claims of knowledge about the true hierarchy of being (about the ends for which man is designed by God and by nature) rather than the usual skepticism about the ends of life expressed by liberal philosophers. But the Christian constitutionalism that I have been sketching is more limited than the theocracy of the early American Puritans and more limited than contemporary liberalism in its ambitions for the earthly city.

For liberalism, as I have argued, is dogmatic and hegemonic in its worldly ambitions, despite its denials. While pretending to be neutral and open-ended, it has very definite ideas about where society ought to be going and promotes its vision of the Good Life with all the weapons of cultural hegemony and state power. Indeed, the dominant form of liberalism today—the 'Big Government' of the modern welfare state—is highly intrusive in the imposition of secular liberal values. It establishes public schools that systematically indoctrinate young people in secular humanism and prohibit the free expression of religion; it attempts to redefine masculinity and femininity by changing the culture of the family, the workplace, and the military; it launches its own versions of moral crusades, such as antismoking, which prohibit smoking in the workplace and even in some barrooms; it requires universities to change their admissions policies for affirmative action and their athletic spending for women; it is trying to restructure a 'private association' such as the Boy Scouts to diminish its moral opposition to homosexuality and to repudiate its religious roots; and in some European countries, the welfare or 'nanny state' has begun to reconstitute the family by prohibiting parents from spanking their children, nationalizing day care, and requiring men to be resocialized for homemaking. Overall, a Christian theory of constitutionalism, though asserting the common spiritual destiny of mankind and promoting orthodoxy in the spiritual realm, is more open to the diversity of political regimes than liberalism, which demands a homogeneous world culture of secular democracy and free-market capitalism or the welfare state and imposes it with all the political, military, and economic means at its disposal (not excluding the prospect of a system of international law that will coercively impose a regime of secular liberalism under the United Nations or the European Union).

Temporal Authority and Christian Prudence

While the spheres of spiritual authority are directed to eternal life and are determined by divine law, the spheres of temporal authority have more modest ends and are determined by lesser laws. That is because temporal authority, though sanctioned by God, is not specifically spelled out by divine revelation; it exists as a consequence of the Fall and as an outgrowth of man's political and rational nature. Though divine law indirectly effects temporal affairs, it allows a fair amount of latitude for prudence to determine the organization of the state, the economy, society, and military matters. In approaching these matters, however, prudence in its proper Christian sense is not reducible to political expediency. Genuine prudence relies on an objective idea of the goods of the temporal realm and of the capacities of human beings for political life, which theologians have formulated into theories of natural and human law. To understand this approach, we need to understand what is meant by Christian prudence and how it works in the temporal realm.

Prudence, of course, is practical wisdom. It is the ability to choose the right course of action in a given situation, as distinguished from theoretical wisdom which aims at knowledge for its own sake. Though prudence is not an inherently Christian notion, it can be found in the Bible, for example, in the book of Wisdom, ch. 8:7, where it is listed along with courage, moderation, and justice as one of the four virtues of a righteous life (reminding one of Plato). It is also described in the opening chapters of Proverbs, where prudence is given the more Hebraic sense of worldly wisdom informed by fear of the Lord. Whether the authors of these books of the Bible were influenced by Greek philosophers is difficult to determine; but the Greek philosophers were the first to offer systematic expositions of prudence that deeply influenced later Christian theologians. The two most influential examples are Aristotle and Aquinas, whose classic definitions will guide our discussion.

In the *Nicomachean Ethics* (chapter six), Aristotle defines prudence as "deliberating well about the good life," which involves choosing the best possible means for attaining happiness. This formulation emphasizes the practical nature of prudence and distinguishes it from pure theory or science, but it does not show one how to make the right choices. Aristotle's doctrine of the Golden Mean (in chapter two) is a more helpful guide to choosing well because it shows that the path to happiness lies in habitual dispositions which avoid the extremes of passion. Those habits, known as the moral virtues, enable one to choose the right behavior in the right circumstances. But even the Mean is often too formal for making concrete choices. Aristotle's *Politics* actually provides the most help in understanding prudence because it raises the most comprehensive practical question—the question of the best regime or the best form of government—and answers it by presenting a standard of perfection while leaving the concrete decision to the acting statesman or legislator. The standard is "the good life," a self-sufficient existence in which the best citizens enjoy the leisure to exercise the full range of virtues in political activity and philosophy. Since the good life is rarely attained in its fullest degree, Aristotle ranks political regimes by their ability to approximate it: The best regimes are kingship or aristocracy because they attain the good life in large measure; the decent or average regimes are polity or democracy because they realize it very imperfectly; and the worst regimes are oligarchy and tyranny because they actively repress it. By sketching a hierarchy of perfection and stressing the instability and shortcomings of all regimes, Aristotle teaches the prudent statesman to seek the best possible regime for attaining the good life that circumstances will permit. Aristotelian prudence is thus the 'art of the possible'—the quest for perfection in the imperfect world of politics.

Christian prudence builds on Aristotelian prudence by deepening its understanding of the good life and the imperfections of the world. This may not be obvious at first glance because Aristotle's greatest student, St. Thomas Aquinas, follows the Philosopher with only a few modifications of the formal definitions. Aquinas defines prudence as choosing the best possible means for attaining the end of happiness and the application of the universal principles of morality to particular circumstances (*S. Th.*, II-II, 47.3 and 47.15). Though seeming to add little to the classical conception of prudence, Christian political thinkers nevertheless give it a new and, in a way, greater significance than the classical philosophers. For, as we have seen, Christianity is guided by the distinction between the Two Cities—a doctrine that highlights the disparity between the perfections of the city of God or heavenly city and the imperfections, corruptions, and vanities of all activities in the earthly city or fallen world. As every Christian is keenly aware, decisions in the earthly city are approximations of higher goods that are impossible to attain fully in this life and thus require prudential accommodations to the fallen world.

Christian anthropology also deepens the classical view of human nature by bringing out more emphatically than the Greek philosophers the dual nature of man—the duality in every human being, not only between the rational and irrational parts of the soul, but also between the divine part that is made in the image of God and the lower part corrupted by sin and inclined toward depravity. Christian prudence takes its bearings from the division of the Two Cities and the dual natural of man, seeking the best approximation of perfection 'this side of Heaven' before the Second Coming when the divisions will be overcome by the return of the Messiah and the establishment of the kingdom of God. As Oliver O'Donovan shows in his book, *The Desire of the Nations: Rediscovering the Roots of Political Theology*, Christian politics is inherently prudential because it takes place during the *saeculum,* the time of incomplete redemption from the birth of Christ to the end of the world. In this period, which is literally the secular or temporal age (the age of time), all political power is conditional and all political judgments are imperfect approximations of an elusive perfection.[13] Thus, Christianity deepens and expands the classical conception of prudence by extending the hierarchy of perfection from this world to the next and by developing a keen sense of the imperfections of this world due to original sin that will not change until the end of time.

In the Christian hierarchy of perfection, the highest good is salvation, the happiness of those who enjoy the everlasting vision of God in Heaven (the beatific vision). As the final end of the spiritual realm, eternal happiness is dimly approximated on earth by an order of charity, holiness, and grace that can be found in the church, the family, the works of charity, contemplative prayer, and works of art that glorify the beauty of God's creation. Since the spiritual realm is spelled out by divine law in absolute terms, prudence would seem to have no role here. Yet even in the spiritual realm, prudential applications of divine law are needed because the perfection that is commanded is often impossible to carry out to the fullest degree on earth.

This may be inferred from the greatest statement of Christian ethics, the Sermon on the Mount. In this sermon, Jesus gives a new definition of righteousness that seems impossible to attain and may be deliberately designed to humble His most devout followers. Jesus says, for example, that we should pluck out our eyes if they bring sexual temptation, but He does not say if this is meant to be applied literally. He says that we should not resist an evildoer, but He does not say what should be done if a child is threatened by injury or harm. He says that we should make no plans for tomorrow in order to depend entirely on the providence of the heavenly Father, but He does not say how we are to provide for our families. And, in the most difficult command of all, He says that we should "be perfect even as the heavenly Father is perfect," but He does not say how we can be as perfect as God. As statements of perfection, these ideals are impossible to achieve fully in this life by mortal human beings, even by the most holy and saintly. The Sermon on the Mount thereby reveals Christianity's radical spirituality and radical otherworldliness. It also makes prudence of some kind necessary in order to apply the highest spiritual ideals in the fallen world, on the assumption that approximations are possible and that mercy and forgiveness will be granted for the inevitable shortcomings.

If this is the role of Christian prudence (and mercy) in the spiritual realm, how does prudence work in the temporal realm where expectations are lower? The ends or goods of the temporal realm are lower than those of the spiritual realm because they do not directly concern eternal salvation or the order of charity, holiness, and grace. The temporal realm deals with worldly things, such as politics, economics, social status, and war. Surprisingly, the lower ranking of the goods of temporal welfare make them more difficult to identify than the goods of spiritual welfare because the Gospels and Epistles have little to say about temporal matters. Prudence is therefore needed not only to determine the means for attaining the goods of the temporal realm but also to identify the temporal goods themselves.

In chapter four, I referred to passages in the New Testament (1 Peter 2 and Romans 13) and to Augustine and Aquinas in order to argue that the temporal realm is concerned with three basic goods, understood as a hierarchy of goods. They are: (1) civil peace or "the tranquillity of order" (in Augustine's words), which involves the control of man's sinful nature, the restraint and punishment of criminals, and national security within and without the state; (2) moral virtue, meaning the inculcation of a few basic moral qualities in citizens, such as courage, moderation, and justice so they can work for the common good and exercise some measure of responsible freedom (in conformity with the admonition in 1 Pet. 2:16 to "Live as freemen, yet without using your freedom as a pretext for evil"); and (3) civic piety, meaning the reverence for political authority as God-given rather than as a creation of a human social contract. Civic piety makes obedience to the state a religious duty but does not require a confessional state (imposing Christian orthodoxy), though it does require the state to acknowledge the sovereignty of God and to promote the unhindered flourishing of spiritual life as part of God-given political authority. These three temporal goods are appropriate to the temporal realm because they are limited goods in the sense of being secondary to eternal salvation and in the sense of accepting the existing nature of man as a fallen but partly rational being.

The task of Christian prudence is to mix and balance such ends in order to form the temporal common good as well as to combine them judiciously with the higher ends of spiritual life. The challenge is to continuously weigh all four goods—civil peace, moral virtue, civic piety, and otherworldly salvation—in such a way that the integrity of each good is preserved while giving more or less importance to the others, depending on the circumstances (for example, it may be necessary in periods of chaos and instability to give greater emphasis to establishing order than to promoting virtue; but in periods of stability and material prosperity, such as our own times, it may be wise to cause a certain amount of disorder in order to remind citizens of their spiritual destiny). The practical difficulty of the challenge is indicated by the fact that even the greatest Christian theologians differed on the proper balance and status of the temporal goods: Luther took a minimalist view, emphasizing civil peace or order as the primary end of the temporal realm; Augustine and Aquinas were more positive than Luther, with Aquinas offering a natural law theory of the proper ends of rational creatures that included preservation, procreation, and rational perfection through society and knowledge of God; and Calvin advocated the most intrusive and activist view of government, a sort of theocratic welfare state as I called it in chapter two, that is responsible for civil peace, virtuous conduct, care for the poor, widows, and orphans, and defending Calvinist orthodoxy in worship and beliefs.

However one formulates the three basic goods of the temporal realm (peace, virtue, and piety) this approach offers a genuine alternative to Christian politics in the present age. While most modern Christians have adopted a Kantian approach—a 'politics of absolute moral imperatives'—the approach that I have sketched of the premodern Augustinians requires a 'politics of prudence' (a phrase I have borrowed from Russell Kirk).[14] The two approaches are quite different. A 'politics of moral imperatives' deduces political principles directly from a Kantianized version of the *Imago Dei* that makes temporal affairs an extension of divine law. It sets unconditional rules with little or no flexibility in application and requires one legitimate regime for all nations, a liberal democracy based on human rights, which is thought to be just in itself because it is the only regime consistent with the dignity of man in his full moral maturity.

By contrast, a 'politics of prudence' means choosing the best possible regime for attaining the limited goods of the temporal realm and balancing them with the highest goods of the spiritual realm. This approach respects the distinction between the universality of the church and the particularity of nations and allows a variety of legitimate political regimes—monarchies, mixed regimes, limited authoritarian regimes, constitutional republics—which are legitimate because they are able to approximate reasonably the temporal common good. The prudential approach presupposes the metaphysics of Platonic-Aristotelian Christianity, according to which a higher order of being is the source of lower orders and the lower orders gain their legitimacy by approximating the higher order without being absorbed by it. This implies that liberal democracy is not legitimate as an end-in-itself but only insofar as it approximates a higher order of being; it also implies that other regimes may be more legitimate than democracy insofar as they attain more perfectly the hierarchy of being.

In comparing the two approaches to politics—the Kantian vs. the prudential—I believe that it is possible to show the superiority of the latter, although I am aware that prudence has acquired a bad reputation today. For many people, prudence is equated with political expediency or pragmatism or the calculation of self-interest in a world of realpolitik. Prudence is also thought to be too pessimistic to inspire loyalty, promoting a cynical view that simply tries to avoid the worst outcomes in the nasty and brutal world of politics. Compared to such pessimism, Kantian-like imperatives require all nations to move toward a moral order of peace and justice that respects human rights. For many people, the Kantian vision is more attractive than prudence because it makes democracy the culmination of historical progress or a major step toward the coming of the kingdom of God on earth.

The unflattering view of prudence, however, is based on a misunderstanding that separates prudence from an objective hierarchy of ends and leaves it in a moral vacuum where expediency reigns supreme. The correct view of Christian prudence is not amoral expedience. It presupposes the essential truth of the Two Cities and an objective order of ends; it requires one to choose the highest possible temporal goods that circumstances permit in the fallen world. In this light, prudence rises above expediency and aims at the greatest good while recognizing that the greatest good is rarely, if ever, attainable and that one must settle for approximations of the best. Genuine prudence is therefore 'principled prudence': It admits flexible means for attaining an objective order of ends and often settles for what is lower without denying the existence of higher goods. It enables one to compromise with harsh reality and to pursue a necessary or even a brutal course in politics without becoming cynical because the higher ends, however unrealizable they may be at the moment, are never forgotten, and ultimate redemption beyond politics remains the highest object of faith and hope. A further advantage of the prudential approach is that, in the modern age of democracy when only one legitimate form of government seems possible, it enables people to live in their times without being imprisoned by the horizons of their time. It enables one to distinguish the temporary from the eternal and to elevate the temporal realm without escaping into utopian fantasies. In sum, Christian prudence in the precise sense is *choosing the best means to temporal happiness in the conditions of the fallen world;* and this approach is superior to uncompromising ethical idealism or unprincipled political expedience.

THE BEST GOVERNMENT: MONARCHY OR DEMOCRACY?

What, then, does prudence recommend as the best form of government in the temporal realm? The answer may come as a surprise to those living in the present age: The best regime on grounds of Christian prudence is not liberal democracy but a mixed regime, with the best choice being 'constitutional monarchy under God.' This was the view of many great Christian theologians in the premodern age. They were guided in part by Scripture, which in the New Testament says that one should obey Caesar as a human authority ordained by God. They were also guided by judgments of prudence which indicated that, if it were possible to set up a new government, the best choice for the temporal realm would be a mixed regime consisting of monarchy, aristocracy, and democracy or of aristocracy and democracy in order to form a balanced corporate hierarchy that combined the wisdom and virtue of the few with the freedom and stability of the many. As I said in chapter two, this teaching can be found in Thomas Aquinas and other Catholic theologians of the Middle Ages and in John Calvin and many early Protestants.[15] Is it possible that their arguments are still valid today, despite all that we have learned about the need to democratize Christianity over the past three or four hundred years?

The answer, I think, is yes. The movements to transform Christian politics in a democratic direction over the past several centuries have corrected some of the excesses of an authoritarian past and given greater attention to the material well-being of the great majority of people than the regimes of the past. But the democratic movements have become one-sided or one-dimensional themselves, tying Christianity too closely to liberal democracy and associated structures, such as capitalism, that are not always hospitable to Christian spiritual and moral life and that are not necessarily the best choice for the temporal realm. What has been lost in the democratic age is respect for the hierarchical principle of authority and its beneficial effects in ordering and elevating the human soul.

This is not an easy argument to make in the present age, but a few courageous thinkers have tried to make the case. For example, Edward Goerner argues in *Peter and Caesar*: "The refusal of discipline implicit in the democratic denial of hierarchy inescapably excludes public realization of those sharp excellences of the spirit that . . . demand an ascetic moment in their process of realization. Only by virtue of some hierarchical articulation can a people pursue such objects." While Goerner also notes that democracies are frequently capable of heroic exertions for the necessities of war and national security, he argues that "an equivalent effort in the name of high culture and civilization is hardly likely on any considerable scale."[16] And Aidan Nichols argues in *Christendom Awake*, a remarkably independent and unfashionable work that truly challenges the prejudices of our age, that "the significance of a religiously sanctioned monarchy lies in the fact that it alone of all possible State forms represents the essential notion that authority descends [from above]. *A me reges regnant* ('By me kings reign') is the subscription of the Christ image on the crown made in c. 962 for the Holy Roman Emperor Otto II and is still preserved in the Viennese Hofburg."[17] According to these thinkers, the deficiency of democratic or republican forms is the inability to sustain the high culture and civic piety that monarchical and aristocratic forms once cultivated as a matter of course and that helped to sustain a Christian civilization with loftier aspirations than bourgeois culture.

Because such concerns are legitimate aspects of temporal power, the arguments of someone like Thomas Aquinas on behalf of mixed or constitutional monarchy are not outdated. In fact, they have a more permanent appeal than unconditional or one-sided arguments for liberal democracy. Aquinas's arguments are, in principle, still convincing today if we can recognize that majority rule and human rights are not the only standards for measuring the temporal common good. The goods of the temporal realm—including justice itself—must be formulated in terms of a hierarchy of ends rather than in terms of consent or human rights. As we have seen, those temporal ends begin with civil peace and stability; but they also include moral virtue and civic piety or the creation of an atmosphere that nurtures virtue and piety in a comprehensive 'high culture' that elevates rather than degrades the human soul. The prudential arguments of thinkers like Aquinas (and the classical philosophers who influenced him) retain their validity because they indicate that mixed monarchy or mixed aristocratic regimes are better than liberal democracy for realizing the proper ends of the temporal realm. Even if there is no possibility of implementing mixed regimes today or in the near future, the arguments for them give us the true perspective on politics by indicating that liberal democracy is a second or third choice compared to more hierarchically arranged regimes.

This ranking is implicit in Aquinas's arguments for the best regime. If we consult his early treatise *On the Government of Princes* and his later remarks in the *Summa Theologiae* on the best constitution, we see that Thomas favors limited kingship or mixed monarchy in which three elements are combined—monarchy, aristocracy, and democracy. According to this theory, the monarch exists to promote unity and virtue, understood as magnanimity or royal grandeur and a just concern for the common good of the realm. Along with the king, Thomas expects the aristocratic element to provide an avenue for virtue, understood as the practical wisdom or experienced leadership of a political class of rulers (modeled on the hereditary nobility of the Roman Senate or the elected chiefs of the tribes of ancient Israel). Whatever the precise structure of the monarchical and aristocratic elements, they need to be held in check and limited by a democratic element that enables the people to participate in politics. This mixture not only prevents the king and nobles from degenerating into tyranny or oligarchy, but it also encourages active elements among the people to assert themselves and to develop civic friendship. As Thomas says, the people deserve a role in choosing rulers because "all are eligible" to make some decisions, and the stability of the regime is enhanced when everyone has some share in the government. While Thomas denies that the people are sovereign as a matter of right, he does say that including the people along with the aristocratic and monarchical elements is a wise measure for obtaining the political goods of stability and moral virtue. And he adds that the entire temporal realm must be balanced with the authority of the church and its priesthood so that temporal rulers recognize the higher goods of the spiritual realm. The result is a mixed and balanced constitution where specific roles are designed to the people, the aristocracy, the monarchy, and an independent priesthood.[18]

In support of Aquinas's view, one can argue historically that this arrangement is similar to the constitutions of two long-lasting and impressive regimes, ancient Sparta and modern England. Ancient Sparta was a mixed monarchy that combined elements of monarchy, aristocracy, and democracy. At the top was kingship, consisting of two kings who exercised priestly and military duties and who were believed to be hereditary descendants of Hercules; in the middle was the *gerousia* or body of venerable elders, consisting of an elected council of thirty gentlemen over the age of sixty who were the guardians of morals and the constitution; and last but not least were the *ephors*, consisting of five citizens elected every year by people's assemblies with considerable power in determining matters of war, morals, and foreign policy and possessing the authority to criticize the kings.[19] Following a similar pattern, the English constitution (from about the Elizabethan age to the end of the British Empire after World War II) was a mixed monarchy that combined the prerogatives of the king with the powers of the House of Lords and the House of Commons in a constitutional sharing of power that included the established Church of England. The best case for the English Constitution can be found in Edmund Burke's "Appeal from the New to the Old Whigs" (1791), which shows how the goal of "ordered and virtuous liberty" is sustained by the English constitutional mixture of three elements and the conception of the people as a corporate body. As Burke says, it is the best political order because it is most in accord with human nature and civilized society.[20]

Additional arguments for the superiority of mixed monarchy are provided by Plato and Cicero. In Plato's *Laws*, the Athenian Stranger (whom everyone recognizes as Socrates), makes the following observation: "There are, as it were, two mothers of regimes . . . one [is] monarchy and the other democracy. . . . Almost all other regimes . . . are woven from these. Both of them should and must be present if there is to be freedom and friendship, together with prudence . . . [and] no city will ever have a fine political life if it lacks a share in either of these" (693d). Following this logic, the Stranger proposes a blueprint for a practical regime that combines the monarchical principle, which he equates with wisdom, and the democratic principle, which he equates with consent. In his account, the right mixture of wisdom and consent begins with the actions of a wise founder who lays down the laws of the constitutional order; it is then duly administered by the best political members of the city—the elder chieftains of a few notable families—and they share power with the common people who are given responsibility in governing through numerous offices and roles in public events. Though a council of censors strictly regulates morals, the intended result is a vibrant public life which is arguably more 'democratic' than many modern liberal democracies because of the high degree of active participation by all citizens in the political life of the community.

In similar fashion, Cicero presents a famous argument for the mixed regime in the *Republic,* where his character Scipio says: "You are right to ask which I consider the best of three [regimes], for I do not approve of any of them when employed by itself, and consider the form which is a combination of all of them superior to any single one. But if I were compelled to approve one single unmixed form, I might choose kingship [for] the name of king seems like that of father to us . . . [and is] sustained by the care of one man who is the most virtuous and most eminent. But here [also] are the aristocrats, with the claim that they can do this more effectively and that there will be more wisdom in the counsels of several than in those of one man. . . . And here also are the people, shouting with a loud voice that they are willing to obey neither one nor a few, [and] that nothing is sweeter than liberty. . . . Thus, kings attract us by our affection for them, aristocracies by their wisdom, and popular governments by their freedom" (I, 35.54–56). Such arguments, presented by Plato and Cicero, highlight the advantages of a mixed regime in promoting a stable and balanced order that combines freedom and virtue in the citizen body with feelings of filial affection and piety for the foremost ruler. The only point that is missing in the classical philosophers is a proper distinction between the spiritual and temporal realms that the Greeks and Romans (and non-Christian cultures in general) were unable to grasp in all its implications. Though the classical philosophers knew that politics was not the highest realm, because philosophy or theoretical wisdom was the highest good, they lacked the New Testament and its critical insight that God's realm and Caesar's realm are distinct though not entirely separate realms, requiring the supremacy of the church over the state and proper respect for the independence of the state as it serves the temporal common good.

Taking into account the important amendment to Plato and Cicero required by the New Testament, Christians today should be able to see that their arguments, along with those of the later Scholastic theologians for a constitutional monarchy under God, are still valid today. I am aware that this statement sounds a bit un-American (and though I am an American patriot, I am a bit like Alexander Hamilton in loving my country while preferring an old Whig view of politics rather than an unreservedly republican view). For loving one's country does not preclude the awareness of higher possibilities in politics. Does not prudence point to the superiority of mixed monarchical regimes or the need for aristocratic elements while living in a democratic regime that bears all the imperfections of the present age? This question is unsettling to most Americans and contemporary Christians because they think that popular sovereignty and human rights are the only legitimate principles of government and the culmination of historical progress. Yet, they are rarely called upon to justify this view and simply assume that the case is closed because Thomas Jefferson proclaimed it to be "self-evident" to all enlightened minds. But Christian faith and intellectual honesty require us to reopen the case and to ask if constitutional monarchy or mixed regimes combining the rule of the one, the few, and the many, and duly limited by reverence for the sovereignty of God, are not better than liberal democracy.

The main advantage of constitutionally mixed regimes, as the classical and Scholastic thinkers indicate, lies in combining a significant role for the people with hierarchical elements that not only strengthen the stability of the regime over the long run but also, and more important, direct the souls of citizens upwards to the higher goods of virtue and piety that are not ordinarily promoted by the popular culture of a liberal democratic society. This is not to deny that liberal democracies can be stable or cultivate a certain type of moral virtue and civic piety in the citizen body. While most Americans justify democracy with the official doctrine of natural rights, they also understand and often use prudential arguments about the goods of the temporal realm: that middle-class property ownership promotes civic order and stability by giving the majority a stake in the regime; that democratic participation promotes certain moral virtues among the people—especially in local self-government and military service where virtues such as moderation, courage, rationality, and justice (understood as political equality, teamwork, and fairness) are learned. There is also a democratic version of civic piety, expressed in the Flag Salute and the national holiday of Thanksgiving which remind the American people that they live in a nation under God.

But most Americans would be reluctant to admit how much the temporal goods of order, virtue, and piety that they have achieved in the course of their history have relied on the influence of hierarchical elements from older aristocratic and monarchical traditions that survived in the democratic age. Without these undemocratic elements, the people acting on their own instincts would have succumbed quickly to the two great evils of modern liberal democracy—the corrosive skepticism of liberalism carried by the culture of rights and the leveling effects of mass democracy. Historically, these evils were postponed (some critics argue until the late 1960s) by hierarchical elements from the past, embodied in undemocratic religious traditions, the social leadership of upper classes, elite institutions of higher learning, and patriarchal authority figures that served as checks on the irresponsible freedom and equality of a mass democracy. The hierarchical traditions and institutions served as checks and restraints on the democratic soul, repressing the lower impulses toward instant gratification and self-expression and nurturing higher parts of the soul—the parts that require greater patience and depth of feeling as well as more dignified and decorous behavior than are commonly found in pure democracies.

For those who might doubt this argument, one should recall the teaching of Plato: "The regime in the city shapes the regime in soul," by which Plato meant that the political order ultimately shapes the minds, hearts, and souls of its citizens. A hierarchical political regime produces hierarchies in the soul, whereas a democratic regime produces an indiscriminate equality of pleasures in the soul and lets loose a wild variety of lower desires. Since virtue is a well-ordered soul—a soul in which reason rules over the lower passions with the help of pride—virtue is best promoted in a political community where higher elements can rule over and control lower and baser elements. When the community as a whole is able to look up to its rulers as embodiments of wisdom and virtue, the souls of all are elevated. Even when the rulers do not live up to these high ideals (as they often do not) but still profess admiration for rational and spiritual perfection rather than simply letting people be themselves, the effects can be beneficial. For, as Plato also argues, the means by which nobler elements control the unruly elements is by making them feel ashamed of their lower impulses—by making base and vulgar actions seem beneath the dignity of a decent human being to publicly or privately express. When deviant behavior is gradually released from shame by treating all social hierarchies and conventions as unjust or repressive (the process that former Senator Daniel Patrick Moynihan has described as "defining deviancy down"), then democracy slides into coarseness and crudeness and eventually into anarchy, brutality, and animal behavior.[21] The ennobling effect on the human soul of looking up with reverence to traditional authority figures and with deference to higher goods creates a predisposition in favor of monarchy and aristocracy in the temporal realm.

Of course, one may object that corrupt monarchies or dissolute aristocracies can be more degraded and damaging to souls than a healthy republic; this is a true historical observation that must be duly weighed in the balance. Hence, in practical terms, one would want a constitutional order that prevents the monarch and other ruling bodies as well as the people from doing whatever they pleased. But the possibility of corrupt elites damaging healthy souls does not invalidate another truthful observation: that moral decline in democratic societies is most often caused by an excess of democracy, meaning the liberation of the people as well as the educated classes from the undemocratic

constraints that have held their lower natures in check. To acknowledge this 'politically incorrect' observation, one needs to be reminded
of the aristocratic (and even monarchical) elements that have existed
in American history and that have operated in a positive fashion to
check the excesses of democracy. Those elements were most alive
during the colonial period and the founding generation, whose greatest leaders (such as John Winthrop and John Cotton among the early
Puritans and Washington, Adams, Madison, Jefferson, and Hamilton
among the revolutionary and constitutional generation) were inspired
by a notion of leadership that combined the ideal of a Christian gentleman politician with a dedication to republican principles. Their
leadership created a 'mixed regime' by combining the practical
wisdom and noble character of a quasi-aristocratic class of rulers with
the formal mechanisms of a republican constitution.[22]

The same may also be said of many other kinds of social and political elites throughout American history: for example, 'society ladies'
(from former first ladies to Emily Post) who served as arbiters of good
manners and social graces in contrast to democratic informality and
vulgarity; patriarchal father figures who stood as revered and sometimes intimidating heads of families, governing them like monarchs
while checking the aggression of their sons and protecting the purity
of their daughters; the old-fashioned Protestant minister who acted as
a moral authority and censor of immoral behavior rather than limiting himself to the role of social worker or sympathetic counselor; the
officer corps in the military academies and all branches of the armed
services who were trained as "officers and gentlemen" in accordance
with a code of honor and duty traceable to medieval ideas of chivalry;
the educated ladies and gentlemen turned out by the liberal arts universities in order to serve as a cultured elite for setting a high tone for
the tastes of society; the artists who promoted the ideal of 'high culture' in the arts instead of the 'popular culture' of Hollywood and
mass entertainment; and the architects who were faithful to the noble
classical style in public buildings (especially in our beautiful capital,
Washington, D.C.) and who built churches and cathedrals in the
Gothic style rather than succumbing to the utilitarian-functional style
of democratic modernism. These were some of the hierarchical elements that mixed with American democracy and acted for decades as

supports for higher civilization and as counterforces to the surrounding mass culture. They had the positive effect of elevating souls in the temporal sphere and even influenced the spiritual realm by a kind of carryover effect, repressing and sublimating lower desires to higher ones and raising the overall tone of society.

Are such hierarchical elements in the city and in the soul still necessary today? I would argue that they are needed now more than ever, both in the temporal realm for promoting civil peace, moral virtue, and civic piety and as an aid to the spiritual realm by nurturing high culture and keeping open the higher possibilities of the soul. Christians need to recognize that they have as great a stake in political and social hierarchies that elevate culture as they do in democratic structures that empower the people and serve the needs of the least advantaged members of society. It is certainly worth pondering whether Americans who have no sense of monarchical and aristocratic traditions will eventually lose the reverence, awe, and deference to higher authority that is necessary for maintaining a genuine spiritual order. The obvious test case is the Roman Catholic Church in America and in the European democracies of today.

Because of a belief in the absolute sovereignty of the people in every aspect of life, many Catholics in America find the pope and the bishops of the Church to be archaic and illegitimate; they also grow increasingly impatient with the formal ceremonies of mass and sacramental life. The hierarchies of the Church and the entire spiritual order are increasingly difficult to combine with a democratic temporal order—not impossible, I hasten to add, but extremely difficult. It is actually a big gamble by the Catholic Church (as well as by the other episcopal churches such as the Anglican and the Eastern Orthodox and even the high Presbyterianism of genuine Calvinism) to embrace modern democracy as closely as they have. The church hierarchy must continually remind the flock, and often its own bishops and priests, that democracy may be acceptable in the state, but it is not acceptable in the church or the family or educational institutions where public opinion polls do not determine the truth. Even such spiritual notions as "Christ the King" or "God the Father" or "God the Almighty Creator and Lord of the Universe" are harder to grasp in democratic ages when, as Tocqueville observed, people insist on less awesome conceptions of God (inclining them toward pantheism, in which God as a transcendent Creator is rejected and the divine presence is seen as equally present everywhere in the universe, from bugs and trees to the human soul and holy sacraments). Democratic customs also subvert traditional forms of worship such as kneeling in church or genuflection, which appear to be relics of court manners that seemingly insult the 'dignity' of democratic citizens (which undoubtedly explains why kneelers have been removed from many modern Catholic churches and priests are increasingly referred to as 'presiders' rather than as the duly ordained celebrants of sacred mysteries). These trends in the spiritual realm are all traceable to democratic resentment of hierarchy.

In addition to preserving notions of deference and awe, monarchical and aristocratic regimes usually cultivate notions of leisure in the true sense of unhurried activities that transcend work and play. Leisure is properly understood as more than a time for relaxation from work. It is time for the cultivation of nonproductive activities like the refinement of beauty and the detachment from the world in the contemplation of eternity—that is, in the quest for philosophical and spiritual wisdom. In a world of middle-class democracy where market productivity is considered the primary measure of worth and technical knowledge the only valuable knowledge and speed and efficiency the highest priorities, it is hard to develop the spirit of voluntary charity and otherworldly asceticism that nurtures contemplative prayer, religious orders, and monasticism (not to mention the great desert hermits like St. Anthony). Yet, few things are as important today for spiritual revival than Christian otherworldliness (what used to be called 'contempt for the world') and the radical spirituality that are often found in strange mystical personalities who are not encumbered by conventional notions of normalcy or productivity and who are looked upon with awe rather than dismissed as useless and weird. Can these attitudes and personalities be cultivated without limiting democracy and capitalism?

In raising these questions, I want to emphasize my central point in order to avoid confusion: These are prudential judgments rather than absolute ethical imperatives. They are arguments about choosing the best institutions in an imperfect world to serve the temporal common good and to keep open a sense of transcendence and reverence for sacred mysteries in the spiritual realm. No political regime does this job particularly well. All prudential judgments about politics involve trade-offs that are difficult to weigh. On the one hand, monarchies and aristocracies are prone to dissolute behavior that makes them decadent and unjustly contemptuous of the well-being of the masses; yet, they are often concerned, sometimes out of sheer vanity, with monuments of grandeur and the production of high culture that are less deadening to the soul than the mundane pursuits of modern mass society. On the other hand, social stability, a reasonable standard of living for most people, and minimal standards of decency and self-respect are great goods in temporal affairs; and modern democracies deliver these necessary, though modest, goods very well. But the main point that needs emphasizing for our present age is that the higher inclinations of the soul need cultivation in addition to the mundane ones; and modern liberal democracies do not do a good job of cultivating the higher ones. In fact, all the pressures in a democratic society are in the opposite direction, leaving the higher impulses to fend for themselves in an atmosphere of hostility or indifference and even encouraging the educated classes to treat them with irony or contempt: The missing ingredient in modern democracy is the hierarchical principle that helps to sustain high culture over popular culture. Yet, Christians and all concerned citizens have an important stake, both political and spiritual, in the predominance of high culture and therefore must attend more carefully to promoting it. Otherwise, our fate is to live in a stable democratic world which feeds and entertains us very well but whose culture is degraded by the accumulated products of middle-class consumerism combined with a rebellious avant-garde and a raucous youth culture that deadens our souls and pollutes our moral and spiritual atmosphere.

Because of the difficult trade-offs involved in prudential judgments, I infer that the best temporal regime is one that combines democratic, aristocratic, and, if possible, monarchical institutions. As T. S. Eliot says in describing such a vision in *Christianity and Culture*, "what is important is a structure of society in which there will be, from 'top' to 'bottom,' a continuous gradation of cultural levels."[23] It should be one in which the people have sufficient amounts of power to be active and responsible citizens and to protect the material interests of the least advantaged, combined with hierarchical institutions which allow a wide variety of elites (social, political, military, artistic, philosophical, and spiritual) to have authoritative roles in society and to form a culture that keeps the human soul open to higher goods than the popular activities of work, entertainment, sports, and technical mastery. Thus, Christian prudence indicates that, if circumstances make it possible to establish, the best regime for the temporal order would be a mixed constitutional monarchy under God rather than a liberal democracy.

The problem today, of course is that most traces of hierarchical authority have vanished. Even in early America, only faint echoes existed, primarily in the social customs of leading citizens and in relics of classical and medieval culture that I described above. These elements have now disappeared as a result of two hundred years of democratic leveling and the expansion of individual rights to proportions that the American founders would never have imagined when they proclaimed an inalienable right to the pursuit of happiness. In a genuine irony of history, certain kinds of inequalities and social hierarchies are still permitted to exist today and even to flourish unabashedly—I mean the inequalities of wealth generated by capitalism as well as the bureaucratic hierarchies of the welfare state and the judges of the United States Supreme Court. But these inequalities are not constructive hierarchies; they do not elevate the soul like traditional authority figures or like classical and medieval culture. The great financial successes of entrepreneurs like Bill Gates or the fame of Hollywood entertainers and sports figures simply whet the appetite for material consumption and shallow celebrityhood, while the bureaucrats of the welfare state and the judges of the court system act in highly undemocratic fashion to impose a stifling equality on an often reluctant public. The only kinds of elitism that liberal democracies tolerate today are those that accentuate materialism or advance the process of democratic leveling and permissive freedom.

Given these circumstances, it is obvious that some version of democracy is the only practical option in the present age for the ordering of temporal affairs. We no longer have the range of options of earlier ages. As Tocqueville noted, we are in the grip of a powerful tide of history that is moving the whole world toward democracy on the Western, mainly the American, model. Although Tocqueville mistakenly thought that the democratic tide was providential, he was nevertheless correct to see it as the dominant trend in the modern age extending over several centuries. Though no one can say how long the trend will last, it is safe to say that the only choice for the foreseeable future is not between monarchy and democracy but between different kinds of democracy: either a degraded and tyrannical version in which equality would destroy liberty (and with it, any hope for virtue and piety) or a noble version in which equality would be balanced with ordered liberty (and with it, the higher aspirations of the soul).

While many of Tocqueville's suggestions for ennobling democracy are commendable, they will not be sufficient if we persist in the error that Tocqueville himself and most modern Christians make—the belief that God has anointed democracy as the only form of government consistent with His will because it alone recognizes the rights and dignity of the individual. This is the error of Kantian Christianity that I have criticized, not for emphasizing human dignity, but for confusing dignity with autonomy of personality and for equating Christian charity with legally protected external freedoms, while forgetting the biblical notion that true dignity lies in the possession of an immortal soul with a supernatural destiny and the more subtle Scholastic notion that dignity lies in the possession of a rational soul that is ordained to know and to love the eternal being that is its Creator and Savior. Instead of perpetuating the Kantian error, we need a more sober argument that treats democracy, not as the only legitimate regime and the high point of historical progress, but as a second choice that is a reasonable option in the present age. To make such an argument, one must return to the Augustinian and Thomistic conception of politics, according to which democracy is not an absolute but a conditional good—a political and social order that is not just in itself but is legitimate insofar as it serves a higher order of perfection and reflects its transcendent glory, however dimly.[24] From this perspective, a tempered version of democracy that publicly acknowledges the sovereignty of God—a 'constitutional democracy under God'—is an acceptable second choice for Christians and for all reasonable people in the present age, with the provision that its excesses be resisted by strengthening every kind of constructive hierarchy as much as possible.

To defend constitutional democracy under God as a realistic second choice, one must use prudential reasoning rather than the abstract ideologies of human rights or theories of inevitable historical progress. What would prudential reasoning look like in this case? I already presented a prime example in discussing Alexander Solzhenitsyn in the previous chapter. Solzhenitsyn derives his political views from the Two Cities and develops a clear ranking of political regimes from worst to best. In his scheme, the worst regime is totalitarian communism whose all-powerful state imposes atheism and systematically destroys the lives and souls of its people. It must be resisted: "When Caesar, having exacted what is Caesar's, demands still more insistently that we render to him what is God's—that is a sacrifice we dare not make!" For Solzhenitsyn, however, the alternative is not modern Western democracy based on human rights. Instead, Solzhenitsyn speaks favorably of traditional Russian tsarism which he says was bearable because it kept the state within certain limits by convincing even the most autocratic rulers that they were responsible to God. Though tsarism oppressed the serfs and reduced the Russian Orthodox Church to a position of servility, it did not destroy the soul of the Russian people and even allowed the flourishing of spiritual, artistic, and family life for centuries. (A disturbing fact, worthy of deep reflection, is that the greatest Russian artists and saints were products of the tsarist period.) Nevertheless, Solzhenitsyn indicates that constitutionally limited regimes are better than traditional tsarism. The best regime in Russian history was the constitutional monarchy that existed briefly from 1905–1911 under Tsar Nicholas II and Prime Minister Peter Stolypin, whose agenda was constitutional and land reform. Since this regime is unavailable in present circumstances, Solzhenitsyn argues in *Rebuilding Russia* (1991) for constitutional democracy as a reasonable approximation. But he chooses democracy "not as an end in itself . . . but to avoid tyranny"; and he insists that it is merely a state structure, not "a universal principle of human existence, almost a cult." His aim is to mix political freedom with Christian self-sacrifice in order to serve the higher ends of moral and spiritual development. Solzhenitsyn offers a powerful example of prudential reasoning by showing that constitutional democracy under God, though a second choice compared to constitutional monarchy, is the best available option in the present circumstances of Russia, given its tragic history and the conditions of the modern world.

In terms more familiar to us, one can find a prudential argument for democracy in the political thought of Sir Winston Churchill and Reinhold Niebuhr. Everyone has heard of Churchill's famous statement that democracy is the worst form of government except for all the others. But not everyone is sure what Churchill meant. His precise quotation has an Augustinian flavor about politics in the fallen world: "Many forms of government have been tried . . . in this world of sin and woe. No one pretends that democracy is perfect or all-wise. Indeed, it has been said that democracy is the worst form of government, except for all the other forms that have been tried from time to time" (Speech to the House of Commons, November 11, 1947). Churchill is giving a prudential argument for democracy rather than one based on popular sovereignty or human rights. His point is that politics takes place in a flawed and sinful world where evil tends to predominate. Statesmen must be prudent, basing their judgments and actions on realism about the human condition and rejecting illusions that the world can be changed fundamentally before the Second Coming. Much of prudent politics is devoted to avoiding the worst outcomes by opposing tyranny and waging just wars. In this sad condition, democracy looks pretty good, a regime worth dying for. It may even be better than striving for perfection because utopian schemes require trusting power to ideological fanatics who often pervert power for self-righteous ends.

Nevertheless, Churchill did not think that democracy based on universal suffrage was the best form of government. Like Edmund Burke, he thought that constitutional or mixed monarchy was better because it united people around the symbolic authority of the king, allowed the gentlemen class to govern, and gave adequate consideration to the welfare of the great masses of people and often inspired in the people a heroic temper. For Churchill, a purely democratic world without the glory and grandeur of the British Empire would be a poorer world. So when he spoke of defending democracy as the least objectionable form of government in the fallen world, he was actually overstating the pessimism of his prudential outlook because he believed that constitutional monarchy was better. Or perhaps he was speaking loosely and had in mind all constitutionally limited regimes, knowing that their very acceptance of imperfection made them superior to the twisted utopias of fascism and communism. However his famous words are interpreted, Churchill provides another example of a prudential approach to politics that treats democracy, not as an end in itself, but as a second choice among stable constitutional orders that is nevertheless worth great sacrifices in defending it against its mortal enemies.

In similar tones but with a more positive judgment on democracy, Reinhold Niebuhr defended the proximate justice that can be found in democracy—the closest approximation of the high ideals of love and justice that exists in the fallen world of politics. To clarify this point, he wrote *The Children of Light and the Children of Darkness: A Vindication of Democracy and a Critique of Its Traditional Defense* (1944). The thesis is that democracy cannot be adequately defended by appealing to an optimistic view of human nature or to property rights or to an automatic harmony of interests—views commonly found among Enlightenment rationalists, bourgeois materialists, and liberal Christians. Instead, one must acknowledge the Augustinian doctrine of original sin: that man is a creature corrupted by the Fall and driven by self-love, aggression, and the lust for power. While some political thinkers, such as Luther and Hobbes, claim that the pessimistic view of man points to authoritarianism (to the need for strong rulers who will control the people), Niebuhr argues that the doctrine of original sin points to constitutional democracy—to distrust of powerful rulers and to the need for limits on the state. In the fallen world where all regimes are corruptible and incline to tyranny, constitutional democracy based on Christian realism is the safest bet.

Yet, this argument sounds too cynical as a defense of democracy. So Niebuhr tempers it with his famous statement: "Man's capacity for justice makes democracy possible; but man's inclination to injustice makes democracy necessary." The significance of this balanced phrase is the recognition that man is not so depraved that he lacks any sense of justice but he is sufficiently depraved that one should not count on it and allow oneself to trust in the justice or benevolence of rulers. The ambivalence of Niebuhr about human nature, I argued in chapter three, led him to compensate for his Augustinian pessimism by adding elements of Kantian idealism, which means he defended democracy not only as a prudent choice for fallible and sinful men but also as a moral imperative that recognizes the essential equality of humanity. Despite the addition of ethical idealism, Niebuhr deserves credit for educating Christians as well as the American public in sober prudential reasoning. As Robert Kaufman points out, Niebuhr showed that "the cardinal moral virtue for a statesman was prudence: the art of applying general principles to particular circumstances informed by a realistic assessment of man's nature, the nature of the international environment, . . . and the probable consequences of alternative courses of action."[25]

This quote sums up nicely the prudential politics that one finds in the Christian realism of Solzhenitsyn, Churchill, and Niebuhr and indicates its advantages over approaches based on unconditional moral imperatives. By appealing to prudence, they see democracy as a means to higher ends rather than as an end-in-itself, even if it rarely attains those higher ends. They thereby avoid the temptation of worshiping the democratic state as a kind of religion or idol that overshadows the higher spiritual realm and subverts the divinely ordained spheres of church, family, and charity. The prudence of Christian realism is thus a better guard against totalitarian tyranny than the appeal to human rights because its brutal honesty about human nature prevents one from giving in to utopian fantasies. And such prudence is also the best safeguard against democratic decay or democratic tyranny. For, in our times, these dangers are mainly due to the indefinite expansion of rights, which creates pressure for increasing the power of the centralized state beyond reasonable limits and encourages permissive morality in the private sphere. The prudential approach to politics derived from the Two Cities works against the evils of centralized power and permissive freedom by reminding citizens that the state is instituted by God for the limited ends of the temporal realm and for the unhindered flourishing of the higher spiritual realm rather than for satisfying the ever-expanding list of entitlements that are now claimed as human rights.

ECONOMY, SOCIETY, AND MILITARY

While the state is the most important institution for ordering the earthly city, other spheres of temporal authority exist and pose difficult choices. How should the economy in a Christian polity be organized? Should it be based on private property or communal sharing, on capitalism or socialism, or on some mixture of the two? How should social classes be arranged? Can a Christian society permit inequalities of wealth and status, or does it require equality of result or, at least, equality of opportunity? In matters of war and peace, is Christianity essentially pacifist, or does it provide grounds for just wars, military duty, and even a code of chivalry for Christian soldiers? Obviously, these debates cannot be resolved with any degree of thoroughness in the present context. All that I wish to demonstrate is that the issues fit into the Christian theory of constitutionalism that I have been sketching because, as spheres of temporal authority, they are limited in scope and are best determined by prudence in accordance with man's fallen but rational nature. Like political structures, the institutions of economic, social, and military life should strive to attain the goods of the temporal realm while preserving an openness to spiritual transcendence in the midst of the harsh realities and mundane pursuits of the fallen world.

Consider the best organization of the economy and the best arrangement of social classes. At first glance, these matters seem to go beyond prudence because many passages in the New Testament address them directly, implying that the revealed will of God and the divine law of Christian charity are guides to economic and social policy rather than prudential reasoning. In many places, the Gospels and Epistles speak directly about economic and social relations. For example, Christ repeatedly condemns the rich and blesses the poor:

"It is easier for a camel to pass through the eye of a needle than for a rich man to enter the kingdom of God"; "go, sell what you possess and give it to the poor"; and it is not possible to serve "God and mammon" (Matt. 7:24; 19:21–24). Paul also says that "the love of money is the root of all evil" (1 Tim. 6:10). And Mary, in praising the Lord's power and righteousness, says, "He has scattered the proud in the imagination of their hearts, He has put down the mighty from their thrones, and exalted those of low degree; He has filled the hungry with good things and the rich He has sent away empty" (Luke 1:51–53). And James, in his Epistle (2:1–9), condemns class distinctions, saying that partiality should not be shown in public gatherings to those who are rich and well-dressed because such favoritism dishonors the poor whom "God [has] chosen to be rich in faith and heirs of the kingdom." One could also cite the example of early Christians, described in the Book of Acts, who practiced the communal sharing of property. Do these statements point directly to a specific economic and social order as the necessary application of Christian divine law?

The answer is yes, according to advocates of the social gospel such as Walter Rauschenbusch and to Christian socialists such as Jürgen Moltmann and to proponents of liberation theology such as Gustavo Gutiérrez. In their eyes, social democracy is a direct inference from the Christian concepts of charity and justice. They see the economy and social relations as branches of moral theology, the direct application of the law of God to social norms: Since Christ came to bring good news to the poor and the oppressed, he must have wanted the economy and society to be arranged in a way that equalizes wealth and empowers the poor. In a word, Christianity implies socialism.

The main objection to the Christian socialists is that the New Testament never takes the last step of calling for social revolution or a radical restructuring of society because it recognizes that all attempts to translate commands of love into structures of power collide with the fallen nature of man. While this may be evident to us in light of the twentieth-century experience with socialism, the lesson can also be found in the New Testament itself. As noted above, the Book of Acts (4:32–5:11) describes an experiment in the communal sharing of goods by the first Christians under the directorship of the Apostles:

"Now the company of those who believed were of one heart and soul, and no one said that any of the things which he possessed was his own, but they had everything in common . . . and there was not a needy person among them." Interestingly, the account also includes the story of a man named Ananias and his wife, Sapphira, who withheld from the apostolic leadership the profits they had made on the sale of a piece of property. When Peter found out they were hoarding, he condemned them as selfish agents of Satan and as liars before God, at which point both Ananias and Sapphira fell down and were struck dead! Without drawing a lesson, Scripture simply says, "And great fear came upon the whole church." Is the story recommending communal sharing as an expression of Christian charity, or is it sending a warning about the perils of such schemes due to the inevitable problem of selfish hoarding?

As I see it, the Book of Acts is describing an ideal that is nearly impossible to achieve (even on a small scale under the close scrutiny of the Apostles) because it does not accord with man's sinful nature. This does not mean that Christian sects from time to time have not tried to implement such schemes, such as the Hutterites who used peaceful means to equalize property or the Muntzerites who did so by violent revolution. But the lesson of Scripture seems to be that such communal sharing is a noble but unrealistic arrangement and that other options for the distribution of property and wealth are legitimate. Certainly, Acts provides an opening for more conventional notions of property than communal sharing or for mixtures of private and communal property that are better suited to the fallen nature of man (which will be with us until a 'new heaven and new earth' are established at the end of time by divine intervention). Until that time, one must be realistic, while also preserving glimpses of a radically transformed world that enables people to see that property and social status are not the true measures of human worth.

This seems to be Paul's position in those passages of his epistles which address economic and social issues. In 1 Tim. 6:7–17, Paul begins by condemning money outright: "Money is the root of all evil," because the craving for money causes loss of faith. Besides, he adds, we came into the world with nothing and we take nothing out, so why crave possessions? Even after these strong moral condemnations, however, Paul never argues that money and ownership should be abolished; instead, they must be seen as conditional goods for temporal use and the craving for them must be moderated: "If we have food and clothing, with these we shall be content"; and, "as for the rich in this world, charge them not to be haughty . . . they are to be rich in good deeds, liberal and generous." Though Christian socialists might regard this advice as a failure of nerve for not trying to eradicate the root of all evil through revolution, Paul seems satisfied with a moral and spiritual response: Instead of calling for the rich and powerful to be overthrown, he calls on them to be generous and charitable to their servants and to the poor. Nor does Paul spell out detailed commands, like those of the Old Testament which say, "If you lend money to any of my people who is poor, . . . you shall not exact interest from him" (Exod. 22:25), though presumably Paul would include this command in his calls for generosity and charity.

At the same time, Paul makes harsh remarks about lazy and unproductive behavior that modern-day capitalists could approve. In fact, Lady Margaret Thatcher quotes Paul approvingly to show that he had the good sense to advocate her own economic philosophy in 2 Thess. 3:6–12: "If a man will not work, he shall not eat. For we hear that some of you are living in idleness . . . not doing any work. Now such persons we command and exhort in the Lord Jesus Christ to do their own work and to earn their own living."[26] For Mrs. Thatcher, Paul expresses the kind of Protestant work ethic that supports her brand of Victorian capitalism and opposition to the welfare state. Yet, she errs by emphasizing only one side of Paul, forgetting his words (as well as Christ's and Mary's quoted above) that strongly condemn love of money and the accumulation of riches. Such statements make a full-throated endorsement of capitalism impossible to sustain on scriptural grounds. The most accurate summary of Scripture's teaching on economics and social classes would be mixed: Like socialism, Scripture condemns riches, wealth, money, and class distinctions from the perspective of ideal charity and justice; but, like capitalism, it permits private property, money, inequalities, and requires people to work for a living as realistic concessions to our fallen condition, while attempting to moderate the craving for mammon by commanding generosity, sharing, and charity.

From this mixed perspective, I infer that both socialists and capitalists are wrong if they treat economics and social relations in terms of divine law or even as branches of moral theology that culminate in unconditional moral imperatives. The challenge is more subtle and complex: Christian charity and justice influence economic and social teaching by setting moral boundaries, but the choice of institutions and policies requires prudential judgments about how best to attain certain temporal goods in the conditions set by the fallen world. Thus, it would be unjustified to speak of Christian socialism (which, as Pope Pius XI said, is a contradiction in terms); but it would be equally unjustified to speak of Christian capitalism. Such labels do not pay sufficient attention to the difference between the spiritual and temporal realms designated by the Two Cities. As I have argued, the Two Cities doctrine should be the guiding star for Christian reflection on the world. It indicates that the label "Christian" may be properly applied only to the spheres of spiritual authority— to the institutions of church, family, and charity, and possibly to the artistic sphere of beauty (because a specifically Christian view of beauty does exist, exemplified above all by iconography, a visible image of an invisible beauty). But the Two Cities makes it difficult or impossible to speak of Christian democracy or the Christian economy or even of the Christian ordering of class relations any more than one can speak of Christian plumbing or Christian carpentry or Christian football (except, perhaps, in Texas!). These activities are included in spheres of temporal authority that pertain to the best use of temporal goods, such as power, wealth, honor, pleasure, and security. The proper ordering of such goods depends less on divine law than on natural and human law. And the best possible order in many circumstances may rise no higher than social convention or positive right which one may try to reform but which may not be overthrown unless the arrangements are egregiously unjust. This view is sober in recognizing that Christian love cannot transform every institution of the fallen world. Yet, this view is also uplifting because it prevents one from absolutizing the goods of this world or from taking them at full face value (as the pagans have always been tempted to do). The divine light of the transcendent God shines through to the fallen world, however dimly; but much of the temporal realm goes on daily in ordinary fashion by its own secondary causes, and compromises with weak and fallible human nature must be negotiated by practical wisdom.

Reflecting the distinction of realms, Aquinas says, "Human law is ordained for one kind of community and divine law for another kind, because human law is ordained for the civil community . . . but the community for which the divine law is ordained is that of men in relation to God, either in this life or in the life to come" (*S. Th.*, I-II, 100.2). And since "it belongs to the human law to be derived from the law of nature" (*S. Th.*, I-II, 95.4), the major decisions of the civil community are arrived at by prudential reasoning which applies natural law to concrete situations and codifies them into human or civil law (positive law). Such realism does not mean that decisions of human law are arbitrary or amoral because, as I have stated repeatedly, genuine Christian prudence is not merely expedience or pragmatism. Genuine Christian prudence is choosing the best means to temporal happiness according to an objective hierarchy of ends—starting with the lower ones that pertain to civil peace and a modicum of moral virtue, including justice and the harmony of classes, and preserving an opening for piety and spiritual transcendence without expecting to meet the highest levels of charity or love in temporal affairs except in rare instances. As every rational person knows (when not deluded by utopian fantasies), economics deals with the mundane business of producing, distributing, and consuming material goods, from which profit making and even usury cannot be entirely removed. This condition can be moderated and ameliorated, but it cannot be abolished or radically transformed by Christian charity in the earthly city or fallen world.

Following such prudential wisdom, it would be a mistake to treat the economy and society as spheres of spiritual authority or as moral imperatives, as both Christian socialists and Christian capitalists are prone to do. Two prime examples of this mistake are Gustavo Gutiérrez in *A Theology of Liberation* and Michael Novak in *The Spirit of Democratic Capitalism*. Although both admit that Christianity does not require a particular economic and social system and that no system can be equated with the kingdom of God, Gutiérrez claims that the "kingdom" is built through economic and social systems, and Novak argues that doctrines like the Trinity and the Incarnation provide spiritual analogies for his economic policies. To argue these points, both have refined the rhetorical art of being suggestive without being definitive in order to create the impression that divine imperatives support their economic and social theories.

Gutiérrez's tactic is to argue for a new theology that links salvation with liberation and merges Christ the Savior with Christ the Liberator. His theology of "liberating praxis," as he calls it, emphasizes the building of Christ's kingdom in this world and equates the kingdom with temporal happiness: "The growth of the Kingdom is a process which occurs historically in liberation, insofar as liberation means greater human fulfillment."[27] For the most part, Gutiérrez does not spell out what the kingdom of human fulfillment might mean, except to say that it will require "a new way to be human" and "a permanent cultural revolution" or "a dynamic and historical conception of the human person." Since the new humanity is supposed to bring an end to oppression, exploitation, and alienation, Gutiérrez points to socialism, though he generally avoids specific proposals. One of the few references to a program is in the middle of *A Theology of Liberation* where he says almost haphazardly, "This transformation ought to be directed toward a radical change in the foundation of society, that is, the private ownership in the means of production."[28] Though obviously using a Marxian reference to abolishing capitalism, Gutiérrez offers no further elaboration, leaving the reader with a burning desire to rectify injustice without a clear blueprint for action and without showing that the proposed solution will work better than the existing arrangements. In his attempt to spiritualize socialism, Gutiérrez gives us grand moral passion without much practical wisdom.

For Michael Novak, the rhetorical strategy is different. He admits socialism has an advantage over capitalism by offering a moral vision that has tremendous appeal to Christians who long for social justice. Novak's challenge is to find an equally appealing justification for capitalism that removes its tarnished image as a materialistic system driven by self-interest and greed: What is needed is a spiritual argument "appropriate to democratic-capitalism as it is."[29] In this regard, his writings provide compelling replies to left-wing critics by showing that democratic capitalism is nobler in practice than it is in theory: Capitalism protects liberty by keeping the state from absorbing the market and the private sector; capitalism raises the living standard of the masses and is often driven by the desire to provide for one's family and to seek self-improvement rather than by greed; capitalism requires virtues like industry, rationality, thrift, creativity or inventiveness, and provides the financial means for exercising private charity; capitalism also presupposes a communitarian-individual who is both cooperative and self-reliant rather than an isolated and lonely self.

The problem with Novak's defense is that he moves from these sharp prudential arguments to a "theology" of capitalism that seeks to spiritualize the marketplace and to baptize the business corporation. He cites several theological doctrines that supposedly support capitalism by analogy with the spiritual realm. For example, he says, the Trinity provides a divine analogy for the structure of political economy, because the doctrine of Three Persons in One God is analogous to building a community (unity) without destroying human individuality (distinction of persons). Or the Incarnation, in which God entered the fallen world in order to redeem it, provides an analogy for capitalism's acceptance of the sinful world in order to improve it. Or Isaiah's description of the Christlike suffering servant, who is mocked and crucified, provides a metaphor for the mocked and despised business corporation among liberal academics.[30] But are these theological analogies appropriate for capitalism? I doubt it. They even sound a bit blasphemous, a quest for spiritual arguments to support a mundane economic system. Why baptize economics and sociology with spiritual meaning?

In light of the Two Cities, a better approach is to see the economic and social spheres as having moral boundaries set by the spiritual sphere while the major policy and institutional decisions are made by prudential judgments about temporal goods and human nature as we know it. In this way, the economy and social relations will remain under broad spiritual guidelines while not being determined by divine law, placing them properly in the semi-independent zone of temporality that has secondary significance compared to the spiritual realm. The premodern Christian theologians generally understood this point better than the modern ones because they never lost sight of the Two Cities and its notion that temporal goods are part of a hierarchy of ends that are distinct but not entirely separate from spiritual goods, permitting carefully graduated judgments that do not collapse one sphere into the other.

To illustrate the superiority of the premodern theologians in the application of practical wisdom, one may cite Aquinas's views of economy and society which articulate different degrees of perfection rather than inflexible absolutes. In Aquinas's scheme, divine law sets the outer boundaries for property ownership because the Bible teaches that God has sovereign dominion over all material things and gave man conditional dominion over the earth and its lower creatures as a grant or blessing for human use. This grant establishes the principle of "natural dominion" over external things but leaves everything in common for all mankind. Because natural dominion is held in common, natural law does not specify a clear title to ownership or a precise distribution of property. Instead, it leaves ownership to the "best use" for rational creatures. To determine the "best use" of property, one must use prudential reasoning about human nature as we know it.

As Thomas says, sounding like Milton Friedman and other modern-day capitalists, prudence indicates that private ownership is best in most cases: Everyone takes better care of the property that belongs to him; individual responsibility is the most efficient use of property; and private property produces fewer quarrels about ownership than communal property. But, Thomas continues, sounding like a socialist and even like Robin Hood, the common good is higher than the private good, which means the political community can command the rich to share with the poor when inequalities become too great. And, in cases of extreme necessity, the poor may steal from the rich because all property reverts to common use when survival is threatened. Nevertheless, "moderate profits" through legitimate trade and honest business are morally acceptable most of the time, as long as profit serves ends beyond acquisition, such as providing for one's family and community.[31] A further qualification is that even moderate profits should not be based on usury (although Thomas finally admits that "human law allows usury, not because it is just, but to avoid interference with the useful activities of many people").[32] On the highest level, of course, Thomas recognizes that Christianity teaches detachment from material possessions and contempt for worldly goods. But the renunciation of all material possessions is not a universal command in the present circumstances. It is, rather, a counsel of divine law that certain religious orders practice under vows of "voluntary poverty."[33] Their example provides a glimpse of the original innocence of man and of the coming kingdom of God, a reminder that property and social status are irrelevant to man's last end—the everlasting vision of God in the world-to-come.

Thomas's position on property is thus a carefully graduated account of the hierarchy of perfection that is implicit in divine, natural, and human law. He justifies private property and commerce in order to meet people's basic material needs in this world. He requires a just concern for the common good and a charitable concern for the poor (not excluding redistribution of wealth to alleviate dire poverty or the demand for a just and living wage, but not demanding absolute equality either). And he recommends complete detachment from material possessions for a saintly minority. Through a graduated response, Thomas reconciles the seemingly inconsistent demands of capitalism, socialism, and asceticism not by a false synthesis but by a prudent application of the hierarchy of being and the degrees of perfection tailored to different people and circumstances. He thereby rejects the elevation of private ownership to the status of an inalienable natural right (as modern doctrines demand) while offering lawful protections for private property and for differences of wealth. He also permits flexibility on which claims of acquisition should be legally recognized—inheritance, the first use of property, or the mixing of labor with raw materials; all three titles may be established by human law. And he leaves open the momentous practical question of whether an agricultural society with a limited and static economy is better for the common good than an industrial society with a dynamic economy of unlimited growth. This, too, is a prudential judgment.

While it is hard to say how Thomas would judge modern practices, I suspect that he would favor private ownership over socialism because, as he says, the former better fits the best use of property by fallible but rational men who are inclined to act by enlightened self-interest. Yet, Thomas's endorsement of capitalism would come with huge qualifications (which many modern Catholic encyclicals and Protestant statements have tried to articulate). Such qualifications include warnings that the affluence and materialism of modern industrial societies are bad for the moral health of the whole society, that free markets are callous and unfair to the poor who fall into the lower twenty percent of income brackets, and that uncontrolled industrial development is dangerous to the natural environment which man must manage as a steward in accordance with the conditional grant of dominion given by God over the creatures of the earth.

This complex mixture of attitudes may be the best formula for the prudent management of economy and society in a modern Christian polity, though it does not fit neatly into any contemporary categories of right or left. It is adamant in defending private ownership for households and families ("petty bourgeois" or middle class in contemporary language); it is critical of huge economic inequalities that have no higher purpose than the accumulation of wealth; it is opposed to environmental destruction (somewhat "socialist" or "green" in contemporary terms); and it is antimaterialistic or nonpossessive at the highest levels for saintly people dedicated to the proper use of leisure in charitable works, contemplation, and prayer (meaning the highest respect is reserved for ascetic or voluntary poverty, for which there is no appropriate modern terminology). If one still wants to call this mixed package "Christian economics" or "Christian sociology," one may do so if it is understood to be reasonably derived from the hierarchy of being implicit in the Christian doctrines of Creation and Fall, rather than a direct deduction from Christian divine law or the doctrine of the kingdom of God or an egalitarian theory of social justice. The best label for Thomas's economic and social theory is a teaching of Christian prudence about the best use of temporal goods—a careful balance of the efficiency of capitalism, the priority of the common good, and the perfection of voluntary poverty.

By following a similar pattern of reasoning, one can arrive at a proper perspective on the last aspect of temporal government, the issues of war and peace. The proper pattern is equally complex because the New Testament contains numerous statements that directly bear on questions of war and peace, suggesting that Christian charity or love should be an adequate guide rather than the prudent application of natural law. In the Sermon on the Mount, Christ blesses the peacemakers as the children of God; and, in His most radical statements, He preaches nonresistance to evil, turning the other cheek, and loving one's enemies. Of course, Christ also displays righteous anger at times—expelling money changers from the temple, saying those who corrupt little children should have millstones tied to their necks and be drowned in the sea, condemning Judas His betrayer as someone who should not have been born, withering a fig tree, and announcing that He comes not to bring peace but the sword that will set His followers against their family's wishes. But the overall thrust of Christian love or charity (*agape*) is to put war, violence, and coercion on the defensive and to elevate milder virtues above martial virtues and military glory.

In applying these teachings, some early Christians inclined toward pacifism, although, as Paul Ramsey points out, they may have opposed military service in order to avoid the emperor worship required of Roman soldiers rather than to avoid killing and violence as such.[34] After all, Christ commanded obedience to Caesar in the things that are Caesar's, which the Apostles Peter and Paul interpreted to mean that the Roman emperor is a human authority who "does not bear the sword in vain . . . [for he] is the servant of God to execute his wrath on wrongdoers" (Rom. 13:4). Presumably, Paul meant that the sword may be justly applied to domestic and foreign wrongdoers, sanctioning military duty as well as police work. If this is correct, then Christ and the Apostles began the accommodation with the world by sanctioning the coercive power of the state while commanding a better way to treat neighbors and enemies than violent punishment. Within these conflicting demands, the church and the theologians have worked out theories of just war that permit the legitimate use of force under certain conditions. Such theories are a prudent concession to the fallen world that raise the threshold for justifiable violence to a high level without forbidding it entirely. Over the centuries, Christian theologians have spelled out the precise conditions for the proper use of force or violence in a just war—such as public authorization; the motive of redressing an injury or punishing a wrongdoer or providing for self-defense; the proportionate use of force; the exhaustion of other means; the avoidance of killing innocent noncombatants, and the aim of restoring peace.

Our task here is not to dispute the precise conditions for a just war but to explain why the Christian accommodation to the fallen world is justified. In the first place, as St. Augustine points out in *The City of God*, the universality of Christian love and the recognition of a common humanity have not eliminated national or tribal loyalties. Since the Tower of Babel, mankind has been divided into different languages and peoples; and the divisions will continue until the end of time. As St. Augustine also indicates, the possibility of establishing one world government, on the model of the Roman Empire, can be imagined; but it could not be realized without terrible wars of conquest or a world tyranny in which the *Pax Romana* were imposed by force on all nations.[35] Therefore, St. Augustine does not argue that Christian love and the duties of universal brotherhood should be translated into a structure of power that establishes world government, as King Charlemagne mistakenly assumed when he read St. Augustine's *City of God* as a blueprint for the Holy Roman Empire or as Dante later claimed in sketching a worldwide monarchy that would unite all humanity.

Following Augustine's logic and rejecting Charlemagne's and Dante's views, one could argue that Christian love does not require the modern equivalent of world government, whether it evolves out of the United Nations or a system of international law. One could still argue on prudential grounds, claiming that world government or a regime of international law would help to prevent war. But then one must face the realist argument that it is the balance of power maintained by the Western alliance that best preserves the peace of the world rather than the United Nations. A wiser line of argument than defending world government is to insist that the universality of Christian love, insofar as it has an institutional embodiment, is found in the universal church rather than in a universal political and military structure. But, even this divinely ordained universal institution is itself divided into Catholic, Orthodox, and Protestant churches and has just begun, through small and slow steps in an ecumenical dialogue, to move toward eventual unity. And, of course, there is the ongoing rivalry between Christianity and Islam as the principal claimants to the title of universal religion. It is therefore reasonable to assume that the division of mankind into competing national and religious groups will continue indefinitely in the fallen world with the ever present possibility of war and the necessity for coercive power combined with the hope for peaceful resolution of differences. While the biblical command to "welcome the stranger" obviously implies a duty to temper nationalism and to allow immigration, it does not mean that healthy patriotism and national loyalty must be abolished in the name of Christian charity.

Faced with this reality, Christians can acknowledge that the duty to love one's neighbor does not rule out the possibility of war and requires some version of just war theory. In support of this view, Reinhold Niebuhr argued in a powerful essay on the eve of World War II, "Why the Christian Church Is Not Pacifist," that the Gospels not only preach the law of love but, they also teach the fact of sin. Hence, Niebuhr said, "Most modern forms of Christian pacifism are heretical . . . they have really absorbed the Renaissance faith in the goodness of man and have rejected the Christian doctrine of original sin as an outmoded bit of pessimism." With devastating logic, Niebuhr goes on to criticize those Christian pacifists who take Gandhi as their model of nonviolent resistance. Gandhi, he says, was not obeying the command of nonresistance to evil preached by Christ in the Sermon on the Mount; Gandhi was still resisting evil, but he chose nonviolent means to do so. Gandhi was seeking power and justice in the world like other politicians, which means his pacifism did not transcend politics, like Christ's suffering and death, which were undertaken for the salvation of souls. Nonviolent resistance is therefore not morally superior to violent resistance; both are exercises in power and should be judged by their effectiveness in worldly terms. This is a test of prudence, which indicates that pacifism may work in certain circumstances to bring about justice—usually, when the oppressors, like the British in India whom Gandhi faced, have a moral conscience which can be shamed by passive resistance; but it will not work against Hitler or Stalin or criminal gangsters who feel no shame in killing unarmed people. Thus, when the "law of love" collides with the "fact of sin," the law of love permits justified violence unless one totally renounces the world and offers one's suffering as atonement for sin rather than as a tactic for political resistance.

Interestingly, Niebuhr approves of Christian pacifism when it is practiced as spiritual perfectionism by saintly people who voluntarily renounce politics. Niebuhr cites medieval ascetic perfectionism and the Protestant sectarian perfectionism of the Anabaptist churches for "the effort to achieve a standard of perfect love . . . that is not presented as a political alternative." This kind of pacifism is not a Christian heresy because it does not claim to discover a method for eliminating conflict and warfare. "It regard[s] the mystery of evil as beyond its power of solution. It [is] content to set up the most perfect and unselfish individual life as a symbol of the Kingdom of God. It kn[ows] that this could only be done by disavowing the political task and freeing the individual of all responsibility for social justice." The pacifism of the Mennonites, Amish, and others is a suffering spirituality that withdraws from the political world into separate political communities and renounces oaths of loyalty, military service, and all pretenses of power solely to stand as pure examples of nonresisting love (often at great cost in terms of suffering, persecution, and renunciation) that are signs of the kingdom of God in the present fallen world. This mitigates violence by reminding people that there is a higher vision, without demanding that everyone imitate their example because they freely offer their lives as a sacrifice with no expectation of worldly success.[36]

For the rest of Christian society and its citizens, war is a responsibility that cannot be avoided. Hence, they must accept the legitimacy of armed forces and military institutions and their special requirements. One of those requirements is a hierarchical command structure with generals and admirals at the top and lower ranks beneath them. Experience shows that there is no alternative to a corporate hierarchy for organizing the military. Democratic models of military command structures do not work, although different degrees of formality and informality and varying amounts of independent judgment by local commanders have proven effective in different political cultures. Nor is there any alternative to the essentially masculine warrior ethos of the military, despite the introduction of women to many aspects of modern military life (with combat roles for women being the most controversial and where a prudent regard for human nature as we know it counsels against it). In an institution such as the military with its special requirements for command, discipline, and comradery that must be geared toward fighting and winning wars, the question arises whether any standard beyond the rational consideration of human nature is relevant. Do Christian ethics have any direct bearing on the formation of soldiers and their conduct in war?

Here I offer two suggestions for consideration. The first is to train officers in the old-fashioned ethos of chivalry—the code of honor passed down from the Christian Middle Ages which combines the pagan notion of pride in serving one's country with the Christian idea of using one's strength to protect the weak and the vulnerable against harm. In the training of military leaders, Western societies have traditionally followed the model of "an officer and a gentleman" whose code of duty and honor is an expression of chivalry. But this model has withered in democratic cultures where narrow professional training and ideological indoctrination in political correctness are favored. Though the pride of a gentleman and the humility of a Christian sometimes conflict with each other, they can be reconciled in the code of honor known as chivalry which motivates honorable men to protect their country and the victims of aggression like medieval knights protected the weak and the vulnerable from harm as well as their lords and ladies. The instinct for chivalry actually motivates more American soldiers than one might think, for the feeling of pride that American soldiers experience in fighting a war to right the wrongs of an unjust aggressor is essentially chivalric. It is motivated by the ideal of protecting 'the good guys from the bad guys' and is often inspired by images of soldiers liberating innocent children from oppressors and preserving them from harm. The code of honor known as chivalry should be cultivated deliberately in military services because it is the noblest expression of masculine pride which, contrary to contemporary ideologies, is not socially constructed but natural. It is wiser to accept masculine pride, with its instinct to protect and to provide for others, and to channel it in a constructive direction than to try to repress it by insisting on gender neutrality (which will break down in battle as men protect women from dangers and risks). Even in the modern age, chivalry suits a Christian military for its missions far better than the democratic ideas of narrow professionalism and ideological indoctrination.

A second suggestion for the training of Christian soldiers is more controversial and would be more difficult to implement in the modern world. I think that it would be valuable to restore the ancient idea of ritual purification for soldiers after battle—a rite of personal and public atonement for taking lives even in a just and necessary war. Oddly, one might find some useful analogies in the modern pop psychology of 'grief counseling' after the experience of tragedy or death. The aim of such practices is to bring 'closure' to terrible experiences in order to get on with life. This is similar to what military chaplains have dealt with for years—namely, guilt feelings for taking a life or for surviving unharmed after close comrades have perished. How many soldiers have returned from war and refused to speak about their experiences because of buried feelings of grief and guilt? Religiously speaking, purification or expiation is needed to resolve the peculiar tensions of respecting and loving life while recognizing the necessity of taking life that must lie at the heart of every decent human being and certainly of every Christian soldier. In the Bible (Num. 31:19), we read of a holy war that God commanded Moses and the Israelites to undertake in order to punish the Midianites for their offenses. After a terrible slaughter, the soldiers are told, "whoever of you has killed any person, and whoever has touched any slain, purify yourselves and your captives on the third day and the seventh. You shall purify every garment, every article of skin, all work of goats' hair, and every article of wood." Obviously, this would need updating; but the idea is to cleanse the body and the soul of the blood of warfare and ask forgiveness for doing an impure deed, even when commanded by God in a righteous and holy war.

Ritual purification might be even more necessary in modern warfare because such wars can be so high-tech and impersonal—such as the recent NATO war in Serbia where no ground troops were introduced and none of the combat pilots ever saw or touched the blood of the slain enemy, not to mention the blood of noncombatants accidentally killed through miscalculations. It trivializes life and death to treat the whole experience as an artificial video game or to refer to the accidental deaths as 'collateral damage.' One must strive to grasp the awesome moral challenge of the biblical statement regarding the punishment of unjust aggressors: "Whoever sheds the blood of man, by man shall his blood be shed; for God made man in His own image" (Gen. 9:6). The paradox is that respect for human life, grounded in the *Imago Dei*, sometimes requires the taking of life as a just punishment in order to restore the moral order. But to prevent the 'good guys' from sinking to the level of the 'bad guys,' one needs more than a righteous motive, such as redressing an injury. One also needs some kind of ritual purification to express sorrow for an impure deed, as necessary and as just as the deed may be. Catholics, of course, have confession and penance for expiation; but the problem of killing in a just war is not the same as contrition for committing a sin. It is grief or guilt for doing something required by a legitimate authority as a consequence of our fallen condition. War veterans, such as the Vietnam veterans, have the memorial wall for expressing grief. But why not have a public ceremony after wars in which some soldiers symbolically wash their hands and pour blood into the ground in order to invoke the awe and sorrow one should feel when honorable men violate the divine image in man in order to protect the divine image in man? I mention this as a suggestion for expressing a Christian view of war that realistically accepts our fallen condition while finding a way to transcend the harsh realities of the earthly city.

CONSTITUTIONALISM WITHOUT LIBERALISM

This completes my sketch of a Christian theory of constitutional government. It is designed to challenge prevailing constitutional theories based on Kantian liberalism and to replace them with an Augustinian approach derived from the doctrine of the Two Cities and a Christian version of political prudence. The best label I can suggest for this approach is *'constitutionalism without liberalism'* because it aims at protecting people from tyranny and permits controlled political freedom; but it does so as a religious obligation—as a type of piety that recognizes the inherently limited ends of the temporal realm in the overall hierarchy of being—rather than as an assertion of natural or human rights.

The crux of my argument for 'constitutionalism without liberalism' is the proper distinction between the two realms—between the spiritual spheres of authority (consisting of the Christian church, the Christian family, and the institutions and practices of Christian charity that are derived from divine law) and the temporal spheres of authority (consisting of the state, the economy, social classes, the military, and rules of warfare that Christianity leaves to prudence or practical reasoning about human nature). The advantage of this theory is that it offers a more truthful and effective grounding for political authority than Kantian liberalism because it upholds the state as an institution from God while limiting its powers by an objective hierarchy of ends. The Christian theory of constitutional government under God thereby preserves what is best in modern politics while avoiding its harmful and subversive features.

THE SPIRITUAL SIGNIFICANCE OF THE MODERN DEMOCRATIC AGE

Since the beginning of the book, I have tried to challenge the thinking of two groups of people—the secularists who believe that Christianity should have no public role because it is the enemy of democracy and freedom and the religious believers who think that Christianity and modern democracy share a common moral vision. I took the position that both groups were mistaken. Instead of outright hostility or essential harmony, we confront a difficult dilemma: Modern liberal democracy needs Christianity to support its basic moral principles, but Christianity is not necessarily a liberal or a democratic religion. I argued that the dilemma could be resolved by recovering St. Augustine's doctrine of the Two Cities and applying it to the modern age. It shows that Christianity is a transpolitical faith—an otherworldly religion—that is not tied to any particular form of government or social order as a matter of divine law; accordingly, it permits a variety of political regimes as long as they publicly acknowledge the sovereignty of God and strive to attain the limited ends of the temporal realm while facilitating or at least not hindering the spiritual life of Christian believers. This makes stable constitutional order, rather than democracy or human rights *per se,* the litmus test of legitimate government for Christians. And it permits a practical accommodation with the modern world without turning the Christian faith into a mirror image of political liberalism.

In exploring the dilemma and seeking a solution, I drew attention on numerous occasions to a crucial question: What is the spiritual significance of the modern democratic age? How should one judge the empowerment of the majority in a democratic order, the politics of human rights, the opening of the world to individual talent, the economic and social order of industrial capitalism and modern technology, the popular culture of the Enlightenment and modern mass society? These questions forced us to evaluate the dominant political and social realities of our times. Some criticize the whole order as spiritually empty and unheroic—the uninspiring ethos of bourgeois civilization—while others praise it as the most just and humane era in history for bringing the common man to power, ending slavery, emancipating women, raising the living standards and extending the life span of the great masses of people, and giving everyone a sense of their dignity as free and responsible human beings.

In a recent and provocative essay, *A Catholic Modernity?*, Charles Taylor shows why it is so difficult to make a fair judgment about the spiritual significance of our modern democratic age. In some respects, he says, it seems devoid of spiritual meaning: It is post-Christian and even anti-Christian because it has performed "a spiritual lobotomy" on many people. Modern culture has cut out the highest part of the human soul, the part that longs for eternity and for spiritual transcendence of the here and now, the part that seeks the presence of the Incarnate God in worship and daily life and even hopes for a dim reflection of the city of God in social and political institutions. Instead of focusing on eternal life, we have become absorbed in one-dimensional materialism, trivialized life and death, and learned to avoid thinking or talking about life after death. In part as a reaction to the shallowness of modern democratic life, many have been seduced by utopian experiments that have tried to transform finite reality by establishing Heaven on earth, producing instead the nightmare of totalitarian tyranny and the worst atrocities of human history. Yet, in other respects, the present age seems more infused with Christian values than ever before. There is widespread recognition of our common humanity and awareness of the duties of universal benevolence and charity, often reflected in respect for universal human rights and personal dignity and in the practices of such humane organizations as Doctors without Borders and the various agencies of the United Nations. For Taylor, "the Christian roots of all this run deep"; yet, he admits, "the break with Christendom was necessary for this great extension of Gospel-inspired actions."[1] If both tendencies are present, what is the spiritual significance of the modern democratic age?

I think the best answer is the most modest one: We do not know for sure whether the modern age represents progress or decline in the overall plan of salvation history. Since we cannot be sure, we must treat it in Augustinian fashion as merely another phase in the rise and fall of the earthly city, with as many flaws as virtues, rather than viewing it in Kantian or progressive fashion as the high point of history and as morally superior to previous ages because people are now more free, prosperous, and enlightened than their ancestors. This judgment makes it difficult to view modern liberal democracy as the best (not to mention the *only* legitimate) arrangement for temporal affairs on grounds of Christian ethics. One cannot say with confidence that the present structures are better than the corporate hierarchies of the Christian Middle Ages or the struggles of the early church in the pre-Constantinian age of persecution and martyrdom. Those ages were cruel in many respects. But they also produced many great saints and martyrs, monks and mystics, theologians and philosophers, clergymen and nuns, popes and reformers, Christian kings and knights, cathedrals and icons, hymns and chants, prayers and liturgies, as well as piety and virtue among ordinary faithful people. These people and their monuments often make the religion of our tolerant, democratic age look spiritually flat or indifferent. They remind us, as Tocqueville said, that a democratic age tends to elevate the average or the mediocre above the extraordinary without producing either great sinners or great saints.

Moreover, this age will not last forever, and no one knows if the following age—the so-called 'postmodern' age—will be worse or better. Speaking broadly, one might speculate that the depressing spectacle of widespread religious indifference in modern Western democracies, especially in formerly Christian nations such as France, England, the Scandinavian countries, and now Italy and Spain, could very well be followed by strange developments once the forces of modern culture are fully played out over the next one hundred years or so. After all, the political idealism that once excited modern hearts and that took the place of religion (from the French Revolution of 1789 to the fall of the Berlin Wall in 1989) is now dead. The last two centuries have been dominated by politics, but the next ones will likely be dominated by religion. But what kind of religion?

We are presently in a temporary period of stability in which immersion in middle-class careerism, creature comforts, and high-tech gadgets diverts people from the abyss of nihilism in the surrounding modern cultures. Once economic recession pricks this bubble or the inner emptiness of the present holding pattern becomes unbearable, we could see the void of atheistic humanism being filled by waves of strange New Age religions and doomsday cults mixed with environmental pantheism and science fiction. Such developments will make organized Christianity and Islam look like bastions of sanity and moral order. The wisest course is therefore to accept a practical or prudent alliance with the present democratic regimes as second-best choices compared to more spiritual orders and hierarchical constitutions, while trying to improve the present order as much as possible without deluding one's self about an inner affinity between Christianity and modern liberal democracy. One must also keep open the option of withdrawing from the present order and living in separate religious communities if modern democracies become too decadent to live in or to reform.

As Oliver O'Donovan suggests in his challenging book, *The Desire of the Nations: Rediscovering the Roots of Political Theology*, the relation of Christians to the temporal order is always conditional because we live in the *saeculum* or temporary period between the birth of Christ and the Second Coming of Christ, when nothing fundamental changes in the earthly city because the redemption of fallen man has been fully satisfied by the sacrificial death and resurrection of Christ, but the recognition of that redemption is incomplete.[2] In this period, we are necessarily guided by prudence and the thought of hunkering down until the Second Coming. No inevitable progress occurs during this period, even if the modern democratic world has a greater sense of universal humanity than ever before and even if the whole world has recently celebrated the dawn of the third millennium and thereby implicitly recognized the birth of Christ as the universal measure of time. Are these events spiritually significant or merely tributes to Western technology and advertising? No one can be sure if this is progress or decline in the coming of the kingdom of God, because backsliding is always possible in democratic cultures that overemphasize autonomy and mastery in their conceptions of human dignity and because the failed utopianism and religious indifference of the present period may be followed by new forms of barbarism, not to mention natural cataclysms.

Yet, it is also possible that the 'postmodern age' will be a religious one that is purer and more noble than those of the past because, after centuries of experience, we really have attained a mature sense of freedom and responsibility. Even someone as tough-minded as Alexander Solzhenitsyn has spoken of spiritual renewal based on voluntary religious obligation, which he describes as a new and higher anthropological stage, comparable to the historical changes from the Middle Ages to the Renaissance and Enlightenment—a postmodern Christian civilization.

The major point is that no one knows for sure if the present and future course of the earthly city constitutes progress or decline. It is therefore presumptuous to read in the signs of our times a providential endorsement for the modern democratic age. Instead, we must learn to manage the enduring tensions of the Two Cities, keeping our hearts open to the beauties of the heavenly city while seeking the best possible arrangements of the earthly city and recognizing that the two orders will not be reconciled until the end of time. Living with the tensions of dual citizenship is a more difficult task than assuming an inevitable convergence of Christian faith and modern democratic life, but it is the only honest course for the pilgrims of the earthly city.

NOTES

INTRODUCTION

1. See, for example, James Hastings Nichols, *Democracy and the Churches* (Philadelphia: Westminster Press, 1951). Nichols argues that most Roman Catholics, Anglicans, Lutherans, and Eastern Orthodox churches were distrustful of democracy and that "radical Puritans" were the only reliable carriers of democratic principles. See also, Ernst Troeltsch, *The Social Teaching of the Christian Churches*, trans. Olive Wyon (New York: Macmillan, 1931), 2: 577: "At the present day, Calvinism feels itself to be the only Christian ecclesiastical body which is in agreement with the modern democratic and capitalistic development, and, moreover, the only one which is suited to it."

2. Elaine Pagels, *The Gnostic Gospels* (New York: Vintage, 1989), ch. 2. And Brian Tierney, *The Idea of Natural Rights: Studies on Natural Rights, Natural Law, and Church Law, 1150–1625* (Atlanta: Scholars Press, 1997), p. 215: "Perhaps there was always a possibility that Christian teaching on the inherent value of each individual person could be reformulated as a doctrine of subjective natural rights. But, certainly, through most of Christian history, the possibility was not realized."

3. Paul Johnson, "Is There a Moral Basis for Capitalism?" in *Democracy and Mediating Structures: A Theological Inquiry*, ed. Michael Novak (Washington, D.C.: American Enterprise Institute, 1980), p. 51. See also Paul E. Sigmund, "Catholicism and Liberal Democracy," in *Catholicism and Liberalism: Contributions to American Public Philosophy*, ed. R. Bruce Douglass

and David Hollenbach (Cambridge: Cambridge University Press, 1994), pp. 217–42.

4. See Robert H. Murray, *The Political Consequences of the Reformation* (London: Benn, 1926), p. 105. Murray finds an unbroken line running from Luther's liberty of conscience to the political liberty of the Declaration of Independence. For a recent statement, see John Witte, Jr., *Religion and the American Constitutional Experiment: Essential Rights and Liberties* (Boulder: Westview Press, 2000), p. 17: "Protestant doctrines of the person and society were cast into democratic social forms."

5. H. Richard Niebuhr, *The Kingdom of God in America* (Chicago: Willett, Clark, & Co., 1937), ch. 1, pp. 17–44. This idea goes back to nineteenth-century historians, such as George Bancroft who said: "My nation's enthusiasm for freedom was born from its enthusiasm for Calvinism," in *History of the United States from the Discovery of the American Continent,* 15th ed. (Boston, 1853), 1: 464.

6. See Henri Bergson, *The Two Sources of Morality and Religion,* trans. R. Ashley Audra and Cloudesley Brereton (New York: H. Holt and Co., 1935); Graham Maddox, *Religion and the Rise of Democracy* (London: Routledge, 1996); John W. De Gruchy, *Christianity and Democracy: A Theology for a Just World Order* (Cambridge: Cambridge University Press, 1995); Glenn Tinder, *The Political Meaning of Christianity: An Interpretation* (Baton Rouge: Louisiana State University Press, 1989); Alexander D. Lindsay, *The Churches and Democracy* (London: Epworth, 1934) and *The Modern Democratic State* (London: Oxford University Press, 1943).

7. Desmond M. Tutu, "Religious Human Rights and the Bible," in "Religious Human Rights in the World Today: A Report on the 1994 Atlanta Conference," Emory International Law Review 10:1 (spring 1996): 67–68.

8. Friedrich Nietzsche, *Beyond Good and Evil: Prelude to a Philosophy of the Future,* trans. Walter Kaufmann (New York: Vintage, 1966), #202.

CHAPTER ONE

1. This, of course, is the controversial thesis of Francis Fukuyama in *The End of History and the Last Man* (New York: Free Press, 1992).

2. John Paul II, *Centesimus Annus,* par. 46, Vatican trans. (Sherbrooke, Quebec: Editions Paulines, 1991). See also James V. Schall, "A Reflection on the Classical Tractate on Tyranny: The Problem of Democratic Tyranny," *American Journal of Jurisprudence* 41 (1996): 1–19.

3. The comparison of ancient and modern republics was a crucial part of the debate about the origins of liberalism and can be found in such works as Thomas Hobbes, *Leviathan*, ch. 21; *The Federalist Papers*, nos. 9–10; Benjamin Constant, "The Liberty of the Ancients Compared with That of the Moderns," in *Political Writings*, trans. Biancamaria Fontana (Cambridge: Cambridge University Press, 1988), pp. 307–28.

Among contemporary scholars, the debate has been revived by Hannah Arendt, *On Revolution* (New York: Viking, 1963); Paul A. Rahe, *Republics Ancient and Modern: Classical Republicanism and the American Revolution* (Chapel Hill: University of North Carolina Press, 1992); Thomas L. Pangle, *The Spirit of Modern Republicanism: The Moral Vision of the American Founders and the Philosophy of Locke* (Chicago: University of Chicago Press, 1988); and Gordon Wood, *The Creation of the American Republic, 1776–1787* (Chapel Hill: University of North Carolina Press, 1969).

4. See Aristotle, *The Athenian Constitution*, trans. P. J. Rhodes (Harmondsworth, England, and New York: Penguin, 1984), sect. 42–69.

5. Rahe, *Republics Ancient and Modern*, pp. 42–45.

6. See A. H. M. Jones, *Athenian Democracy* (New York: Praeger, 1960), pp. 17–20, 92; and Josiah Ober, *Mass and Elite in Democratic Athens* (Princeton: Princeton University Press, 1989), pp. 53–103.

7. Herodotus, *The Persian Wars*, trans. George Rawlinson (New York: Modern Library, 1942), bk. V, sect. 78.

8. M. I. Finley, *Democracy Ancient and Modern* (New Brunswick, N.J.: Rutgers University Press, 1973), pp. 50–51.

9. Fustel de Coulanges, *The Ancient City* (Baltimore: The Johns Hopkins University Press, 1980), pp. 197–211.

10. A. H. M. Jones, *Athenian Democracy*, pp. 41–42.

11. Ober, *Mass and Elite in Democratic Athens*, pp. 68–79.

12. Jean-Jacques Rousseau, *The First Discourse and Second Discourses*, trans. Roger D. Masters (New York: St. Martin's Press, 1964), p. 51.

13. Georg W. F. Hegel, *The Philosophy of History*, trans. J. Sibree (New York: Dover, 1956), p. 446, emphasis added.

14. Milton Viorst, ed., *The Great Documents of Western Civilization* (New York: Bantam, 1965), pp. 122–29, emphasis added.

15. Speech on the Kansas-Nebraska Act at Peoria, Illinois (1854), in *The Portable Abraham Lincoln*, ed. Andrew Delbanco (New York: Penguin, 1992), p. 63.

16. Viorst, *Documents of Western Civilization*, pp. 185–89.

17. For a subtle and insightful analysis of this point, see David Walsh, *The Growth of the Liberal Soul* (Columbia, Mo.: University of Missouri Press, 1997), pp. 1–76.

18. James Madison, Alexander Hamilton, and John Jay, *The Federalist Papers*, ed. Clinton Rossiter (New York: Mentor, 1961), no. 1, p. 33.

19. Letter to William Short, Jan. 3, 1793, emphasis added, in *The Portable Jefferson*, ed. Merrill D. Peterson (New York: Viking, 1975), p. 464

20. Ernest L. Fortin, *Human Rights, Virtue, and the Common Good,* in *Collected* Essays, three volumes, ed. J. Brian Benestad (Lanham, Md.: Rowman and Littlefield, 1996), 3: 11.

21. *Democracy in America,* ed. J. P. Mayer, trans. George Lawrence (New York: Harper, 1969), p. 692.

22. Friedrich Nietzsche, *Thus Spoke Zarathustra,* I.5 in *The Portable Nietzsche,* trans. Walter Kaufmann (New York: Viking, 1968).

23. José Ortega y Gasset, *The Revolt of the Masses* (New York: Norton, 1960), chs. 6–11.

24. John Locke, *An Essay Concerning Human Understanding,* Bk. 2, ch. 27.10, ed. Alexander C. Fraser (New York: Dover, 1959), 2 vols., 1: 449.

25. John Stuart Mill, "Utilitarianism," in *Utilitarianism and Other Writings,* ed. Mary Warnock (New York: Meridian, 1962), p. 281: "The ultimate sanction, therefore, of all morality . . . [is] a subjective feeling in our own minds."

26. For a more fully developed and incisive analysis of liberalism's fatal tendency to produce unconstrained willful autonomy, see Pierre Manent, *The City of Man,* trans. Marc A. Le Pain (Princeton, N.J.: Princeton University Press, 1998).

27. Richard Rorty, "Postmodern Bourgeois Liberalism," in *Hermeneutics and Praxis,* ed. Robert Hollinger (Notre Dame, Ind.: University of Notre Dame Press, 1985), p. 220.

28. As Nietzsche saw it, the rejection of God and eternity by modern skeptics gave them a guilty conscience which they hoped to assuage by insisting on a heightened sensitivity to a diluted version of Christian morality. See *Twilight of the Idols,* "Skirmishes of an Untimely Man," no. 5 in *The Portable Nietzsche,* p. 515: "They are rid of the Christian God and now believe all the more firmly that they must cling to the Christian morality."

29. Vàclav Havel, "Civilization's Thin Veneer," Harvard Commencement Address (1995) published in *Harvard Magazine,* July–Aug. 1995, pp. 32–35, 66.

30. For those familiar with Christian apologetics, the arguments that I have used here are variations on the traditional "cosmological" and "teleological" arguments for God found in Aquinas, Pascal, and Leibniz rather than the "ontological" or "psychological" arguments found in St. Anselm and Descartes. For some thoughts on how convincing cosmological and teleological arguments for God can be to modern philosophers and scientists, see "Is Natural Theology Still Viable Today?" by W. Norris Clarke, S.J. in *Explorations in Metaphysics: Being-God-Person* (Notre Dame, Ind.: University of Notre Dame Press, 1994), pp. 150–82. And Stanley L. Jaki, "God and Man's Science: A View of Creation," in *The Christian Vision: Man and Society* (Hillsdale, Mich.: Hillsdale College Press, 1984), pp. 35–49.

CHAPTER TWO

1. David Walsh, *The Growth of the Liberal Soul,* p. 201

2. Daniel J. Elazar, *The Covenant Tradition in Politics,* 4 vols. (New Brunswick and London: Transaction Publishers, 1996–1998). See, for example, 2:3, *Covenant and Commonwealth,* where Elazar says, "The covenants of the Bible are the founding covenants of Western civilization . . . the covenant idea has within it the seeds of modern constitutionalism."

3. See Thomas L. Pangle, "The Hebrew Bible's Challenge to Political Philosophy: Some Introductory Remarks," in *Political Philosophy and the Human Soul: Essays in Memory of Allan Bloom,* (Lanham, Md.: Rowman and Littlefield, 1995), 67–82. I am indebted to this chapter for many of the insights I present here about the politics of the Hebrew Bible.

4. Paul Johnson, *A History of the Jews* (New York: Harper and Row, 1987), p. 27.

5. *Summa Theologiae,* I-II, 105.1

6. Aaron Wildavsky, *The Nursing Father: Moses as a Political Leader* (Tuscaloosa: University of Alabama Press, 1984), p. 24.

7. See Gustavo Gutiérrez, *A Theology of Liberation: History, Politics, and Salvation,* trans. Sister Caridad Inda and John Eagleson (Maryknoll, N.Y.: Orbis, 1971), pp. 86–91; and Michael Walzer, *Exodus and Revolution* (New York: Basic Books, 1985).

8. Adam Garfinkle, "The Two Religions of American Jews: A Provocation for the Sake of Heaven," *Conservative Judaism* (fall 1996): 3–22.

9. Martin Buber, *The Kingship of God* (New York: Harper and Row, 1967), p. 25.

10. Graham Maddox, *Religion and the Rise of Democracy* (London: Routledge, 1996), pp. 34–45.

11. Max Weber, *Ancient Judaism*, trans. H. H. Gerth and D. Martindale (Glencoe, Ill.: The Free Press, 1952), p. 278.

12. See Umberto Cassuto, *A Commentary on the Book of Genesis*, 2 vols., part 2, trans. Israel Abrahams (Jerusalem: Magnes Press, 1984), 2:127.

13. See the discussion by Wolfgang Huber and Roberto Papini in *Christianity and Democracy in Global Context*, ed. John Witte, Jr. (Boulder, Colo.: Westview Press, 1993), pp. 31–64. And Brian Tierney, *The Idea of Natural Rights*, p. 215, cited above in the Introduction, note 2. And John A. Henley, "Theology and the Basis of Human Rights," *Scottish Journal of Theology* 39 (1986):367, which notes the "silence of much of the Christian tradition on the subject" of human rights.

14. Hugo Rahner, S.J., *Church and State in Early Christianity*, trans. Leo Donald Davis, S.J. (San Francisco: Ignatius Press, 1992), pp. 1–132.

15. St. Augustine, *The City of God*, trans. Henry Bettenson (New York: Penguin, 1976), 5.17. All citations are to the Penguin edition.

16. John Cotton, Letter to Lord Say (1636), in *The People Shall Judge: Readings in the Formation of American Policy*, 2 vols. (Chicago: University of Chicago Press, 1949), 1:10.

17. *Life and Letters of John Winthrop: Governor of the Massachusetts Bay Company*, ed. Robert C. Winthrop, 2 vols. (Boston: Ticknor and Fields, 1864–67), 2:430.

18. *A Vindication of the Government of New England Churches*, ch. 2.3, in *The People Shall Judge*, 1:37.

19. Quoted in Daniel W. Howe, *Making the American Self: Jonathan Edwards to Abraham Lincoln* (Cambridge, Mass.: Harvard University Press, 1997), pp. 39–40.

20. Quoted in Earnest R. Taylor, *Methodism and Politics, 1791–1851* (Cambridge: Cambridge University Press, 1935), p. 44.

21. See Søren Kierkegaard, "The Present Age," in *A Kierkegaard Anthology*, ed. Robert Bretall (Princeton: Princeton University Press, 1946), pp. 258–70; and *Journals*, no. 179, Dec. 31, 1837, quoted in Erik von Kuehnelt-Leddihn, *Liberty or Equality: The Challenge of Our Time* (Caldwell, Idaho: Caxton Printers, 1952), p. 133.

22.   Alexander Schmemann, *The Historical Road of Eastern Orthodoxy*, trans. Lydia W. Kesich (New York: Holt, Rinehart, and Winston, 1963), pp. 116–18, 150–219; and Timothy Ware, *The Orthodox Church* (Baltimore: Penguin, 1963), pp. 48–50.

23.   See Wolfgang Huber, "Christianity and Democracy in Europe," in *Christianity and Democracy in Global Context*, pp. 40–42.

24.   James Hastings Nichols, *Democracy and the Churches* (Philadelphia: Westminster Press, 1951), pp. 9–11. And Ernst Troeltsch, *The Social Teaching of the Christian Churches*, trans. Olive Wyon (New York: Macmillan, 1931) 2 vols., 2:577; emphasis added.

25.   Joseph Canning, *A History of Medieval Political Thought, 300–1450* (London and New York: Routledge, 1996), p. 4.

26.   The crucial passages on the Apostolic Succession from these authors are neatly selected and presented in *Documents of the Christian Church*, third edition, ed. Henry Bettenson and Chris Maunder (Oxford: Oxford University Press, 1999), pp. 74–81. The passages include Clement of Rome (*Letter to the Corinthians*, sect. 42, 44), Irenaeus (*Against the Heresies*, III, ch. 3.1–3.4; IV, ch. 26.2), Tertullian (*Rulings on Heresies,* sect. 20, 21, 32), Cyprian (*On the Unity of the Catholic Church*, sect. 4–6; and *Letter* 33.1), and Eusebius (*Ecclesiastical History*, IV, chs. 19–27).

27.   For the conciliarist, Nicholas of Cusa, the decisions of a council were made by bishops, with lower clergy and laity permitted to consent to what the bishops decreed. And bishops derived their authority from the Apostolic Succession: "The faith will never fail in the church, for Christ . . . will remain with the successors of the Apostles until the end of the world." In *The Catholic Concordance*, trans. Paul E. Sigmund (Cambridge: Cambridge University Press, 1991), 2, par. 118, 138–139, 247.

28.   See John Calvin, *The Institutes of the Christian Religion*, 2 vols., trans. Ford L. Battles and ed. John T. McNeill (Philadelphia: Westminster Press, 1960), Bk. IV, ch. 4.4 and 5.2.

29.   Gregory of Nyssa, *On the Making of Man*, in *A Select Library of Nicene and Post-Nicene Fathers of the Christian Church*, vol. 5, trans. Philip Schaff and Henry Wace (Grand Rapids, Mich.: Eerdmans, 1988), ch. 4.1.

30.   Augustine, *City of God*, 12.2.

31.   Ibid., 11.16, 11.23–26.

32.   St. Thomas Aquinas, *Summa Theologica*, 5 vols., trans. Fathers of the English Dominican Province (Westminster, Md.: Benziger Bros., 1948; Christian Classics, 1981), I-II, Q. 1, Prologue. All citations are to this edition.

33. St. Thomas Aquinas, *Summa Contra Gentiles,* 5 vols., vol. 2, trans. James F. Anderson (Notre Dame, Ind.: University of Notre Dame Press, 1975), II, ch. 45.2–8.

34. *The Celestial Hierarchy,* ch. 3.1–3.2, in *Pseudo-Dionysius: The Complete Works,* trans. Colm Luibheid and Paul Rorem (New York: Paulist Press, 1987).

35. Calvin, *Institutes of the Christian Religion,* I, 14.4–14.9.

36. Dante, *Monarchy,* trans. Prue Shaw (Cambridge: Cambridge University Press, 1998), I.9.

37. See James M. Blythe, *Ideal Government and the Mixed Constitution in the Middle Ages* (Princeton: Princeton University Press, 1992). Speaking of medieval theologians, Blythe says: "Most favored limited monarchy with some or all of the characteristics of a mixed constitution . . . usually they [found] this form to be ideally best or best in most circumstances" (p. 180).

38. For some of the references to "the city of God" as the pilgrim church on earth, the angels in Heaven, the saints, all of humanity, all righteous people in the Bible, see Augustine, *The City of God,* 1.35; 8.24 ("Indeed, the city of God, which is the holy Church, is now being built in the whole world"); 10.7; 15.26; 16.3; 17.1; and 18.54.

39. See *The City of God,* 19.13–14. Herbert Deane misses this point and overstates the similarities between Hobbes's and Augustine's conception of politics; but he rightly criticizes McIlwain and others who make Augustine an advocate for theocracy and a Christian state, see Herbert A. Deane, *The Political and Social Ideas of St. Augustine* (New York: Columbia University Press, 1963) pp. 123, 234–37.

40. Saint Augustine, *Confessions,* trans. R. S. Pine-Coffin (New York: Penguin, 1961), III.7–9; emphasis added. These passages refer not only to eternal law but also to something like natural law as the standard for judging human law; but the concept of natural law remains undeveloped in Augustine.

41. *On Free Choice,* I. 5.11–6.15, in Augustine, *Political Writings,* trans. Michael W. Tkacz and Douglas Kries (Indianapolis: Hackett, 1994), pp. 216–17.

42. See John Finnis, *Aquinas: Moral, Political, and Legal Theory* (Oxford: Oxford University Press, 1998). In chapters 7 and 8, Finnis ably defends the proposition that Aquinas limits the ends of the state to peace, justice, and some moral virtues; but Finnis does not trace Aquinas's position to his Augustinian conception of politics in the fallen world. This causes Finnis to overstate Aquinas's similarity with modern liberalism: "[Aquinas's] position is not readily distinguishable from the 'grand simple principle' . . . of John Stuart Mill's *On Liberty*" (p. 228).

43. *S. Th.*, II-II, 66.2, 66.6, 77.4, and 78.1: "[H]uman law has permitted interest taking, not that [it] can be harmonized with justice, but lest the advantage of many be hindered."

44. As Thomas says, "In those things pertaining to the salvation of souls, . . . one should obey the spiritual rather than the secular power. But in those things which pertain to civic welfare, one should obey the secular rather than the spiritual power: 'Render to Caesar the things that are Caesar's' [Mt. 22:21]. Unless, per chance, the secular power is joined to the spiritual power, as in the case of the Pope, who holds the supremacy of both powers. . . ." From the *Commentary on the Sentences*, II, dist. 44, *expositio textus*, ad. 4; quoted in St. Thomas Aquinas, *On Law, Morality, and Politics*, ed. William P. Baumgarth and Richard J. Regan, S.J. (Indianapolis: Hackett, 1988), p. 259.

45. John Emerich Edward Dalberg-Acton, *Selected Writings of Lord Acton*, vol. 1, *Essays in the History of Liberty*, ed. J. Rufus Fears (Indianapolis: Liberty Classics, 1986), p. 34.

46. Martin Luther, "On Secular Authority," in *Luther and Calvin on Secular Authority*, ed. Harro Hopfl (Cambridge: Cambridge University Press, 1991), pp. 30–31.

47. See John W. De Gruchy, *Christianity and Democracy* (Cambridge: Cambridge University Press, 1995), pp. 119–21.

48. See Ralph C. Hancock, *Calvin and the Foundations of Modern Politics* (Ithaca: Cornell University Press, 1989), especially pp. 129–40 for the interpretation of Calvin's "spiritualized worldliness."

49. As far as I can tell, covenantal political theory is not mentioned by Calvin but was developed by some of his followers in France, such as Phillipe Mornay, in the *Vindiciae, Contra Tyrannos* (1579), ed. George Garnett (Cambridge: Cambridge University Press, 1994) and by followers of Zwingli in Switzerland, preeminently Heinrich Bullinger, in *The One and Eternal Testament or Covenant of God* (1534) in *Fountainhead of Federalism: Heinrich Bullinger and the Covenantal Tradition*, ed. Charles S. McCoy and J. Wayne Baker (Louisville, Ky.: Westminster-John Knox Press, 1991).

CHAPTER THREE

1. This phrase is taken from Nathan O. Hatch, *The Democratization of American Christianity* (New Haven, Conn.: Yale University Press, 1989).

2. John Emerich Edward Dalberg-Acton, *Selected Writings of Lord Acton*, vol. 1, *Essays in the History of Liberty*, ed. J. Rufus Fears (Indianapolis:

Liberty Classics, 1986), "The History of Freedom in Christianity," p. 34. And M. Stanton Evans, *The Theme Is Freedom: Religion, Politics, and the American Tradition* (Washington, D.C.: Regnery, 1994).

3. Brian Tierney, *The Idea of Natural Rights* (1997) and *Religion, Law, and the Growth of Constitutional Thought, 1150–1650* (Cambridge: Cambridge University Press, 1982); Richard Tuck, *Natural Rights Theories: Their Origin and Development* (Cambridge: Cambridge University Press, 1979); for a more qualified view, see Paul E. Sigmund, *Nicholas of Cusa and Medieval Political Thought* (Cambridge, Mass.: Harvard University Press, 1963).

4. Paul E. Sigmund, *Nicholas of Cusa and Medieval Political Thought*, pp. 310–14.

5. Nicholas of Cusa, *The Catholic Concordance*, trans. Paul E. Sigmund (Cambridge: Cambridge University Press, 1991) Bk. I, 7.40.

6. Tierney, *The Idea of Natural Rights*, pp. 22–36.

7. John N. Figgis, *The Divine Right of Kings,* (Gloucester, Mass.: Peter Smith, 1970), pp. 4–6, 90–92.

8. See Robert H. Murray, *The Political Consequences of the Reformation: Studies in Sixteenth Century Political Thought* (London: Ernest Benn Limited, 1926), pp. 104–5: "There is only one liberty, and it is liberty of conscience. All other forms are its offspring. . . . The line of succession runs from Martin Luther to John Calvin, . . . to Philippe Mornay, . . . to John Knox , . . . to John Milton, . . . to John Locke, . . . to Alexander Hamilton. Obviously, the view that every layman is a priest is of the most far reaching order." This thesis is at least as old as Hegel; it has been restated many times, as noted above, by Tocqueville, Troeltsche, and A. D. Lindsay.

9. See Perry Miller, ed., *The American Puritans: Their Prose and Poetry* (New York: Columbia University Press, 1956), pp. 2–3, 78–79.

10. Phillipe Mornay, *Vindiciae, Contra Tyrannos*, trans. and ed. George Garnett (Cambridge: Cambridge University Press, 1994), pp. 14–76; and Heinrich Bullinger, *The One and Eternal Testament or Covenant of God* in *Fountainhead of Federalism: Heinrich Bullinger and the Covenantal Tradition*, ed. Charles S. McCoy and J. Wayne Baker (Louisville, Ky.: Westminster-John Knox Press, 1991).

11. Milton Viorst, *The Great Documents of Western Civilization*, pp. 160–61.

12. Quoted in Jerry H. Combee, "The Religious Roots of the Rights of Man in America," in *Religion and Politics*, ed. Fred E. Bauman and Kenneth M. Jensen (Charlottesville: University Press of Virginia, 1989), pp. 79–80.

13. For a more judicious assessment of trends, see John Witte, Jr., *Religion and the American Constitutional Experiment*, pp. 14–21. Witte says that Protestants did not "invent" democracy or rights; but they did take theological doctrines of equal persons before God (in their dignity and depravity) and "cast them into democratic forms designed to protect rights." For a sharper distinction between Protestantism and liberalism, see Stanley Hauerwas, *A Community of Character: Toward a Constructive Christian Social Ethic* (Notre Dame, Ind.: University of Notre Dame Press, 1981), chs. 4 and 5; and Barry Alan Shain, *The Myth of American Individualism: The Protestant Origins of American Political Thought* (Princeton, N.J.: Princeton University Press, 1994). Both Hauerwas and Shain argue that Protestants rejected liberal individualism but nurtured democracy in corporate communities of character.

14. Joseph H. Fichter, *Man of Spain: Francis Suarez* (New York: Macmillan, 1940), p. 306.

15. Francisco Suarez, *On Laws and God the Lawgiver*, Bk. III, 2.3–4.11, in *Selections from Three Works*, vol. 2, trans. and ed. Gwladys L. Williams, Ammi Brown, and John Waldron (Oxford: Clarendon Press, 1944).

16. Francisco Suarez, *Defense of the Catholic and Apostolic Faith*, Bk. III, 1.2, in *Extracts on Politics and Government*, trans. and ed. George Albert Moore (Chevy Chase, Md.: Country Dollar Press, 1950).

17. *On the Three Theological Virtues: Faith, Hope, and Charity* (1621), "On Charity," XIII, 8.2, in *Extracts on Politics and Government*, where revolution against tyrants is justified as part of just war (a right of self-defense) and as part of contract theory which makes the whole commonwealth superior to the king. Even private men, in some cases, may kill a tyrant.

18. See Brian Tierney, *The Idea of Natural Rights*: "Suarez . . . did not construct a complete modern theory of rights and the state . . . [but] helped to establish the substructure on which later theories of rights would be built" (p. 315).

19. *On Faith*, XVIII, 4.9, in *Selections from Three Works*.

20. See David Berman, "Deism, Immortality, and the Art of Theological Lying," in *Deism, Masonry, and the Enlightenment: Essays Honoring Alfred O. Aldridge*, ed. J. A. Leo Lemay (Newark: University of Delaware Press, 1987), pp. 61–78.

21. See Walter Nicgorski, "The Significance of the Non-Lockean Heritage of the Declaration of Independence," *American Journal of Jurisprudence* 21 (1976): 156–77.

22. Paul Johnson, "God and the Americans," *Commentary*, January 1995, pp. 25–45.

23. Alexis de Tocqueville, *Democracy in America*, trans. George Lawrence and ed. J. P. Mayer (New York: Harper, 1969), p. 12.

24. For further analysis of Tocqueville's deism and view of God in history, see Robert P. Kraynak, "Alexis de Tocqueville on Divine Providence and Historical Progress," in *Political Philosophy and the Human Soul: Essays in Memory of Allan Bloom* (Lanham, Md.: Rowman and Littlefield, 1995), pp. 203–28.

25. Jean-Marie Cardinal Lustiger, "Liberty, Equality, and Fraternity," in *First Things* 76 (Oct. 1997): 38–45. See also, Pierre Manent, "Christianity and Democracy: Some Remarks on the Political History of Religion, or, on the Religious History of Modern Politics," in *Modern Liberty and Its Discontents*, ed. and trans. Daniel J. Mahoney and Paul Seaton (Lanham, Md.: Rowman and Littlefield, 1998), pp. 97–116.

26. See Ernest L. Fortin, *Collected Essays,* vol. 3, *Human Rights, Virtue, and the Common Good*, ed. J. Brian Benestad (Lanham, Md.: Rowman and Littlefield, 1996), chs. 16, 20, 21 for three brilliant articles tracing the genesis and influence of the term "social justice."

27. Francisco de Vitoria, *On the American Indians*, I, 6.23, in *Political Writings*, ed. Anthony Pagden and Jeremy Lawrance (Cambridge: Cambridge University Press, 1991).

28. *Indian Freedom: The Cause of Bartolomé de las Casas, 1484–1566: A Reader*, trans. Francis Patrick Sullivan, S.J. (Kansas City, Mo.: Sheed and Ward, 1995), p. 253.

29. Bartolomé de Las Casas, *In Defense of the Indians*, trans. Stafford Poole, C.M. (De Kalb, Ill.: Northern Illinois University Press, 1974), ch. 33, "Cannibalism not intrinsically evil"; and chs. 34–37, "Human sacrifice is not always evil to those who commit it," pp. 212–42.

30. *S. Th.,* I-II, 94.5, ad. 3; and II-II, 57.3, ad. 2.

31. Las Casas, *In Defense of the Indians*, ch. 3, p. 39.

32. Vitoria, *Commentaria a la secunda secundae de Santo Tomas*, 6 vols., 3:340, quoted and translated in Brian Tierney, *The Idea of Natural Rights*, p. 75.

33. See Las Casas, *The Only Way of Attracting All People to the True Faith*, in *Indian Freedom*, pp. 200–22; and *In Defense of the Indians*, ch. 3.

34. Gustavo Gutiérrez, *Las Casas: In Search of the Poor of Jesus Christ*, trans. Robert R. Barr (Maryknoll, N.Y.: Orbis, 1993), p. 382.

35. Ibid., pp. 385–89; and Las Casas, *In Defense of the Indians*, ch. 60, p. 353: "After they first know the true God through belief in the Gospel, they may at last freely subject themselves to the king of Castille (from

whom they have received such a benefit) as to their supreme prince and emperor, while the rights of their natural lords are retained."

36. David B. Davis, *The Problem of Slavery in Western Culture* (Ithaca, N.Y.: Cornell University Press, 1966), pp. 316–23, 348–69.

37. *S. Th.*, II-II, 57.3; and I-II, 94.5: "the distinctions of possessions and slavery were not brought in by nature but devised by human reason for the benefit of human life."

38. For some memorable portraits, see Thomas Bokenkotter, *Church and Revolution: Catholics in the Struggle for Democracy and Social Justice* (New York: Doubleday, 1998). For a sympathetic Protestant view, see John W. De Gruchy, *Christianity and Democracy: A Theology for a Just World Order,* especially pp. 95–128.

39. Pope Leo XIII, *Rerum Novarum* (1891), in Claudia Carlen, *The Papal Encyclicals*, 5 vols. (Raleigh, N.C.: Pierian Press, 1990), II: 241–60, esp. par. 5–23.

40. Walter Rauschenbusch, *A Theology for the Social Gospel* (New York: Macmillan, 1917), pp. 5, 178.

41. See Noel D. Cary, *The Path to Christian Democracy: German Catholics and the Party System from Windhorst to Adenauer* (Cambridge, Mass.: Harvard University Press, 1996), p. 184.

42. Konrad Adenauer, *Memoirs, 1945–53,* trans. Beate Ruhm von Oppen (Chicago: Regnery, 1966), p. 45.

43. Quoted in Thomas Bokenkotter, *Church and Revolution: Catholics in the Struggle for Democracy and Social Justice* (New York: Doubleday, 1998), p. 466.

44. Leo XIII, *Immortale Dei,* "On the Christian Constitution of States" (1885), par. 36, in *The Papal Encyclicals, II:* 115.

45. See "Free and Equal in Dignity and Rights: The Universal Declaration of Human Rights," in *PS: Political Science and Politics* 31:3 (Sept. 1998): 505–34.

46. Desmond M. Tutu, "Religious Human Rights and the Bible," in "Religious Human Rights in the World Today: A Report on the 1994 Atlanta Conference," *Emory International Law Review* 10:1 (spring 1996): 67–68.

47. Pope John XXIII, *Pacem in Terris* (1963), par. 9–14, in *The Gospel of Peace and Justice: Catholic Social Teaching since Pope John* (Maryknoll, N.Y.: Orbis, 1976).

48. Immanuel Kant, *Fundamental Principles of the Metaphysics of Morals,* trans. Thomas K. Abbott (New York: Macmillan, 1949). This second

formulation of the categorical imperative is the crucial principle for modern moral theology. In Kant's words it says (pp. 45–46): "Nonrational beings [have] only a relative value as means, and are therefore called *things;* rational beings . . . are called *persons* because their very nature points them out as ends in themselves . . . possess[ing] absolute worth. . . . Accordingly, the practical imperative will be as follows: *So act as to treat humanity, whether in thine own person or in that of any other, in every case as an end withal, never as a means only*" (Kant's emphasis).

49. Immanuel Kant, *The Metaphysical Elements of Justice*, par. 52. (emphasis added), trans. John Ladd (Indianapolis: Library of Liberal Arts, 1965).

50. See W. Norris Clarke, S.J., *Explorations in Metaphysics: Being-God-Person* (Notre Dame, Ind.: University of Notre Dame Press, 1994), pp. 211–12; and Josef Ratzinger, "Concerning the Notion of Person in Theology," *Communio* 17 (1990): 438–54.

51. All references are to *The Documents of Vatican II*, ed. Walter M. Abbott, S.J. and trans. ed. Joseph Gallagher (New York: American Press, 1966).

52. All references are to the *Catechism of the Catholic Church*, English trans. (United States Catholic Conference, 1994).

53. Martin Luther King, Jr., "Letter from Birmingham Jail," in *What Country Have I? Political Writings by Black Americans*, ed. Herbert J. Storing (New York: St. Martin's Press, 1970), pp. 117–31, emphasis added.

54. Glenn Tinder, *The Political Meaning of Christianity: An Interpretation* (Baton Rouge: Louisiana State University Press, 1989), pp. 13, 178, 203, 208. Tinder notes his indebtedness to Dietrich Bonhoeffer, who also incorporated Kantian elements in his analysis of the "person" which he sees as a being who lives with the burden of "absolute moral responsibility" toward others; see Dietrich Bonhoeffer, *The Communion of Saints: A Dogmatic Inquiry into the Sociology of the Church*, trans. R. Gregor Smith (New York: Harper and Row, 1960), pp. 30–31.

55. As for Eastern Orthodox trends, see Nicholas Berdyaev, *The Destiny of Man* (New York: Scribner, 1937), esp. pp. 69–79. Influenced by Jacques Maritain, Berdyaev developed a version of Christian "personalism" for the Russian Orthodox tradition. He defined the person as a creature made in the image of God who possesses the existential freedom and dignity of a "creative being."

56. Pope John Paul II, *Crossing the Threshold of Hope*, ed. Vittorio Messori (New York: Knopf, 1994), pp. 196–203.

57. Karol Wojtyla, *The Acting Person*, trans. Andrzej Potocki and ed. Anna-Teresa Tymieniecka (Boston: D. Reidel Co., 1979), Preface, p. xiv. And, *Crossing the Threshold of Hope*, pp. 200–201: "The personalistic principle . . . is an attempt to translate the commandment of love into philosophical ethics . . . [into] Kantian ethics. . . . Nevertheless, Kant did not fully interpret the commandment of love."

58. Pope John Paul II, *The Splendor of Truth* (Sherbrooke, Quebec: Editions Paulines, 1993), par. 80–83.

59. December 16, 1997, Speech to the United States Ambassador to the Vatican, the Honorable Lindy Boggs; the text is quoted as "John Paul on the American Experiment," in *First Things* 82 (Apr. 1998): 36–37.

60. Pope John Paul II, *The Gospel of Life* (New York: Random House, 1995), par. 70.

61. *The Essential Reinhold Niebuhr: Selected Essays and Addresses*, ed. Robert McAfee Brown (New Haven, Conn.: Yale University Press, 1986), pp. 135–41, 147.

62. Reinhold Niebuhr, *The Nature and Destiny of Man: A Christian Perspective*, vol. 1, *Human Nature* (New York: Scribner, 1964), pp. 55, 150–63.

CHAPTER FOUR

1. For a good summary of these points, see John Witte, Jr., *Christianity and Democracy in Global Context* (Boulder, Colo.: Westview Press, 1993), pp. 1–13.

2. See Reinhold Niebuhr, *The Children of Light and the Children of Darkness: A Vindication of Democracy and a Critique of its Traditional Defense* (New York: Scribner, 1950), pp. 70–110; and see above, chapter three, pp. 162–164.

3. Robert P. George, *Making Men Moral: Civil Liberties and Public Morality* (Oxford: Clarendon Press, 1993), pp. 189–229.

4. John Locke, *The First Treatise of Government*, par. 86, in *Two Treatises of Government*, ed. Peter Laslett (New York: Mentor, 1965).

5. Gordon Graham, *The Idea of Christian Charity: A Critique of Some Contemporary Conceptions* (Notre Dame, Ind.: University of Notre Dame Press, 1990), pp. 98–101, 159.

6. See, for example, the list of rights in the United Nations Universal Declaration of Human Rights (1948)—which includes the right to freedom of conscience and speech, to participation in politics, to work, to

recognition as a person, to leisure, to housing, to education, to health care, to the "full development of the human personality," in *PS: Political Science and Politics* 31:3 (Sept. 1998): 522–23. See also the critique of infinite and absolute rights in Mary Ann Glendon, *Rights Talk: The Impoverishment of Political Discourse* (New York: Free Press, 1991); and James V. Schall, "Human Rights as an Ideological Project," *American Journal of Jurisprudence* 32 (1987): 47–62.

7. For a devastating critique of such trends, as well as suggestions for renewal, see Aidan Nichols, *Christendom Awake: On Re-Energizing the Church in Culture* (Grand Rapids, Mich.: Eerdmans, 1999), ch. 3, "Re-enchanting the Liturgy."

8. Leszek Kolakowski, *God Owes Us Nothing: A Brief Remark on Pascal's Religion and on the Spirit of Jansenism* (Chicago: University of Chicago Press, 1995).

9. Martin Luther, "On Secular Authority," in *Luther and Calvin on Secular Authority*, trans. Harro Hopfl (Cambridge: Cambridge University Press, 1991) p. 20.

10. See Kenneth R. Craycraft, Jr., *The American Myth of Religious Freedom* (Dallas: Spence Publishing Co., 1999), especially chs. 1, 6. And, David R. Carlin, "The Denomination Called Catholic," *First Things* 77 (Nov. 1997): 18–21.

11. Jacques Maritain, *The Primacy of the Spiritual; or, The Things That Are Not Caesar's*, trans. J. F. Scanlan (London: Sheed and Ward, 1930) and *Christianity and Democracy*, trans. Doris C. Anson (New York: Scribner's, 1943), pp. 59–65.

12. See John Courtney Murray, *We Hold These Truths: Catholic Reflections on the American Proposition* (New York: Sheed and Ward, 1960), pp. 333–35.

13. Stanley Hauerwas, *A Community of Character: Toward a Constructive Christian Social Ethic* (Notre Dame, Ind.: University of Notre Dame Press, 1981), pp. 59–68, 72–86. And, *In Good Company: The Church as Polis* (Notre Dame, Ind.: University of Notre Dame Press, 1995).

14. Glenn Tinder, *The Political Meaning of Christianity*, p. 178.

15. The monotheistic belief in a creator God who is outside of nature is less directly political than paganism or polytheism whose gods and spirits are immanent in nature and in political rulers—which means polytheism tends toward the belief in sacred kings who, as divine figures or priests, mediate between Heaven and earth in order to keep the world going

aright. See Brian Tierney, *Religion, Law, and the Growth of Constitutional Thought, 1150–1650* (Cambridge: Cambridge University Press, 1982), pp. 8–10. See also, Kwame Bediako, "Unmasking the Powers: Christianity, Authority, and Desacralization in Modern African Politics," in *Christianity and Democracy in Global Context*, pp. 207–29.

16. St. Augustine, *City of God*, 19.17.

17. Gerhart Niemeyer, "Augustine's Political Philosophy?" in *The Christian Vision: Man in Society* (Hillsdale, Mich.: Hillsdale College Press, 1984), pp. 72–73.

18. See Walter Ullmann, *Principles of Government and Politics in the Middle Ages* (New York: Barnes and Noble, 1961), pp. 58–86.

19. Alexander Solzhenitsyn, *From Under the Rubble*, trans. under the direction of Michael Scammell (Boston: Little, Brown, and Co., 1974), pp. 24–25, 105.

20. Solzhenitsyn, *The Mortal Danger*, trans. Michael Nicholson and Alexis Klimoff (New York: Harper and Row, 1980), pp. 63–64.

21. Solzhenitsyn, "Lenten Letter," in John B. Dunlop, ed. *Alexander Solzhenitsyn: Critical Essays and Documentary Materials* (New York: Collier, 1973), p. 552. See also, Solzhenitsyn, *The Russian Question at the End of the Century* (New York: Farrar, Straus, & Giroux, 1994), p. 108.

22. Solzhenitsyn, *Rebuilding Russia: Reflections and Tentative Proposals* (New York: Farrar, Straus, & Giroux, 1991), p. 53.

23. Jeane J. Kirkpatrick, *Dictatorships and Double Standards: Rationalism and Reason in Politics* (New York: American Enterprise Institute, 1982), pp. 23–52, 96–140.

24. Solzhenitsyn, *From Under the Rubble*, pp. 23–34, emphasis added; *The Mortal Danger*, p. 60; *The Russian Question*, pp. 106–8.

25. Solzhenitsyn, *Rebuilding Russia*, pp. 54–55; *From Under the Rubble*, pp. 136–37.

26. Solzhenitsyn, *August 1914: The Red Wheel, Knot I*, trans. H. T. Willetts (New York: Farrar, Straus, & Giroux, 1989), p. 530.

27. Solzhenitsyn points to this new stage at the end of his Harvard Address, "A World Split Apart," in Ronald Berman, ed. *Solzhenitsyn at Harvard: The Address, Responses, and Reflections* (Washington, D.C.: Ethics and Public Policy Center, 1976), p. 35.

28. Solzhenitsyn, *August 1914: The Red Wheel*, pp. 568–69, 582–606.

29. Solzhenitsyn, *Rebuilding Russia*, p. 82.

30. Solzhenitsyn, *Rebuilding Russia*, pp. 61–63.

31. Ibid., pp. 49, 53.
32. Ibid., pp. 82–90.
33. Ibid., pp. 96–104.

CHAPTER FIVE

1. See Graham Walker, *Moral Foundations of Constitutional Thought: Current Problems, Augustinian Prospects* (Princeton: Princeton University Press, 1990), chs. 3–4. See also, Gerhart Niemeyer, "Augustine's Political Philosophy?" in *The Christian Vision: Man in Society* (Hillsdale, Mich.: Hillsdale College Press, 1984), pp. 51–75; and Jean Bethke Elshtain, *Augustine and the Limits of Politics* (Notre Dame, Ind.: University of Notre Dame Press, 1995); and Richard John Neuhaus, "Christianity and Democracy," *First Things*, October 1996, pp. 30–36. These authors see a connection between Christianity and constitutional government in the Two Cities doctrine and its teaching about the inherently limited ends of the temporal realm.

2. H. Richard Niebuhr, *Theology, History, and Culture: Major Unpublished Writings*, ed. William S. Johnson and Richard R. Niebuhr (New Haven, Conn.: Yale University Press, 1996), pp. 143–59.

3. See Michael Walzer, *Spheres of Justice: A Defense of Pluralism and Equality* (New York: Basic Books, 1983). Also, "Sphere Sovereignty" and "Uniformity: The Curse of Modern Life" in *Abraham Kuyper: A Centennial Reader*, ed. James D. Bratt (Grand Rapids, Mich.: Eerdmans, 1998), pp. 19–44 and 461–90. See also Herman Dooyeweerd, a Dutch Calvinist and recent interpreter of Kuyper, *Essays in Legal, Social, and Political Philosophy* (Lewiston, N.Y.: Edwin Mellen Press, 1996), especially "The Christian Idea of the State," pp. 121–56. And the doctrine of subsidiarity articulated by Pope Pius XI in *Quadragesimo Anno* (1931), sect. 79–80 in *Five Great Encyclicals* (New York: Paulist Press, 1939) and in *The Catechism of the Catholic Church*, sect. 1883–85, 2209, English trans. (United State Catholic Conference, 1994).

4. Most of the crucial passages on the Apostolic Succession from Irenaeus and other authors can be found in *Documents of the Christian Church*, third edition, ed. Henry Bettenson and Chris Maunder (Oxford: Oxford University Press, 1999), pp. 74–81.

5. Samuel P. Huntington, *The Third Wave: Democratization in the Late Twentieth Century* (Norman: University of Oklahoma Press, 1991).

6. 1 Cor. 11:3; Eph. 5:22; Col. 3:18; 1 Pet. 3:1.

7. "Who Are the Promise Keepers?" *The Weekly Standard*, October 6, 1997, pp. 25–29.

8. See George Gilder, *Men and Marriage* (Gretna, La.: Pelican, 1995), especially chapters 6, 8, 11.

9. Viscount de Chateaubriand, *The Genius of Christianity, or, The Spirit and Beauty of the Christian Religion*, English trans. by Charles I. White in 1856 (New York: Howard Fertig, 1976), pp. 620–32.

10. *Catechism of the Catholic Church*, par. 1881, quoting "The Constitution of the Church in the Modern World" (*Gaudium et Spes*), par. 25.1.

11. Ibid., par. 1886, quoting the encyclical of Pope John Paul II, *Centesimus Annus*, par. 36.2.

12. For the best attempt to justify subsidiarity using the rights and dignity of the human person, see Kenneth L. Grasso, "The Common Good, the State, and the Principle of Subsidiarity in Catholic Social Thought," unpublished paper. As Grasso points out, subsidiarity is now justified by the conception of the human person as a subject of rights prior to state. While this helps to explain Catholic social teaching, it needs to be more solidly grounded on the hierarchy of being implicit in the Two Cities in order to specify the legitimate ends which freedom should serve.

13. Oliver O'Donovan, *The Desire of the Nations: Rediscovering the Roots of Political Theology* (Cambridge: Cambridge University Press, 1996), pp. 211–14. O'Donovan finds the roots of political theology in Augustine's doctrine of the Two Cities which is a division of time periods not merely of metaphysical realms: "The doctrine of the Two [Cities] was . . . a doctrine of two ages . . . Secular institutions have a role confined to this passing age (*saeculum*)." From this doctrine he infers that secular powers exist as temporary, conditional powers between the birth of Christ (the last person to unify roles of priest-king) and the end of time (the coming of the kingdom of God). O'Donovan calls the 'Antichrist' anyone who seeks to unify the two powers by aspiring to be a sacred king, priestly prince, or messiah-ruler.

14. Russell Kirk, *The Politics of Prudence* (Bryn Mawr, Pa.: Intercollegiate Studies Institute, 1993).

15. See James M. Blythe, *Ideal Government and the Mixed Constitution in the Middle Ages* (Princeton: Princeton University Press, 1992). And the recent exchange between Cary J. Nederman and Anthony Black, "Christianity and Republicanism," *American Political Science Review* 92:4

(Dec. 1998): 913–21. Nederman shows convincingly that the early and medieval Christians favored organic or corporate hierarchies, usually in mixed regimes, rather than republican constitutions as Black erroneously claims. Black would also be wrong about the early Protestants; Martin Luther and Richard Hooker favored kings or princes, while John Calvin favored a mixed regime combining aristocracy and democracy (as did American Puritans such as John Winthrop).

16. E. A. Goerner, *Peter and Caesar: The Catholic Church and Political Authority* (New York: Herder and Herder, 1965), p. 209.

17. Aidan Nichols, OP, *Christendom Awake: On Re-Energizing the Church in Culture* (Grand Rapids, Mich.: Eerdmans, 1999), p. 84.

18. *De Regimine Principum* ("On the Government of Princes," 1265) by Thomas Aquinas with Ptolemy of Lucca, trans. James M. Blythe (Philadelphia: University of Pennsylvania Press, 1997), sects. I.2–6 and I.14–15. And *Summa Theologiae* (I-II, 105.1). I have tried to combine the arguments from both works in this brief presentation.

19. See Paul A. Rahe, *Republics Ancient and Modern*, vol. one, "The Ancien Regime in Classical Greece" (Chapel Hill: University of North Carolina Press, 1992), pp. 152–69.

20. See Edmund Burke, *Selected Writings and Speeches*, ed. Peter J. Stanlis (Chicago: Regnery, 1963), pp. 518–46.

21. Daniel Patrick Moynihan, "Defining Deviancy Down," *The American Spectator*, winter 1993, pp. 17–28.

22. I am aware that some consider the U.S. Constitution itself to be a mixed regime because the American Framers did not wish to give the people total power in a pure democracy, so they mixed the democratic principle of consent with individual liberty in order to allow inequalities of wealth, intellect, and ambition to flourish. See, for example, Harvey C. Mansfield, Jr., "Liberal Democracy as a Mixed Regime," in *The Spirit of Liberalism* (Cambridge, Mass.: Harvard University Press, 1978), pp. 6–35. But the Constitution is not a true mixed regime because it does not introduce a higher principle of legitimacy than the will of the people or individual rights. Nevertheless, the existence of a political class of leaders outside the Constitution—a class of liberally educated Christian gentlemen devoted to public service—is an aristocratic element that has been mixed with American republicanism with beneficial effects.

23. T. S. Eliot, *Christianity and Culture: The Idea of a Christian Society and Notes Toward the Definition of Culture* (New York: Harcourt Brace, 1977), p. 121.

24. See James V. Schall, "A Reflection on the Classical Tractate on Tyranny: The Problem of Democratic Tyranny," *American Journal of Jurisprudence* 41 (1996): 17: "Democracy is a means not an end and it takes its judgment of right and wrong not from some decision of a majority, but from what is right."

25. Robert G. Kaufman, "E. H. Carr, Winston Churchill, Reinhold Niebuhr, and Us: The Case for Principled, Prudential, Democratic Realism," in *Roots of Realism*, ed. Benjamin Frankel (London: Frank Cass, 1996), p. 344.

26. Margaret Thatcher, "What Does Christianity Have to Do with Politics?" *Crisis*, March 1991, pp. 39–41.

27. Gustavo Gutiérrez, *A Theology of Liberation: History, Politics, and Salvation*, revised edition. Trans. and ed. Sister Caridad Inda and John Eagleson (Maryknoll, N.Y.: Orbis Books, 1995), pp. 104 and 227, note 103.

28. Ibid., pp. 21, 116. Also, Gustavo Gutiérrez, "Liberation, Theology, and Proclamation," in *The Mystical and Political Dimension of the Christian Faith*, ed. Claude Geffre and Gustavo Gutíerrez (New York: Herder and Herder, 1974), p. 59: "The poverty of the poor is not an appeal for generous action to relieve it, but a demand for the construction of a different social order."

29. Michael Novak, *The Spirit of Democratic Capitalism* (Lanham, Md.: Madison Books, 1982), p. 140.

30. Ibid., pp. 333–60. And Michael Novak and John W. Cooper, eds., *The Corporation: A Theological Inquiry* (Washington: American Enterprise Institute, 1981), pp. 203–17.

31. *Summa Theologiae*, II-II, 66.1–2, 7; and 77.4

32. Ibid., II-II, 78.1.

33. *Summa Contra Gentiles*, book 3, part 2, chapters 130–35. "Those who adopt voluntary poverty in order to follow Christ renounce all things so that they may serve the common welfare, enlightening the people by their wisdom, learning, and examples, or strengthening them by prayer and intercession" (ch. 135, par. 15).

34. Paul Ramsey, *War and Christian Conscience: How Shall Modern War Be Conducted Justly?* (Durham, N.C.: Duke University Press, 1961), pp. xv–xxiv.

35. St. Augustine, *The City of God*, 19.7.

36. "Why the Christian Church Is Not Pacifist" (1940) in *The Essential Reinhold Niebuhr: Selected Essays and Addresses*, ed. Robert McAfee Brown (New Haven, Conn.: Yale University Press, 1986), pp. 102–22.

CONCLUSION

1. Charles Taylor, *A Catholic Modernity? Charles Taylor's Marianist Award Lecture,* ed. James L. Heft, S.M. (New York: Oxford University Press, 1999), pp. 19–26.

2. Oliver O'Donovan, *The Desire of the Nations: Rediscovering the Roots of Political Theology* (Cambridge: Cambridge University Press, 1996), pp. 211–12.

SELECT
BIBLIOGRAPHY

Abbott, Walter M., S.J., general editor. *The Documents of Vatican II.* Translation editor, Joseph Gallagher. New York: America Press, 1966.

Adenauer, Konrad. *Memoirs, 1945–53.* Translated by Beate Ruhm von Oppen. Chicago: Regnery, 1966.

Arendt, Hannah. *On Revolution.* New York: Viking, 1963.

Aristotle. *The Athenian Constitution.* Translated by P. J. Rhodes. New York: Penguin, 1984.

Augustine, Saint. *Political Writings.* Translated by Michael W. Tkacz and Douglas Kries. Indianapolis: Hackett, 1994.

———. *The City of God.* Translated by Henry Bettenson. New York: Penguin, 1976.

———. *Confessions.* Translated by R. S. Pine-Coffin. New York: Penguin, 1961.

Bancroft, George. *History of the United States from the Discovery of the American Continent.* Fifteenth edition. Ten volumes. Boston, 1853.

Berdyaev, Nicholas. *The Destiny of Man.* New York: Scribner, 1937.

Bergson, Henri. *The Two Sources of Morality and Religion.* Translated by R. Ashley Audra and Cloudesley Brereton. New York: Holt and Co., 1935.

Berman, David. "Deism, Immortality, and the Art of Theological Lying." In *Deism, Masonry, and the Enlightenment: Essays Honoring Alfred O. Aldridge.* Edited by J. A. Leo Lemay. Newark: University of Delaware Press, 1987.

Bettenson, Henry and Maunder, Chris, editors. *Documents of the Christian Church.* Third edition. Oxford: Oxford University Press, 1999.

Blythe, James M. *Ideal Government and the Mixed Constitution in the Middle Ages.* Princeton: Princeton University Press, 1992.

Bokenkotter, Thomas. *Church and Revolution: Catholics in the Struggle for Democracy and Social Justice.* New York: Doubleday, 1998.

Bonhoeffer, Dietrich. *The Communion of Saints: A Dogmatic Inquiry into the Sociology of the Church.* Translated by R. Gregor Smith. New York: Harper and Row, 1960.

Buber, Martin. *The Kingship of God.* New York: Harper and Row, 1967.

Bullinger, Heinrich. *The One and Eternal Testament or Covenant of God* (1534). In *Fountainhead of Federalism: Heinrich Bullinger and the Covenantal Tradition.* Edited by Charles S. McCoy and J. Wayne Baker. Louisville, Ky.: John Knox Press, 1991.

Burke, Edmund. *Selected Writings and Speeches.* Edited by Peter J. Stanlis. Chicago: Regnery, 1963.

Calvin, John. *The Institutes of the Christian Religion.* Two volumes. Translated by Ford L. Battles. Edited by John T. McNeill. Philadelphia: Westminster Press, 1960.

Canning, Joseph. *A History of Medieval Political Thought, 300–1450.* London and New York: Routledge, 1996.

Carlin, David R. "The Denomination Called Catholic," *First Things* 77 (Nov. 1997): 18–21.

Cary, Noel D. *The Path to Christian Democracy: German Catholics and the Party System from Windhorst to Adenauer.* Cambridge, Mass.: Harvard University Press, 1996.

Cassuto, Umberto. *A Commentary on the Book of Genesis.* Two volumes. Translated by Israel Abrahams. Jerusalem: Magnes Press, 1984.

Catechism of the Catholic Church. English translation. United States Catholic Conference, 1994.

Chateaubriand, Viscount de. *The Genius of Christianity.* English translation by Charles I. White in 1856. New York: Howard Fertig, 1976.

Clarke, W. Norris, S.J. *Explorations in Metaphysics: Being-God-Person.* Notre Dame, Ind.: University of Notre Dame Press, 1994.

Combee, Jerry H. "The Religious Roots of the Rights of Man in America." In *Religion and Politics.* Edited by Fred Bauman and Kenneth M. Jensen. Charlottesville: University Press of Virginia, 1989.

Constant, Benjamin. "The Liberty of the Ancients Compared with That of the Moderns." In *Political Writings.* Translated by Biancamaria Fontana. Cambridge: Cambridge University Press, 1988.

Coulanges, Fustel de. *The Ancient City.* Baltimore: The Johns Hopkins University Press, 1980.

Craycraft, Kenneth R. *The American Myth of Religious Freedom.* Dallas: Spence Publishing Co., 1999.

Dalberg-Acton, John Emerich Edward. *Essays in the History of Liberty.* In *Selected Writings of Lord Acton,* volume one. Edited by J. Rufus Fears. Indianapolis: Liberty Classics, 1986.

Dante. *Monarchy.* Translated by Prue Shaw. Cambridge: Cambridge University Press, 1998.

Davis, David B. *The Problem of Slavery in Western Culture.* Ithaca, N.Y.: Cornell University Press, 1966.

De Gruchy, John W. *Christianity and Democracy: A Theology for a Just World Order.* Cambridge: Cambridge University Press, 1995.

Deane, Herbert A. *The Political and Social Ideas of St. Augustine.* New York: Columbia University Press, 1963.

Dooyeweerd, Herman. *Essays in Legal, Social, and Political Philosophy.* Lewiston, N.Y.: Edwin Mellen Press, 1996.

Elazar, Daniel J. *The Covenant Tradition in Politics.* Four volumes. New Brunswick, N.J. and London: Transaction Publishers, 1996–1998.

Eliot, T. S. *Christianity and Culture: The Idea of a Christian Society and Notes toward the Definition of Culture.* New York: Harcourt Brace, 1977.

Elshtain, Jean Bethke. *Augustine and the Limits of Politics.* Notre Dame, Ind.: University of Notre Dame Press, 1995.

Evans, M. Stanton. *The Theme Is Freedom: Religion, Politics, and the American Tradition.* Washington, D.C.: Regnery, 1994.

Figgis, John N. *The Divine Right of Kings.* Gloucester, Mass.: Peter Smith, 1970.

Finley, M. I. *Democracy Ancient and Modern.* New Brunswick, N.J.: Rutgers University Press, 1973.

Fichter, Joseph H. *Man of Spain: Francis Suarez.* New York: Macmillan, 1940.

Fortin, Ernest L. *Collected Essays.* Three volumes. Edited by J. Brian Benestad. Lanham, Md.: Rowman and Littlefield, 1996.

Fukuyama, Francis. *The End of History and the Last Man.* New York: Free Press, 1992.

Garfinkle, Adam. "The Two Religions of American Jews: A Provocation for the Sake of Heaven." *Conservative Judaism* (fall 1996): 3–22.

George, Robert P. *Making Men Moral: Civil Liberties and Public Morality.* Oxford: Clarendon Press, 1993.

Gilder, George. *Men and Marriage.* Gretna, La.: Pelican, 1995.

Glendon, Mary Ann. *Rights Talk: The Impoverishment of Political Discourse.* New York: Free Press, 1991.

Goerner, Edward A. *Peter and Caesar: The Catholic Church and Political Authority.* New York: Herder and Herder, 1965.

Graham, Gordon. *The Idea of Christian Charity: A Critique of Some Contemporary Conceptions.* Notre Dame, Ind.: University of Notre Dame Press, 1990.

Grasso, Kenneth L. "The Common Good, the State, and the Principle of Subsidiarity in Catholic Social Thought." Unpublished paper.

Gregory of Nyssa. "On the Making of Man." In *A Select Library of Nicene and Post-Nicene Fathers of the Christian Church,* volume 5. Translated by Philip Schaff and Henry Wace. Grand Rapids, Mich.: Eerdmans, 1988.

Gutiérrez, Gustavo. *Las Casas: In Search of the Poor of Jesus Christ.* Translated by Robert R. Barr. Maryknoll, N.Y.: Orbis, 1993.

———. *A Theology of Liberation: History, Politics, and Salvation.* Translated by Sister Caridad Inda and John Eagleson. Maryknoll, N.Y.: Orbis, 1971.

Hancock, Ralph C. *Calvin and the Foundations of Modern Politics.* Ithaca, N.Y.: Cornell University Press, 1989.

Hatch, Nathan O. *The Democratization of American Christianity.* New Haven, Conn.: Yale University Press, 1989.

Hauerwas, Stanley. *In Good Company: The Church as Polis.* Notre Dame, Ind.: University of Notre Dame Press, 1995.

———. *A Community of Character: Toward a Constructive Christian Social Ethic.* Notre Dame, Ind.: University of Notre Dame Press, 1981.

Havel, Václav. "Civilization's Thin Veneer." Harvard Commencement Address (1995). In *Harvard Magazine* (July–Aug. 1995): 32–35, 66.

Hegel, Georg W. F. *The Philosophy of History.* Translated by J. Sibree. New York: Dover, 1956.

Henley, John A. "Theology and the Basis of Human Rights," *Scottish Journal of Theology* 39 (1986): 367–80.

Huntington, Samuel P. *The Third Wave: Democratization in the Late Twentieth Century.* Norman: University of Oklahoma Press, 1991.

Jaki, Stanley L. "God and Man's Science: A View of Creation." In *The Christian Vision: Man and Society.* Hillsdale, Mich.: Hillsdale College Press, 1984.

Jefferson, Thomas. *The Portable Jefferson.* Edited by Merrill D. Peterson. New York: Viking, 1975.

John XXIII, Pope. *Pacem in Terris.* In *The Gospel of Peace and Justice: Catholic Social Teaching Since Pope John.* Maryknoll, N.Y.: Orbis, 1976.

John Paul II, Pope. "On the American Experiment," *First Things* 82 (Apr. 1998): 36–37.

———. *The Gospel of Life*. New York: Random House, 1995.

———. *Crossing the Threshold of Hope*. Edited by Vittorio Messori. New York: Knopf, 1994.

———. *The Splendor of Truth*. Sherbrooke, Quebec: Editions Paulines, 1993.

———. *Centesimus Annus*. Sherbrooke, Quebec: Editions Paulines, 1991.

Johnson, Paul. "God and the Americans," *Commentary* (Jan. 1995): 25–45.

———. *A History of the Jews*. New York: Harper and Row, 1987.

———. "Is There a Moral Basis for Capitalism?" In *Democracy and Mediating Structures: A Theological Inquiry*. Edited by Michael Novak. Washington, D.C.: American Enterprise Institute, 1980.

Jones, A. H. M. *Athenian Democracy*. New York: Praeger, 1960.

Kant, Immanuel. *The Metaphysical Elements of Justice*. Translated by John Ladd. Indianapolis: Library of Liberal Arts, 1965.

———. *Fundamental Principles of the Metaphysics of Morals*. Translated by Thomas K. Abbott. New York: Macmillan, 1949.

Kaufman, Robert G. "E. H. Carr, Winston Churchill, Reinhold Niebuhr, and Us: The Case for Principled, Prudential, Democratic Realism." In *Roots of Realism*. Edited by Benjamin Frankel. London: Frank Cass, 1996.

Kierkegaard, Søren. *A Kierkegaard Anthology*. Edited by Robert Bretall. Princeton: Princeton University Press, 1946.

King, Martin Luther, Jr. "Letter from Birmingham Jail." In *What Country Have I? Political Writings by Black Americans*. Edited by Herbert J. Storing. New York: St. Martin's Press, 1970.

Kirk, Russell. *The Politics of Prudence*. Bryn Mawr, Pa.: Intercollegiate Studies Institute, 1993.

Kirkpatrick, Jeane J. *Dictatorships and Double Standards: Rationalism and Reason in Politics*. New York: American Enterprise Institute, 1982.

Kolakowski, Leszek. *God Owes Us Nothing: A Brief Remark on Pascal's Religion and on the Spirit of Jansenism*. Chicago: University of Chicago Press, 1995.

Kraynak, Robert P. "Alexis de Tocqueville on Divine Providence and Historical Progress." In *Political Philosophy and the Human Soul: Essays in Memory of Allan Bloom*. Lanham, Md.: Rowman and Littlefield, 1995.

Kuehnelt-Leddihn, Erik von. *Liberty or Equality: The Challenge of Our Time*. Caldwell, Idaho: Caxton Printers, 1952.

Kuyper, Abraham. *Abraham Kuyper: A Centennial Reader.* Edited by James D. Bratt. Grand Rapids, Mich.: Eerdmans, 1998.

Las Casas, Bartolomé de. *Indian Freedom: The Cause of Bartolomé de las Casas, 1484–1566: A Reader.* Translated by Francis Patrick Sullivan, S.J. Kansas City, Mo.: Sheed and Ward, 1995.

———. *In Defense of the Indians.* Translated by Stafford Poole. De Kalb, Ill.: Northern Illinois University Press, 1974.

Leo XIII, Pope. *Rerum Novarum* (1891). In *The Papal Encyclicals.* Compiled by Claudia Carlen. Five volumes. Raleigh, N.C.: Pierian Press, 1990.

Lincoln, Abraham. *The Portable Abraham Lincoln.* Edited by Andrew Delbanco. New York: Penguin, 1992.

Lindsay, Alexander D. *The Modern Democratic State.* London: Oxford University Press, 1943.

———. *The Churches and Democracy.* London: Epworth, 1934.

Locke, John. *Two Treatises of Government.* Edited by Peter Laslett. New York: Mentor, 1965.

———. *An Essay Concerning Human Understanding.* Two volumes. Edited by Alexander C. Fraser. New York: Dover, 1959.

Lustiger, Jean-Marie Cardinal. "Liberty, Equality, and Fraternity," *First Things* 76 (Oct. 1997): 38–45.

Luther, Martin. "On Secular Authority." In *Luther and Calvin on Secular Authority.* Edited by Harro Hopfl. Cambridge: Cambridge University Press, 1991.

Maddox, Graham. *Religion and the Rise of Democracy.* London: Routledge, 1996.

Madison, James, Alexander Hamilton, and John Jay. *The Federalist Papers.* Edited by Clinton Rossiter. New York: Mentor, 1961.

Manent, Pierre. *The City of Man.* Translated by Marc A. Le Pain. Princeton: Princeton University Press, 1998.

———. *Modern Liberty and Its Discontents.* Edited and translated by Daniel J. Mahoney and Paul Seaton. Lanham, Md.: Rowman and Littlefield, 1998.

Mansfield, Harvey C., Jr. *The Spirit of Liberalism.* Cambridge, Mass.: Harvard University Press, 1978.

Maritain, Jacques. *Christianity and Democracy.* Translated by Doris C. Anson. New York: Scribner's, 1943.

———. *The Primacy of the Spiritual; or, The Things That Are Not Caesar's.* Translated by J. F. Scanlan. London: Sheed and Ward, 1930.

Mill, John Stuart. *Utilitarianism and Other Writings*. Edited by Mary Warnock. New York: Meridian, 1962.

Miller, Perry, editor. *The American Puritans: Their Prose and Poetry*. New York: Columbia University Press, 1956.

Mornay, Phillipe. *Vindiciae, Contra Tyrannos* (1579). Edited by George Garnett. Cambridge: Cambridge University Press, 1994.

Moynihan, Daniel Patrick. "Defining Deviancy Down." *The American Spectator* (winter 1993): 17–28.

Murray, John Courtney. *We Hold These Truths: Catholic Reflections on the American Proposition*. New York: Sheed and Ward, 1960.

Murray, Robert H. *The Political Consequences of the Reformation: Studies in Sixteenth Century Political Thought*. London: Ernest Benn Limited, 1926.

Nederman, Cary J. and Anthony Black. "Christianity and Republicanism." *American Political Science Review* 92:4 (Dec. 1998): 913–21.

Neuhaus, Richard John. "Christianity and Democracy," *First Things* (Oct. 1996): 30–36.

Nicgorski, Walter. "The Significance of the Non-Lockean Heritage of the Declaration of Independence." *American Journal of Jurisprudence* 21 (1976): 156–77.

Nicholas of Cusa. *The Catholic Concordance*. Translated by Paul E. Sigmund. Cambridge: Cambridge University Press, 1991.

Nichols, Aidan. *Christendom Awake: On Re-Energizing the Church in Culture*. Grand Rapids, Mich.: Eerdmans, 1999.

Nichols, James Hastings. *Democracy and the Churches*. Philadelphia: Westminster Press, 1951.

Niebuhr, H. Richard. *Theology, History, and Culture: Major Unpublished Writings*. Edited by William S. Johnson and Richard R. Niebuhr. New Haven, Conn.: Yale University Press, 1996.

———. *The Kingdom of God in America*. Chicago: Willett, Clark, & Co., 1937.

Niebuhr, Reinhold. *The Essential Reinhold Niebuhr: Selected Essays and Addresses*. Edited by Robert McAfee Brown. New Haven, Conn.: Yale University Press, 1986.

———. *The Nature and Destiny of Man: A Christian Perspective*. Two volumes. New York: Scribner, 1964.

———. *The Children of Light and the Children of Darkness: A Vindication of Democracy and a Critique of Its Traditional Defense*. New York: Scribner, 1944.

Niemeyer, Gerhart. "Augustine's Political Philosophy?" In *The Christian Vision: Man in Society*. Hillsdale, Mich.: Hillsdale College Press, 1984.

Nietzsche, Friedrich. *Twilight of the Idols.* In *The Portable Nietzsche.* Translated by Walter Kaufmann. New York: Viking, 1968.

———. *Beyond Good and Evil: Prelude to a Philosophy of the Future.* Translated by Walter Kaufmann. New York: Vintage, 1966.

Novak, Michael. *The Spirit of Democratic Capitalism.* Lanham, Md.: Madison Books, 1982.

Novak, Michael and John W. Cooper, editors. *The Corporation: A Theological Inquiry.* Washington: American Enterprise Institute, 1981.

Ober, Josiah. *Mass and Elite in Democratic Athens.* Princeton: Princeton University Press, 1989.

O'Donovan, Oliver. *The Desire of the Nations: Rediscovering the Roots of Political Theology.* Cambridge: Cambridge University Press, 1996.

Ortega y Gasset, José. *The Revolt of the Masses.* New York: Norton, 1960.

Pagels, Elaine. *The Gnostic Gospels.* New York: Vintage, 1989.

Pangle, Thomas L. "The Hebrew Bible's Challenge to Political Philosophy: Some Introductory Remarks." In *Political Philosophy and the Human Soul: Essays in Memory of Allan Bloom.* Lanham, Md.: Rowman and Littlefield, 1995.

———. *The Spirit of Modern Republicanism: The Moral Vision of the American Founders and the Philosophy of Locke.* Chicago: University of Chicago Press, 1988.

Pius XI, Pope. *Quadragesimo Anno* (1931). In *Five Great Encyclicals.* New York: Paulist Press, 1939.

Pseudo-Dionysius. *The Complete Works.* Translated by Colm Luibheid and Paul Rorem. New York: Paulist Press, 1987.

Rahe, Paul A. *Republics Ancient and Modern: Classical Republicanism and the American Revolution.* Chapel Hill: University of North Carolina Press, 1992.

Rahner, Hugo, S.J. *Church and State in Early Christianity.* Translated by Leo Donald Davis, S.J. San Francisco: Ignatius Press, 1992.

Ramsey, Paul. *War and Christian Conscience: How Shall Modern War Be Conducted Justly?* Durham, N.C.: Duke University Press, 1961.

Ratzinger, Josef Cardinal. "Concerning the Notion of Person in Theology." *Communio* 17 (1990): 438–54.

Rauschenbusch, Walter. *A Theology for the Social Gospel.* New York: Macmillan, 1917.

Rorty, Richard. "Postmodern Bourgeois Liberalism." In *Hermeneutics and Praxis.* Edited by Robert Hollinger. Notre Dame, Ind.: University of Notre Dame Press, 1985.

Schall, James V. A Reflection on the Classical Tractate on Tyranny: The Problem of Democratic Tyranny." *American Journal of Jurisprudence* 41 (1996): 1–19.

———. "Human Rights as an Ideological Project." *American Journal of Jurisprudence* 32 (1987): 47–62.

Schmemann, Alexander. *The Historical Road of Eastern Orthodoxy.* Translated by Lydia W. Kesich. New York: Holt, Rinehart, and Winston, 1963.

Shain, Barry Alan. *The Myth of American Individualism: The Protestant Origins of American Political Thought.* Princeton: Princeton University Press, 1994.

Sigmund, Paul E. "Catholicism and Liberal Democracy." In *Catholicism and Liberalism: Contributions to American Public Philosophy.* Edited by R. Bruce Douglass and David Hollenbach. Cambridge: Cambridge University Press, 1994.

———. *Nicholas of Cusa and Medieval Political Thought.* Cambridge, Mass.: Harvard University Press, 1963.

Solzhenitsyn, Alexander. *The Russian Question at the End of the Century.* New York: Farrar, Straus, and Giroux, 1994.

———. *Rebuilding Russia: Reflections and Tentative Proposals.* New York: Farrar, Straus, & Giroux, 1991.

———. *August 1914: The Red Wheel, Knot I.* Translated by H. T. Willetts. New York: Farrar, Straus, and Giroux, 1989.

———. *The Mortal Danger.* Translated by Michael Nicholson and Alexis Klimoff. New York: Harper and Row, 1980.

———. *Solzhenitsyn at Harvard: The Address, Responses, and Reflections.* Edited by Ronald Berman. Washington, D.C.: Ethics and Public Policy Center, 1976.

———. *From Under the Rubble.* Translated under the direction of Michael Scammell. Boston: Little, Brown, and Co., 1974.

———. *Alexander Solzhenitsyn: Critical Essays and Documentary Materials.* Edited by John B. Dunlop. New York: Collier, 1973.

Suarez, Francisco. *Extracts on Politics and Government.* Translated and edited by George Albert Moore. Chevy Chase, Md.: Country Dollar Press, 1950.

———. *Selections from Three Works.* Translated and edited by Gwladys L. Williams, Ammi Brown, and John Waldron. Oxford: Clarendon Press, 1944.

Taylor, Charles. *A Catholic Modernity? The Marianist Award Lecture.* Edited by James L. Heft, S.M. New York: Oxford University Press, 1999.

Taylor, Earnest R. *Methodism and Politics, 1791–1851*. Cambridge: Cambridge University Press, 1935.

Thatcher, Margaret. "What Does Christianity Have to Do with Politics?" *Crisis* (Mar. 1991): 39–41.

Thomas Aquinas, St. *On Law, Morality, and Politics*. Edited by William P. Baumgarth and Richard J. Regan, S.J. Indianapolis: Hackett, 1988.

———. *Summa Contra Gentiles*. Five volumes. Notre Dame, Ind.: University of Notre Dame Press, 1975.

———. *Summa Theologica*. Five volumes. Translated by Fathers of the English Dominican Province. Westminster, Md.: Benziger Bros., 1948; Christian Classics, 1981.

Thomas Aquinas, St., with Ptolemy of Lucca. *De Regimine Principum*. Translated by James M. Blythe. Philadelphia: University of Pennsylvania Press, 1997.

Tierney, Brian. *The Idea of Natural Rights: Studies on Natural Rights, Natural Law, and Church Law, 1150–1625*. Atlanta: Scholars Press, 1997.

———. *Religion, Law, and the Growth of Constitutional Thought, 1150–1650*. Cambridge: Cambridge University Press, 1982.

Tinder, Glenn. *The Political Meaning of Christianity: An Interpretation*. Baton Rouge: Louisiana State University Press, 1989.

Tocqueville, Alexis de. *Democracy in America*. Translated by George Lawrence. Edited by J. P. Mayer. New York: Harper, 1966.

Troeltsch, Ernst. *The Social Teaching of the Christian Churches*. Two volumes. Translated by Olive Wyon. New York: Macmillan, 1931.

Tuck, Richard. *Natural Rights Theories: Their Origin and Development*. Cambridge: Cambridge University Press, 1979.

Tutu, Desmond M. "Religious Human Rights and the Bible." In "Religious Human Rights in the World Today: A Report on the 1994 Atlanta Conference." *Emory International Law Review* 10:1 (spring 1996): 63–68.

Ullmann, Walter. *Principles of Government and Politics in the Middle Ages*. New York: Barnes and Noble, 1961.

United Nations Universal Declaration of Human Rights (1948). *PS: Political Science and Politics* 31:3 (Sept. 1998): 522–23.

Viorst, Milton, editor. *The Great Documents of Western Civilization*. New York: Bantam, 1965.

Vitoria, Francisco de. *Political Writings*. Edited by Anthony Pagden and Jeremy Lawrance. Cambridge: Cambridge University Press, 1991.

Walker, Graham. *Moral Foundations of Constitutional Thought: Current Problems, Augustinian Prospects*. Princeton: Princeton University Press, 1990.

Walsh, David. *The Growth of the Liberal Soul.* Columbia, Mo.: University of Missouri Press, 1997.

Walzer, Michael. *Exodus and Revolution.* New York: Basic Books, 1985.

———. *Spheres of Justice: A Defense of Pluralism and Equality.* New York: Basic Books, 1983.

Ware, Timothy. *The Orthodox Church.* Baltimore: Penguin, 1963.

Weber, Max. *Ancient Judaism.* Translated by H. H. Gerth and D. Martindale. Glencoe, Ill.: The Free Press, 1952.

Wildavsky, Aaron. *The Nursing Father: Moses as a Political Leader.* Tuscaloosa: University of Alabama Press, 1984.

Winthrop, Robert C., ed. *Life and Letters of John Winthrop: Governor of the Massachusetts Bay Company.* Two volumes. Boston: Ticknor and Fields, 1864–67.

Witte, John, Jr. *Religion and the American Constitutional Experiment: Essential Rights and Liberties.* Boulder, Colo.: Westview Press, 2000.

———, editor. *Christianity and Democracy in Global Context.* Boulder, Colo.: Westview Press, 1993.

Wojtyla, Karol. *The Acting Person.* Translated by Andrzej Potocki and edited by Anna-Teresa Tymieniecka. Boston: D. Reidel Co., 1979.

Wood, Gordon. *The Creation of the American Republic, 1776–1787.* Chapel Hill: University of North Carolina Press, 1969.